Advances in Discourse Analysis of Translation and Interpreting

This edited thematic collection features the latest developments of discourse analysis in translation and interpreting studies. It investigates the process of how cultural and ideological intervention is conducted in translation and interpreting using a wide array of discourse analysis and systemic functional linguistic approaches and drawing on empirical data from the Chinese context. The book is divided into four main parts: I. uncovering positioning and ideology in interpreting and translation, II. linking linguistic approach with socio-cultural interpretation, III. discourse analysis into news translation and IV. analysis of multimodal and intersemiotic discourse in translation.

The different approaches to discourse analysis provide a much-needed contribution to the field of translation and interpreting studies. This combination of discourse analysis and corpus analysis demonstrates the interconnectedness of these fields and offers a rich source of conceptual and methodological tools.

This book will appeal to scholars and research students in translation and interpreting studies, cross-linguistic discourse analysis and Chinese studies.

Binhua Wang is Professor of Interpreting and Translation Studies and currently Director of the Centre for Translation Studies at the University of Leeds, UK. His research has focused on various aspects of interpreting and translation studies, in which he has published widely in refereed CSSCI/Core journals and SSCI/A&HCI journals. His latest book is *Theorising Interpreting Studies* (2019).

Jeremy Munday is Professor of Translation Studies at the University of Leeds, UK. His specialisms are linguistic translation theories, discourse analysis (including systemic functional linguistics), ideology and translation, and Latin American literature in translation. He is author of *Introducing Translation Studies* (Routledge, 4th edition, 2016) and *Evaluation in Translation: Critical Points of Translator Decision-Making* (Routledge, 2012).

Routledge Advances in Translation and Interpreting Studies

Translation as Actor-Networking
Actors, Agencies, and Networks in the Making of Arthur Waley's English Translation of the Chinese 'Journey to the West'
Wenyan Luo

Chinese-English Interpreting and Intercultural Communication
Jim Hlavac and Zhichang Xu

Translation and Hegel's Philosophy
A Transformative, Socio-Narrative Approach to A.V. Miller's 'Cold-War' Retranslations
David Charlston

Indigenous Cultural Translation
A Thick Description of *Seediq Bale*
Darryl Sterk

Translating Molière for the English-speaking Stage
The Role of Verse and Rhyme
Cédric Ploix

Mapping Spaces of Translation in Twentieth-Century Latin American Print Culture
María Constanza Guzmán Martínez

A Century of Chinese Literature in Translation (1919–2019)
English Publication and Reception
Edited by Leah Gerber and Lintao Qi

Advances in Discourse Analysis of Translation and Interpreting
Linking Linguistic Approaches with Socio-cultural Interpretation
Edited by Binhua Wang and Jeremy Munday

For more information about this series, please visit: www.routledge.com

Advances in Discourse Analysis of Translation and Interpreting

Linking Linguistic Approaches with Socio-cultural Interpretation

Edited by Binhua Wang and Jeremy Munday

LONDON AND NEW YORK

First published 2021
by Routledge
2 Park Square, Milton Park, Abingdon, Oxon OX14 4RN

and by Routledge
52 Vanderbilt Avenue, New York, NY 10017

Routledge is an imprint of the Taylor & Francis Group, an informa business

© 2021 selection and editorial matter, Binhua Wang and Jeremy Munday; individual chapters, the contributors

The right of Binhua Wang and Jeremy Munday to be identified as the authors of the editorial material, and of the authors for their individual chapters, has been asserted in accordance with sections 77 and 78 of the Copyright, Designs and Patents Act 1988.

All rights reserved. No part of this book may be reprinted or reproduced or utilised in any form or by any electronic, mechanical, or other means, now known or hereafter invented, including photocopying and recording, or in any information storage or retrieval system, without permission in writing from the publishers.

Trademark notice: Product or corporate names may be trademarks or registered trademarks, and are used only for identification and explanation without intent to infringe.

British Library Cataloguing-in-Publication Data
A catalogue record for this book is available from the British Library

Library of Congress Cataloging-in-Publication Data
Names: Wang, Binhua, (Professor of translation), editor. | Munday, Jeremy, editor.
Title: Advances in discourse analysis of translation and interpreting : linking linguistic approaches with socio-cultural interpretation / edited by Binhua Wang and Jeremy Munday.
Description: London ; New York : Routledge, 2020. | Series: Routledge advances in translation and interpreting studies | Includes bibliographical references and index.
Identifiers: LCCN 2020017538 (print) | LCCN 2020017539 (ebook)
Subjects: LCSH: Translating and interpreting—Political aspects—China. | Translating and interpreting—Social aspects—China. | Discourse analysis—China.
Classification: LCC P306.8.C6 A38 2020 (print) | LCC P306.8.C6 (ebook) | DDC 418/.020141—dc23
LC record available at https://lccn.loc.gov/2020017538
LC ebook record available at https://lccn.loc.gov/2020017539

ISBN: 978-0-367-42175-5 (hbk)
ISBN: 978-0-367-82244-6 (ebk)

Typeset in Times New Roman
by Apex CoVantage, LLC

 Printed in the United Kingdom
by Henry Ling Limited

Contents

List of figures   vii
List of tables   viii
List of contributors   x

Introduction   1
BINHUA WANG AND JEREMY MUNDAY

PART I
Uncovering positioning and ideology in translation and interpreting   7

1 Presentation, re-presentation and perception of China's political discourse: an analysis about core concepts on the 'Belt and Road' based on a comparable corpus   9
BINHUA WANG

2 From linguistic manipulation to discourse reconstruction: a case study of conference interpreting at the World Economic Forum in China   24
FEI GAO

3 'The main problems in China-Japan relations lie in <u>the FACT that</u> some leaders in Japan keep on visiting the Yasukuni Shrine': a corpus-based CDA on government interpreters' metadiscursive (re)construction of truth, fact and reality   40
CHONGLONG GU

4 Competing narratives and military interpreters' choices: a case study on China–US disaster-relief joint military exercise   64
QIANHUA OUYANG AND QILIANG XU

PART II
Linking linguistic analysis with socio-cultural interpretation   83

5 Functions of the pronoun 'we' in the English translations
   of Chinese government reports   85
   HAILING YU AND CANZHONG WU

6 Interpreting as institutional gatekeeping: a critical discourse
   analysis of interpreted questions at the Chinese foreign
   minister's press conferences   106
   XIN LI AND RANRAN ZHANG

PART III
Discourse analysis of news translation   129

7 Stance mediation in media translation of political speeches:
   an analytical model of appraisal and framing in news
   discourse   131
   LI PAN AND CHUXIN HUANG

8 Representations of the 2014 Hong Kong protests in news
   translation: a corpus-based critical discourse analysis   150
   YUAN PING

9 Reframing China in conflicts: a case study of English
   translation of the South China Sea dispute   170
   BINJIAN QIN

PART IV
Analysis of multimodal and intersemiotic discourse in translation   187

10 Translations of public notices in Macao: a multimodal
   perspective   189
   XI CHEN

11 Representation of identity in dubbed Italian versions of
   multicultural sitcoms: an SFL perspective   212
   MARINA MANFREDI

   Index   226

Figures

1.1	Thesaurus sketch of the top keyword 'Belt' in the "Sub-corpus of CD on B&R"	18
1.2	Thesaurus sketch of the top keyword 'OBOR' in the "Sub-corpus of TE on B&R"	18
2.1	Positive/negative evaluations of the attitude system, contrasted by STs and TTs	31
2.2	Shifts of intensification/down-toning of the graduation system, contrasted by TT positive and TT negative evaluations	31
3.1	Screenshot of concordance lines featuring *this/the fact that*	50
3.2	Screenshot of the interpreted discourse (re)contextualised on the CNN website	54
3.3	Screenshot of the interpreted discourse (re)contextualised on the *China Daily* website	56
3.4	Screenshot of the interpreted discourse appearing on the official Chinese government website (English)	57
4.1	Analytical framework of the narratives	67
5.1	'We' in English translations of AWR and State of the Union addresses	89
5.2	Concordance plot of 'we' in the 2016 English AWR and Obama address	89
5.3	Occurrences of '*we will*' in each year's English translation of the AWR	94
8.1	A snapshot of the ECNTC in Sketch Engine	153
9.1	Attitudinal realisation strategies	172
9.2	Reframing strategies in different value positions	176
9.3	Deviation patterns of attitude towards China	177
9.4	Attitudinal deviation patterns in ambiguity	178
9.5	Attitudinal deviation patterns in labelling	180
10.1	PN released in 2011	197
10.2	PN released in 2012	198
10.3	PN released in 2014	199
10.4	PN on information publicity	203
10.5	PN on reporting crimes	204
10.6	PN on driving while under the influence of alcohol or drugs	206
10.7	PN on red pocket recycle	207

Tables

1.1	The comparable corpus of discourse on the Belt and Road	12
1.2	Evolution of labelling of the B&R in China's own re-presentation through translation and in the perception by *The Economist*	15
1.3	Comparison of the keyword lists between the two sub-corpora	16
1.4	Concordance Lines Group 1	19
1.5	Concordance Lines Group 2	20
1.6	Concordance Lines Group 3	20
1.7	Concordance Lines Group 4	21
2.1	Attitude system (adapted from Martin and White 2005)	27
2.2	Graduation system (adapted from Martin and White 2005)	27
3.1	Established items and expressions in both sub-corpora	47
4.1	Headlines on MoD and DoD portals	70
4.2	Expert role of interpreters and its instantiations	72
5.1	Diachronic distribution of 'wǒmen' and 'we'	88
5.2	Modality type and value in English	92
5.3	Modality used in clauses containing 'we'	92
5.4	Clauses of material process	98
6.1	Composition of the mini-corpus (Corpus B)	110
6.2	Occurrence of interpersonal shifts in different participation frameworks	112
8.1	Media outlets selected in this study	154
8.2	Corpus information by news outlet	155
8.3	Top 10 content words in the STs and the TTs of each media outlet	157
8.4	Comparison of top 25 keywords in the translated news corpora by different semantic groups	159
8.5	Word sketches of *movement* and its Chinese equivalent 运动 in the news corpora	162
9.1	Omission of positive attitudinal inscriptions	178
9.2	Ambiguity deviation of changing positive attitudinal inscription to token	179
9.3	Labelling deviation of changing positive attitudinal inscriptions to tokens	181

10.1	Reiss's Text Topology and Links to Translation Methods (Munday 2016: 115)	191
10.2	Interpersonal function and its realization in the image	194
10.3	Interpersonal function and its realization in Figures 10.2–10.4	200
11.1	From Disney's *Jessie*, episode 1x11	217
11.2	From Disney's *Jessie*, episode 1x13	217
11.3	From Disney's *Jessie*, episode 1x11	218
11.4	From Disney's *Jessie*, episode 1x15	219
11.5	From *How to Be Indie/Essere Indie*, episode 1x01	219
11.6	From Disney's *Jessie*, episode 1x15	219
11.7	From Disney's *Jessie*, episode 1x11	220
11.8	From Disney's *Bunk'D*, episode 1x01	220

Contributors

Xi Chen is an assistant professor in University International College at Macau University of Science and Technology. She has gained her PhD in English linguistics at the University of Macau. Her recent publication is "Representing Cultures Through Language and Image: A Multimodal Approach to Translations of the Chinese Classic Mulan" (2018) in *Perspectives: Studies in Translatology*.

Fei Gao is currently a PhD researcher at the University of Leeds. She obtained her master's degree at the University of Reading. She is also a lecturer in translation and interpreting studies at the Chongqing Youdian University in China. Her research interests include interpreting studies, multimodality, and corpus-based translation and interpreting studies.

Chonglong Gu holds a PhD in interpreting studies (Manchester) and an MA in conference interpreting and translation studies (Leeds). Currently he is a lecturer (assistant professor) in Chinese Translation Studies at the University of Liverpool. Previously, he had experience teaching interpreting and/or translation in China and the UK. His latest academic writings have appeared in international journals (e.g. *The Translator*, *Target*, *Discourse, Context & Media*, *Critical Discourse Studies*, *Translation and Interpreting Studies*, and *Perspectives*) and book chapters. He has recently guest-edited a special issue of *New Voices in Translation Studies* about power, agency, representation and ideology.

Chuxin Huang is an MA student in translation studies at Guangdong University of Foreign Studies. She has published a co-authored article in *Babel* and given presentations on media and political discourse and translation at international conferences in Hong Kong and Seoul. Her three articles on media translation have also been accepted for publication and are forthcoming in 2020.

Xin Li is an associate professor at the School of Foreign Languages, Shanghai Jiao Tong University. Her research interests include corpus-based translation/interpreting studies, the socio-cultural aspects of interpreting and critical discourse analysis.

Marina Manfredi is a lecturer and researcher in English Language and Translation at the University of Bologna, Italy, at the Department of Modern Languages,

Literatures and Cultures. She is also Director of the Language Centre at the same university. She teaches English linguistics for undergraduate students and English translation for postgraduates. Her main research interests lie in the field of translation studies and include systemic functional linguistics and translation, translation teaching, postcolonial translation, metaphor translation, audiovisual translation (especially of multicultural television programmes for younger audiences), news translation, translation of popular science for press magazines for the web and, most recently, museum translation. She has contributed to national and international conferences on these topics and has published various articles and three books.

Jeremy Munday is Professor of Translation Studies at the University of Leeds. His specialisms are linguistic translation theories, discourse analysis (including systemic functional linguistics), ideology and translation, and Latin American literature in translation. He is author of *Introducing Translation Studies* (Routledge, 4th edition 2016) and *Evaluation in Translation: Critical Points of Translator Decision-Making* (Routledge, 2012).

Qianhua Ouyang is Associate Professor of Translation Studies of Guangdong University of Foreign Studies and an experienced conference interpreter. She received her PhD in Linguistics at the University of Macau. Her research interests include discourse and functional approaches to translation and interpreting studies, interpreting quality assessment and interpreting teaching pedagogy.

Li Pan is Professor of Translation Studies at Guangdong University of Foreign Studies (GDUFS) and director of the Centre for Translation and Communication of GDUFS. She is also a researcher at the Centre for Translation Studies of GDUFS and a visiting academic scholar at the Centre for Translation and Intercultural Studies of the University of Manchester. She received her PhD in translation studies from the University of Macau. Her research interests include media and political discourse and translation, functional approaches to translation studies and multimodality discourse analysis and translation.

Yuan Ping is a PhD candidate in translation studies at the School of Languages, Cultures and Societies at the University of Leeds (UK). He is also a lecturer in English at Hangzhou Dianzi University in China. His research interests include news translation, critical discourse analysis, corpus linguistics and narrative theory.

Binjian Qin is a lecturer in the School of Foreign Studies, Guangxi University for Nationalities, China. His research focuses on discourse analysis, media translation and political discourse translation.

Binhua Wang is Professor of interpreting and translation studies and currently director of the Centre for Translation Studies at University of Leeds. He is also Fellow of the "Chartered Institute of Linguists" (CIOL) and editorial board member of *Babel – International Journal of Translation* and *Chinese Translators Journal*. His research has focused on various aspects of interpreting and translation studies, in which he has published over 50 articles, including around 40 in refereed CSSCI/Core journals and SSCI/A&HCI journals and over a dozen peer-reviewed book chapters. He has authored the monographs *Theorising Interpreting Studies* (2019) and *A Descriptive Study of Norms in Interpreting* (2013). His research has been funded by some major research grants such as the General Research Fund (GRF) of the Hong Kong Research Grants Council and the China Ministry of Education Research Grant for Humanities and Social Sciences.

Canzhong Wu is a senior lecturer in the Department of Linguistics, Macquarie University. He specialises in the development of computational tools for multilingual grammatical reference resources, systemic functional linguistics and translation studies.

Qiliang Xu is Assistant Lecturer of Guangdong Baiyun University and a practicing interpreter. He received his master's degree in translation studies at Guangdong University of Foreign Studies. His research interests lie mainly in interpreting education and pedagogy, as well as discourse-analytical approach to interpreting studies.

Hailing Yu got her PhD from the Department of Linguistics, Macquarie University, Australia in 2017. She is now an associate professor in the School of Foreign Languages, Hunan University, China. Her research interests cover translation studies, multimodal discourse analysis and systemic functional linguistics.

Ranran Zhang is a lecturer at the School of Foreign Studies, East China University of Political Science and Law. Her research interests include systemic functional linguistics and forensic linguistics.

Introduction

Binhua Wang and Jeremy Munday

Within the discipline of translation and interpreting studies, a relatively recent development is the conceptualization of the object of investigation as socially situated activities and translators and interpreters as agents of not only linguistic and communicative mediation but also cultural and ideological mediation. The discipline has adopted a more critical stance towards the relationship between discursive practices and their communicative, social and cultural embeddings, labelled by some scholars (e.g., Wolf 2006) as the 'social turn' or 'sociological turn' of translation and interpreting studies. The social turn, like the cultural turn before it, has successfully expanded the horizon of translation and interpreting studies from micro-analysis into words, sentences and texts to macro-analysis into the role of translators/interpreters and the function of translation and interpreting in society and culture. Yet it remains to be further explored how linguistic analysis can be linked to the wider target text function and how socio-cultural studies can be better validated with detailed textual and discoursal analysis (Wang 2019: 613). This book is a step on that path of exploration.

Discourse analysis in its various definitions and forms deals with language use above the sentence, meaning-making in whole texts in specific social and cultural contexts, the entire act of linguistic and cultural communication and the construction and representation of identity. It has long been applied in translation and interpreting studies to explain the expression of ideology and to track the translator/interpreter's cultural intervention. In the 1970s, discourse analysis moved linguistic inquiry beyond the sentence level to focus on the ways in which language users achieve their communicative goals over a whole text or sequence of talk (Mason 2015: 110); it then came to prominence in translation and interpreting studies in the 1990s, building particularly upon Halliday's systemic functional grammar (Munday 2016: 142). Such an approach has been popular in translation and interpreting research because of a strong interrelation between the linguistic choices, communicative goals and socio-cultural contexts.

This thematic collection originated as a selection of the papers presented in Panel 12 of the 6th Conference of The International Association of Translation and Intercultural Studies (IATIS-6) held at Hong Kong Baptist University in July 2018, which was entitled "Advances in Discourse Analysis in Translation Studies: Theoretical Models and Applications". It was the continuation of the successful discourse analysis panel at the 5th Conference of IATIS in Belo Horizonte and the roundtables held at the University of Macau (2012), the University of Leeds (2014) and the University of New South Wales (2016). These events brought together contributions which were published as the special issue of *Target*, 27: 3 (Munday and Zhang 2015), the special issue of *Perspectives* 26: 2 (Zhang and Munday 2018) and the volume *Systemic Functional Linguistics and Translation Studies* (Kim et al, forthcoming). The IATIS-6 panel featured in the current volume aimed to take stock of recent developments in the field and to explore, through the methodologies of discourse analysis, how cultural and ideological intervention is conducted in translation and interpreting. It attracted 47 submissions.

Included in this themed collection are 11 chapters selected and revised from the panel presentations, which can be categorised into the following four parts: I. "Uncovering Positioning and Ideology in Translation and Interpreting"; II. "Linking Linguistic Analysis With Socio-Cultural Interpretation"; III. "Discourse Analysis of News Translation"; IV. "Analysis of Multimodal and Intersemiotic Discourse in Translation". The book therefore represents some of the latest developments of discourse analysis in translation and interpreting studies; theoretical models and applications are explored with a wide array of methodologies and data covering various genres, as described here.

Binhua Wang's chapter "Presentation, Re-presentation and Perception of China's Political Concepts – An Analysis About Core Concepts on the 'Belt and Road' Based on a Comparable Corpus" examines how core concepts in China's political discourse are re-contextualized in international communication. It focuses on core concepts about the "Belt and Road" (B&R), a grand scheme in China's current development agenda and relevant to many other countries in the world. Two sets of research questions are explored: (a) How is the B&R labelled in the Chinese government's discourse, and how is it re-presented through institutional translation? How is it labelled and perceived in Western media's discourse? (b) Is the image of the B&R constructed by the media in the 'perceived' discourse the same as in the 're-presented' discourse of the translation? Through corpus-based discourse analysis into a comparable corpus of discourse on B&R comprising the "Sub-corpus of China's Translated/Interpreted Discourse on B&R in 2015–2018" and the "Sub-corpus of *The Economist* on B&R in 2015–2018", the chapter uncovers the linguistic manifestations of political and ideological mediation through the agency of translators and interpreters and through the agency of the public media. The study advances the new approach of corpus-based discourse analysis of translation and interpreting.

Fei Gao's chapter "From Linguistic Manipulation to Discourse Reconstruction: A Case Study of Conference Interpreting at the World Economic Forum in China" investigates how conference interpreters manipulate linguistic resources in the source texts to reconstruct the discourse of the target texts. The case study is based on an English/Chinese interpreting corpus of panel discussions at the World Economic Forum. Results reveal that the Chinese interpreters tend to (a) strengthen positive evaluation in relation to Chinese economic policies and (b) mitigate related negative evaluation and 'risky' discourse infused with negativity. Both patterns of discursive reconstruction reveal interpreters' linguistic manipulation of evaluative expressions via adding, omitting and changing positive or negative values. The study sheds fresh light on how inter-disciplinary approaches, integrating a critical discourse analysis (CDA) perspective and a pertinent linguistic theory (appraisal theory) for fine-grained analysis may serve research aims in translation and interpreting studies.

Chonglong Gu's chapter "'The main problems in China–Japan Relations Lie in the Fact that Some Leaders in Japan Keep on Visiting the Tasukuni Shrine': A Corpus-Based CDA on Government Interpreters' metadiscursive (re)construction of truth, fact and reality", based on a corpus of press conferences, explores how China's discourse is (re)configured by interpreters in English through metadiscursive resources semantically related to truth, fact and reality (e.g., expressions such as *in fact, actually, indeed, as a matter of fact*). Through a comparison of metadiscursive devices it is found that the interpreters tend to proliferate the use of these markers in English overall. Discursively, this adds an additional layer of factualness and authority to the Chinese original. In addition, special attention in analysis is focused on the structure 'the fact that', which has remained underexplored in interpreter-mediated political encounters from the perspective of ideology and discourse. Critical comparative analysis points to the interpreters' increased use of this structure. This leads to further political legitimation and the (re)creation of positive self-representation and negative other-representation in interpreting. To illustrate the potential global ramifications of such (re)construction, examples are also presented of the interpreted discourse being taken for granted and invoked, quoted or (re)contextualised verbatim by various media outlets and official sources. This study highlights the interpreters' role as important co-constructors of the 'Chinese story' and vital agents of knowledge for Beijing.

Research on interpreters' decision-making mechanisms has been focusing more on the cognitive regime due to the evanescent nature of the activity, but the social and cultural context that weighs heavily on interpreters' choices has not received equally sufficient attention. **Qianhua Ouyang and Qiliang Xu**'s chapter "Competing Narratives and Military Interpreters' Choices: A Case Study on a China–US Disaster-Relief Joint Military Exercise" employs the lens of narrative theory and brings in different layers of narratives as context for the interpreting process. It aims to unveil the narrative activators of interpreters' choices at critical points where major deviations between the input and output occur. The study investigates the midterm consultation conference of the China–US disaster-relief joint military exercise. Public, conceptual and meta-narratives on China–US relation and military relation are first surveyed with reference to reports on government portals and in the mainstream media in the two countries. A corpus of the transcribed recordings of the event is then built for the analysis. It is found that, in most cases, choices of interpreters are activated by immediate verbal input with reference to the closest narratives. However, when the verbal input competes with the accepted public, conceptual and meta-narratives, interpreters may refer to the latter in their decision-making.

Hailing Yu and Canzhong Wu's chapter "Functions of the Pronoun 'We' in the English Translations of Chinese Government Reports" investigates the use and functions of the first-person plural 'we' in the English translations of the Annual Work Report (AWR) of the Chinese government from 2000 to 2019. The study adopts a two-pronged approach, combining low-level automatic analysis and high-level manual analysis. It has been found that the pronoun 'we' is often added in the process of translation and functions to highlight qualities that are considered desirable on the part of the Chinese government/people. Interpersonally, the use of 'we' in combination with modulation helps to highlight a sense of volition and obligation to undertake the work to build a better future for the country. Experientially, assigning 'we' the role of agent in material processes contributes to establishing an active and dynamic image of the Chinese government/people in both achieving pre-set goals in the last year and carrying out the government's plan for the ongoing year. The discussions show that a methodological synergy between discourse analysis and translation studies can serve as a powerful tool to deconstruct and analyse the transfer of political discourses from one language/culture into another.

Government press conferences (GPC) addressed to the international media play a significant role in the communication of a country's national policies and stances to the international media, yet the crucial role of interpreters in these political communicative events has been under-researched in academia. Although there has been a growing body of literature discussing the mediation of GPC interpreters in the Chinese context, their gatekeeping role remains under-explored. In light of previous studies on community interpreting and GPC interpreting, **Xin Li and Ranran Zhang**'s chapter "Interpreting As Institutional Gatekeeping: A Critical Discourse Analysis of Interpreted Questions at the Chinese Foreign Minister's Press Conferences" examines how, through discursive choices, interpreters working for the Ministry of Foreign Affairs (China) realize their gatekeeping role in interpreting the potentially face-threatening questions raised by journalists at the Chinese foreign minister's press conferences (2016–2018). Again adopting critical discourse analysis informed by systemic functional linguistics (SFL) as the theoretical framework, the study starts with a description of interpersonal shifts in the interpreting before discussing the gatekeeping role and possible ideological factors behind the accompanying linguistic choices.

Li Pan and Chuxin Huang's chapter "Stance Mediation in Media Translation of Political Speeches: An Analytical Model of Appraisal and Framing in News Discourse" draws on appraisal theory developed by Martin and White (2005) as the theoretical framework. It compares the framing of the Chinese president in the English discourse disseminated by the Chinese, British and US news media. Investigation of the appraisal and framing in different media seeks to compare the stance signalled in President Xi's metaphors in his original Chinese speeches with the quotations in English translations that appear in the Anglo-American media. The study is expected to shed light on future research using discourse analysis relating to stance mediation in media translation and contextualisation of political speeches.

Yuan Ping's chapter "Representations of Hong Kong in News Translation: A Corpus-Based Critical Discourse Analysis" investigates how the

2014 Hong Kong protests were represented in the translations of news articles published in the following media outlets: the *Reference News* from the Chinese mainland, the *EJ Insight* from Hong Kong, the *BBC Chinese* from the UK and the *New York Times* (Chinese) from the US. The news corpus is composed of English and Chinese news articles on the 2014 Hong Kong protests from these outlets and their original pieces that were released in a range of mainstream news media. This study adopts a corpus-based critical discourse analysis approach in comparing the keywords, concordances and collocations of the original news discourses with those of their translated versions and, more importantly, between the translated news discourses produced by the different media outlets. It considers the contrastive differences between source and target language conventions and pays particular attention to translation shifts which are related to the ideological stances of the media outlets.

Binjian Qin's chapter "Reframing China in Conflicts: A Case Study of English Translation of the South China Sea Dispute" probes into the news reports on the South China Sea dispute and their English translations by China's multilingual news website Xinhuanet. It aims to examine how China is represented via re-narration of news discourse. The methodology used is another example of the application of appraisal theory, developed by Martin and White (2005), and the reframing strategies summarized by Baker (2006) in the translation-oriented perspective of narrative theory. Such theoretical bases are applied to investigate the embedded attitudinal deviation and the stance re-instantiation in the reframed news stories. This study employs the software NVivo 11 to build a corpus containing 91 pairs of Chinese-English news reports collected from Xinhuanet. The quantitative and qualitative analysis shows that Xinhuanet re-instantiates its news stance in the reframed news discourse: in the Chinese version, China is reported with a positive stance. It is depicted as the more powerful side which gives no compromise in this issue. In the English version, however, although China is still described in a positive stance, its superiority is not mentioned and it is portrayed as a side willing to ease the tension and solve the conflict through negotiation. This chapter argues that the possible causes of such deviation may be attributed to the consideration of different target readerships, to Xinhuanet's institutional protocol as a political mouthpiece and to China's stated sociopolitical beliefs of peaceful rising.

Multimodal analysis is a very promising approach to discourse analysis. Public notices in the Chinese context represent a rich venue for the study of the interaction between the semiotic system of language and that of image in achieving meaning potentials. **Xi Chen**'s chapter "Translations of Public Notices in Macao: A Multimodal Perspective" draws on visual social semiotics (Kress and van Leeuwen 2006) in its analysis of the verbal realisation of the appellative function in the translation of public notices in Macao. The study incorporates the visual realisation of the interpersonal function in the images of public notices and the multimodal cooperation between language and image in public notices.

The last chapter presents another take on multimodal and intersemiotic discourse. **Marina Manfredi**'s chapter "Representation of Identity in Dubbed Italian Versions of Multicultural Sitcoms: An SFL Perspective" investigates the representation of multi-ethnic/multicultural identity in dubbed Italian versions of multicultural sitcoms using an SFL perspective. The main focus is on methodology, which links it to Xi Chen's chapter despite the difference in language pairs. Manfredi employs a functional, user-oriented model which examines identity through lexical choice (at the lexico-grammatical level) and dialect variation (at the phonological level) through analysis into examples of English dialogues in Italian-dubbed multicultural sitcoms. This multimodal framework has potential applications for other language pairs and contexts.

The contributions collected in this book demonstrate an advancement in a wide array of applicable discourse-analytical approaches to translation and interpreting studies including systemic-functional analysis, pragmatic and conversation analysis, critical discourse analysis, narrative analysis and corpus-based discourse analysis (Wang 2019: 625). We believe this book will provide not only meaningful data-based empirical findings through contrastive discourse analysis about translation and interpreting activities but also a rich source of conceptual and methodological tools at the interface of disciplines such as translation and interpreting studies, discourse analysis, linguistic studies and multimodal studies. By focusing on contrastive data analysis into translation and interpreting between Chinese and English, the collected efforts also have unique significance. Discourse analytical approaches have tended to be shaped by monolingual methodologies and analysis. We firmly believe that more effort is needed in exploring methods of conducting "contrastive discourse analysis on non-European languages whose conceptual structure may differ crucially" (Munday 2016: 160).

References

Baker, M. (2006) *Translation and Conflict: A Narrative Account*, London and New York: Routledge.
Kim, M., Munday, J., Wang, P. and Wang, Z. (eds.) (forthcoming) *Systemic Functional Linguistics and Translation Studies*, London and New York: Bloomsbury.
Kress, G. and van Leeuwen, T. (2006) *Reading Images: The Grammar of Visual Design* (2nd ed.), London: Routledge.
Martin, J. R. and White, P. R. R. (2005) *The Language of Evaluation: Appraisal in English*, Houndmills, Basingstoke: Palgrave Macmillan.
Mason, I. (2015) 'Discourse analytical approaches', in *Routledge Encyclopedia of Interpreting Studies*. F. Pöchhacker (ed.), London: Routledge. pp. 111–116.
Munday, J. (2016) *Introducing Translation Studies* (4th ed.), London and New York: Routledge.
Munday, J. and Zhang, M. (2015) 'Introduction: Special issue on discourse and translation', *Target* 27(3): 325–334.
Wang, B. (2019) 'Discourse analysis in Chinese translation and interpreting studies', in *The Routledge Handbook of Chinese Discourse Analysis*. S. Chris (ed.), Abingdon, UK: Routledge. pp. 613–629.
Wolf, M. (ed.) (2006) *Übersetzen – Translating – Traduire: Towards a 'Social Turn'?*, Münster, Hamburg, Berlin, Wien, and London: LIT-Verlag.
Zhang, M. and Munday, J. (2018) 'Introduction: Special issue on innovation in discourse analytic approaches to translation studies', *Perspectives* 26(2): 159–165.

Part I
Uncovering positioning and ideology in translation and interpreting

1 Presentation, re-presentation and perception of China's political discourse

An analysis about core concepts on the 'Belt and Road' based on a comparable corpus

Binhua Wang

Introduction

The important role of translation and interpreting (T&I), in particular the process of re-contextualisation, has remained under-explored in political discourse studies, which has "led to the assumption that information can circulate unaltered across different linguistic communities and cultures" (Bielsa 2009: 14). According to Pérez-González (2012), the reasons for such a phenomenon lie in the following two aspects: On the one hand, the tendency of global media analysts to concentrate on the advantages of the monolingual strategy adopted by powerful Anglophone media corporations (including the instantaneity in the processes of information dissemination) has "obscured the complexities involved in overcoming cultural and linguistic barriers, and made the role of translation in global communications invisible" (Bielsa and Bassnett 2009: 18). On the other hand, there are widespread social misconceptions about T&I which perceive T&I only as a routine and uncritical equivalence-matching process while power differentials between the parties involved in the production and negotiation of meaning are often viewed erroneously as being invariable in T&I (Pérez-González 2012: 172).

Meanwhile, in the field of translation studies, a noteworthy development is the conceptualisation of T&I as socially situated activities and translators and interpreters as agents of not only linguistic and communicative mediation but also cultural and ideological mediation (e.g. Inghilleri 2003). After the emergence of the linguistic school of translation studies from the 1950s to the 1980s that centred on the concept of 'equivalence' between the source text and the target text, there followed the "cultural turn" in the 1990s that expanded its scope of research to include cultural aspects. In the past decade the discipline has shown increasing awareness of the need to adopt a more critical stance towards the relationship between discursive practices and their social embedding, which is labelled by some scholars as the "social turn" (e.g. Wolf 2006; Angelelli 2012), and particularly the role of power in discursive practice, which is proposed by Tymoczko and Gentzler (2002) as the "power turn". Such a perspective is also articulated by Baker (2006: 322), who argues that

> it is far more productive to examine contextualisation as a dynamic process of negotiation and one that is constrained by the uneven distribution of power which characterizes all exchanges in society, including those that are mediated by translators and interpreters.

While the cultural turn and the social turn have successfully expanded the horizon of translation studies from linguistic analysis at the micro-level to socio-cultural and ideological analysis at the macro-level, the following issues remain to be further explored: (1) How may micro-analysis be linked to macro-analysis of the context, to the role of translators and interpreters and to the function of T&I in society and international communication? 2) How may socio-cultural studies be better validated with linguistic, textual and discourse analysis? A notable recent development in translation studies is the effort to link linguistic and discourse analysis with socio-cultural and ideological interpretations, which is represented by the special issue of the *Target* journal on "discourse analysis in translation studies" (Munday and Zhang 2015). Translation "presents a fertile research area for comparative or *multilingual* Critical Discourse Analysis (CDA)" (Al-Hejin 2012: 312). Chilton (2004: xii) has already alluded to that potential, stating that translation "pose[s] more intriguing, and politically urgent, challenges for scholars in a world that is both more global and more fragmented". As Schäffner (2004: 145) also suggests, translations can function as part of wider strategic functions of political language, which she identifies as: *coercion, resistance, dissimulation* and *(de)legitimation*. CDA, whose explicit aim is to "make the ideological loading of particular ways of using language and the relations of power which underlie them more visible" (Wodak and Fairclough 1997: 258), may provide a better understanding of the translation of ideology by elucidating the way discourse shapes and is shaped by ideology (Hatim and Mason 1997: 119).

Most political discourse research has been conducted from the perspectives of political science, communication studies, rhetoric studies, pragmatics, sociolinguistics and discourse analysis. While useful research findings have been produced from those perspectives, the understanding of translated/interpreted political discourse is quite limited because an important factor has often been neglected: the role of translators and interpreters as "unknown agents in translated political discourse" (Schäffner 2004, 2012) and in re-contextualising political discourse for international audiences.

As seen from the perspective of interpreting and translation studies, the presentation, re-presentation and perception of political discourse is not only a site for interlingual, cross-cultural and international communication but also a venue for re-contextualisation and manipulation of values, power and ideology.

This chapter will examine how Chinese political concepts presented by the Chinese government are re-contextualized in English with the presentation, re-presentation and perception of the discourse on the 'Belt and Road'. The Belt and

Road is a grand scheme initially proposed by President Xi Jinping of China in late 2013 to revive the Silk Road on both land and sea, which is not only central in China's development agenda and promotion of its influence and soft power but also relevant to many other countries in Asia, Europe and Africa. The Belt and Road has become a core concept in China's political and economic agenda during the past few years. As it involves huge investment of billions of dollars and lots of development projects along the routes of the Belt and Road, it is also meaningful to many other countries. However, it seems that the process of international communication about its concepts and implementation plans has not been an easy one. For example, CNN in the United States asked in the title of its news report about 'One Belt and One Road' in 2017: "Just what is the One Belt, One Road thing anyway?" .[1] The Xinhua News Agency in China also asked in 2015: "Will poor translation mislead China's Silk Road initiative?"[2] Both point to the confusion over the core concepts about the Belt and Road in their re-presentation and perception in international communication.

Therefore, it will be interesting to examine how the Belt and Road is presented in the original Chinese discourse, re-presented in English translation and perceived by Western media. It will also be interesting to see whether and how the perceptions by Western media have changed during the past few years. In this chapter, two sets of research questions will be explored as follows: (a) How is the B&R labelled in the Chinese government's presented discourse and its re-presented discourse through institutional translation? How is it labelled in the perceived discourse by English media? (b) Is the image of the B&R constructed in the perceived discourse the same as in the re-presented discourse? If different, how is the image of the B&R constructed differently in the perceived discourse with discoursal resources?

Data and methodology

Data: A comparable corpus of discourse on the Belt and Road

In order to examine these research questions, a comparable corpus of discourse on the Belt and Road (B&R) was built on the corpus platform of Sketch Engine,[3] which includes the following two sub-corpora:

1 The "Sub-corpus of China's Translated Discourse on B&R in 2015–2018" (abbreviated as "CD on B&R"), which includes seven addresses and statements presented by top officials of the Chinese government on the Belt and Road published between 2015 and 2018 on the websites of www.china.org.cn and www.xinhuanet.com, two official portals of the Chinese government for publishing its policies. All the addresses and statements were translated (or re-presented in English) by its institutional staff translators. POS-tagged in the Sketch Engine, the size of the sub-corpus of "CD on B&R" is 29,054 words

2 The "Sub-corpus of *The Economist* on B&R in 2015–2018" (abbreviated as "TE on B&R"), including 26 articles on the Belt and Road published between

2015 and 2018 in *The Economist*, an English-language weekly magazine-format newspaper published in the UK with a circulation of 1.5 million worldwide that 'offers authoritative insight and opinion on international news, politics, business, finance, science, technology and the connections between them',[4] which makes it representative among Western media. Parts of speech (POS)-tagged in the Sketch Engine, the size of the sub-corpus of "TE on B&R" is 30,219 words.

Information about the texts collected for the comparable corpus in summarised in Table 1.1. As can be seen from the table, both sub-corpora comprise texts on the same subject matter, that is the 'B&R' and their corpus sizes are nearly the same, which means the two sub-corpora are comparable.

Methodology

While previous literature on the translation and interpreting of China's political discourse tend to be prescriptive or descriptive based on isolated examples rather than being critical based on systematic analysis about complete discourse,

Table 1.1 The comparable corpus of discourse on the Belt and Road

Sub-corpora	Corpus size	Texts collected for the corpora
"CD on B&R"	29,054 words	2015: NDRC, action plan on the China-proposed Belt and Road Initiative; 2015: President Xi Jiping, speech at the Bo'ao Forum for Asia; 2015: State Councillor Yang Jiechi, the session of "Jointly Building the 21st Century Maritime Silk Road" in Bo'ao Forum for Asia; 2016: Chairman of the National People's Congress Zhang Dejiang, speech at the Belt and Road Forum in HK; 2017: President Xi Jinping, speech at the World Economic Forum Annual Meeting; 2017: President Xi Jinping, opening speech of The Belt and Road Forum for International Cooperation; 2018: Foreign Minister Wang Yi, press conference after the 'Two Sessions'
"TE on B&R"	30,219 words	2015: Five articles related to the B&R, e.g., "Where all Silk Roads lead", etc. 2016: Five articles related to the B&R, e.g., "Foreign policy. Our bulldozers, our rules", etc. 2017: 14 articles related to the B&R, e.g., "China's grand project. Where the twain shall meet', etc. 2018 (until June): Two articles related to the B&R, e.g., 'Xi vs. Marshall', etc.

the current study will be based on a relatively large-scale comparable corpus of China's political discourse including presented, re-presented and perceived discourses, which will ensure a solid data-based description, interpretation and explanation of political discourse. As Baker et al. (2008) rightly highlighted, the combination of discourse analysis and corpus linguistics is "a useful methodological synergy".

In terms of methodology, the current study will be characterised with three features: (1) Validating discourse analysis with quantitative data generated through corpus tools in order to offset the weakness of anecdotal example analysis in previous literature; (2) combination of synchronic comparison among presented, re-presented and perceived discourses on the same subject matter and diachronic comparison across different periods of their communication; (3) combination of macro-analysis and micro-analysis, which is a useful form of triangulation in discourse analysis, by combining "close qualitative readings with a corpus linguistics approach" (Baker and Levon 2015). Therefore, the whole study is designed in the "triangulatory approach", which can function "as a means of producing a better (more complete, rigorous, interesting and/or deeper) analysis" (Baker and Levon 2015).

As the first step of analysis, the study will compare the labelling of the B&R in the translated discourse from the Chinese government and in the English discourse from *The Economist* in order to see whether there are any differences in labelling of the B&R between the re-presented discourse of the Chinese government and the perceived discourse of Western media. It will also examine the evolution of labelling of the B&R in the two groups of discourse to see how the labels correspond between the re-presented discourse and the perceived discourse. In other words, the first step of analysis will be featured with synchronic comparison and diachronic comparison.

In the second step of the analysis, a macro-analysis based on the comparable corpus will be conducted through a comparison of the keyword lists generated from the two sub-corpora and a comparison of thesaurus sketch of the top keywords in the two sub-corpora, which intends to compare images of the B&R constructed in the re-presented discourse and in the perceived discourse.

The third step of the analysis will examine how the image of the B&R was constructed differently in the perceived discourse through a micro-analysis into the concordance lines of 'Belt', 'OBOR' and 'BRI' and into semantic prosody of the keywords about the B&R.

Labelling of the B&R

Evolution of labelling of the B&R in the presentation of Chinese government and in the re-presentation through translation

In September 2013 Chinese President Xi Jinping first proposed jointly building "the Silk Road Economic Belt" (丝绸之路经济带) during his visit to the country of Kazakhstan in Central Asia and then "the 21st-Century Maritime Silk Road" (21世纪海上丝绸之路) during his visit to Indonesia in Southeast Asia in October

2013. The two proposals were combined under a single label as "One Belt and One Road" (一带一路) by Chinese official media at the end of 2013.

Soon after that, One Belt and One Road (一带一路) was promoted as "a major development strategy of the country" (国家重大发展战略) by the Chinese government and Chinese media. For example, the "Report on the Work of the Government" (政府工作报告) to China's National Congress in March 2014 highlighted that "we will intensify the planning and building of a Silk Road economic belt and a 21st century maritime Silk Road".

In March 2015, the National Development and Reform Commission (国家发展和改革委员会) of China issued an official document on "Vision and Actions on Jointly Building Silk Road Economic Belt and 21st-Century Maritime Silk Road".

In September 2015, the National Development and Reform Commission together with Ministry of Foreign Affairs and Ministry of Commerce even issued an official document providing guidelines for translation of the core concepts about the Belt and Road,[5] including the following three points: (1) In international communication the complete translation of "丝绸之路经济带和21世纪海上丝绸之路" should be "the Silk Road Economic Belt and the 21st-Century Maritime Silk Road"; "一带一路" can be briefly translated as "the Belt and Road" (Acronym: B&R). (2) As for the labelling of the Belt and Road, the document specifically designated it as 'initiative' (倡议) in singular form while prohibiting the labelling of it as 'strategy', 'program', 'project' or 'agenda'. (3) The document also recommended the translation of "一带一路倡议" as "the Belt and Road Initiative" (abbreviated as BRI) or "the land and maritime Silk Road initiative".

Evolution of labelling of the B&R in the perception by The Economist

Queries for the words of 'Belt', 'OBOR', 'Silk Road', and 'BRI' in the sub-corpus of "TE on B&R" reveals the following evolution of labelling of the B&R in Western media as represented by *The Economist*:

In 2015–2016, the Belt and Road was first labelled as 'new Silk Road' (freq = 7) by *The Economist*. In 2015–2017, it was labelled for most of the time as 'One Belt, One Road' (freq = 21) or 'OBOR' (freq = 46). In 2018, it was labelled as 'Belt and Road Initiative' (freq = 7) or 'BRI' (freq = 12) but the previous label of 'One Belt, One Road' or 'OBOR' (freq = 20) still persisted.

It will be also interesting to compare the evolution of labelling of the B&R between the re-presentation by China's own translation and the perception by *The Economist*, as is shown in Table 1.2.

As can be observed from Table 1.2, there is an obvious time lag and discrepancy in labelling of the B&R between China's own re-presentation and Western media's perception exemplified by *The Economist*. Right after the B&R was initially proposed by the Chinese president in September and October 2013, the first formal labelling of it by the Chinese government and media at the end of 2013 as 'One Belt, One Road' (一带一路) has been the most influential label of the B&R, especially in the perception by Western media. Though the label was introduced by *The Economist* initially with elaboration of its signified meaning, that is, 'new

Table 1.2 Evolution of labelling of the B&R in China's own re-presentation through translation and in the perception by *The Economist*

	Sept. and Oct. 2013–2019	Late 2013–2019	Sept. 2015–2019	
Re-presentation	'the Silk Road Economic Belt' and 'the 21st-Century Maritime Silk Road'	'One Belt and One Road'	'Belt and Road Initiative' or 'BRI'	
			2015–2017	*2018–2019*
Perception			'new Silk Road'; 'One Belt, One Road' or 'OBOR'	'Belt and Road Initiative' or 'BRI'; 'One Belt, One Road' or 'OBOR'

Silk Road', the label of 'One Belt, One Road' and its acronym 'OBOR' persisted in Western media's perception until the end of 2017. The institutional and proactive re-translation or re-labelling of the B&R by the Chinese government in September 2015 was reflected only after over two years in Western media's perception in 2018.

Comparison of images of the B&R constructed in re-presented discourse and in perceived discourse: a macro-analysis based on the comparable corpus

Comparison of the keyword list: positive image in re-presentation vs. neutral to negative image in perception

Keyword lists were generated through the corpus-analytic tool of Sketch Engine from the "Sub-corpus of CD on B&R" and the "Sub-corpus of TE on B&R". The top-35 keyword lists of the two sub-corpora are compared in Table 1.3.

As seen from the keyword list of the "Sub-corpus of CD on B&R", the following keywords of three categories are used in China's own re-presented discourse to describe and define the nature of the B&R:

1 Synonyms of the B&R, such as Belt, Road, Silk (Road), Maritime (Route) and Initiative.
2 Main agents involved in the B&R, such as Xi Jinping, Bo'ao (Forum for Asia) and SCO (Shanghai Cooperation Organisation).
3 Description of the B&R, such as cooperation, inclusiveness, multilateral, economic globalization, win-win cooperation, mutual learning, regional cooperation, common development, practical cooperation, mutual benefit, common destiny, shared future, maritime cooperation, global governance, global growth, economic cooperation, financial cooperation.

16 *Binhua Wang*

Table 1.3 Comparison of the keyword lists between the two sub-corpora

Sub-corpus of CD on B&R			Sub-corpus of TE on B&R		
Item	Score of keyness	Freq	Item	Score of keyness	Freq
Belt	1567.43	213	OBOR	1289.13	46
Silk	719.66	90	AIIB	1008.17	36
cooperation	433.41	281	Xi	906.91	106
Maritime	345.1	40	Jinping	442.01	22
maritime	170.27	28	SOEs	656.88	26
ASEAN	313.88	27	SOE	322.9	12
Cooperation	310.14	32	Soe	284.82	14
Jinping	308.01	14	CPEC	445.73	16
Xi	234.28	25	Silk	350.89	48
Initiative	301.25	91	Xinjiang	311.65	21
Boao	270.77	9	BRI	299.34	12
SCO	239.47	13	Belt	208.68	31
Road	212.33	296	hegemon	181.16	7
inclusiveness	210.26	10	Gwadar	155.77	6
multilateral	206.1	16	multilateral	153.14	13
economic globalization	807.71	27	soft power	645.35	23
win-win cooperation	614.12	20	Chinese investment	561.3	20
mutual learning	504.5	17	direct investment	145.65	9
global economy	472.71	21	state broadcaster	141.07	5
regional cooperation	389.4	13	Chinese money	141.07	5
common development	382.69	13	Chinese firm	113.06	4
practical cooperation	362.71	12	hard power	112.16	4
mutual benefit	313.28	15	high-speed rail	91.84	4
common destiny	292.08	10	Chinese dream	85.05	3
community of common destiny	276.9	9	regional hegemon	85.05	3
maritime cooperation	276.9	9	Asian infrastructure	85.05	3
major-country diplomacy	246.25	8	Chinese government	84.71	6
global governance	246.25	8	Chinese aid	84.37	3
shared future	244.29	8	Chinese president	84.37	3
ancient silk road	242.13	8	economic diplomacy	82.89	3
global growth	235.87	8	Chinese leader	82.89	3

world peace	211.91	11	multilateral system	82.17	3
human civilization	201.3	7	big role	81.46	3
economic cooperation	187.31	7	common destiny	80.76	3
financial cooperation	184.94	6	other infrastructure	78.75	3

The keyword list of the "Sub-corpus of TE on B&R" indicates that in Western media's discourse of perception about the B&R, there are also three types of keywords describing and defining its nature but with rather different implicatures:

1 Synonyms of the B&R, such as OBOR, Silk (Road), BRI, Belt (and Road).
2 Main agents involved in the B&R, such as Xi Jinping, AIIB (Asian Infrastructure Investment Bank), SOE (state-owned enterprises), Chinese firm, Chinese government, Chinese president and Chinese leader.
3 Description of the B&R, such as hegemon, multilateral, soft power, hard power, regional hegemon, Asian infrastructure, economic diplomacy, multilateral system, etc.

Though the discourses in the two sub-corpora are about the same subject matter, that is, the B&R, the comparison between the keyword lists from them represent two different images about the B&R. A rather positive image of the B&R was constructed in the discourse (re)presented by the Chinese government, which is evident especially in the third category of keywords that describes and define the nature of the B&R, for example, 'cooperation', 'inclusiveness', 'common development', 'mutual benefit', etc. In contrast, a neutral to negative image was reconstructed about the B&R in the discourse perceived by *The Economist*, which is also evident particularly in the third category of keywords defining and describing the nature and content of the B&R, for example, 'hegemon', 'soft power', 'hard power', etc.

Thesaurus sketch of the top keywords in the re-presentation and in perception

What is the 'B&R' in China's re-presented discourse? A thesaurus sketch of the top keyword 'Belt' in the "Sub-corpus of CD on B&R" (Figure 1.1) tells vividly that the 'B&R' is first and foremost a 'route', 'road' and 'corridor'. It is mainly about development. It was proposed as an 'initiative' for 'construction'. It proposes such concepts as 'cooperation', 'partnership', 'opening-up' and 'integration'.

What is the 'B&R' in Western media's perceived discourse? A thesaurus sketch of the top keyword 'OBOR' in the "Sub-corpus of TE on B&R" (Figure 1.2) reveals that the 'B&R' is first and foremost about 'AIIB' (Asian Infrastructure Investment

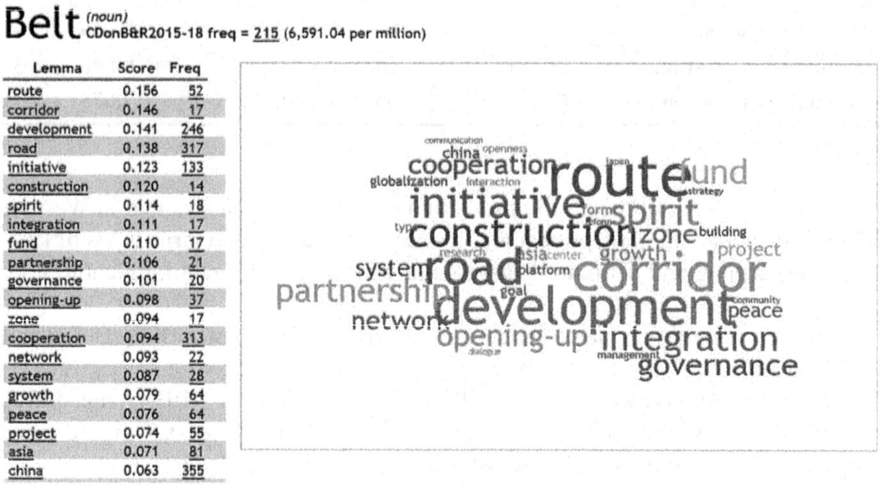

Belt (noun) CDonB&R2015-18 freq = 215 (6,591.04 per million)

Lemma	Score	Freq
route	0.156	52
corridor	0.146	17
development	0.141	246
road	0.138	317
initiative	0.123	133
construction	0.120	14
spirit	0.114	18
integration	0.111	17
fund	0.110	17
partnership	0.106	21
governance	0.101	20
opening-up	0.098	37
zone	0.094	17
cooperation	0.094	313
network	0.093	22
system	0.087	28
growth	0.079	64
peace	0.076	64
project	0.074	55
asia	0.071	81
china	0.063	355

Figure 1.1 Thesaurus sketch of the top keyword 'Belt' in the "Sub-corpus of CD on B&R"

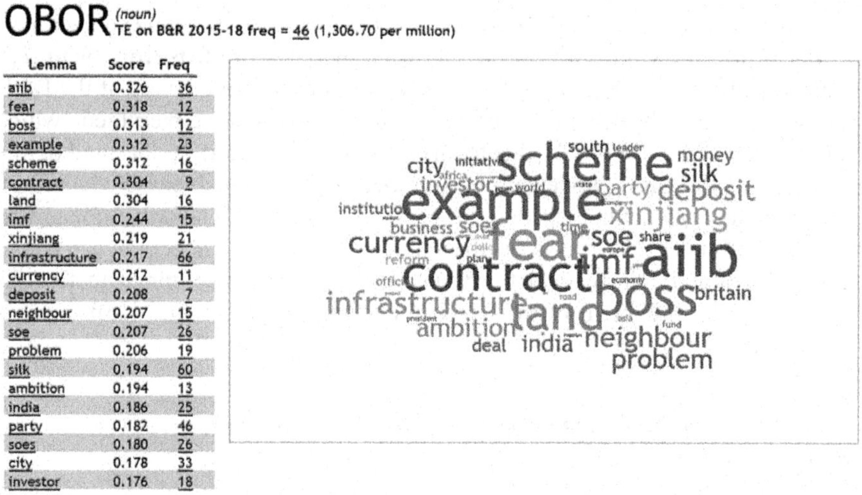

OBOR (noun) TE on B&R 2015-18 freq = 46 (1,306.70 per million)

Lemma	Score	Freq
aiib	0.326	36
fear	0.318	12
boss	0.313	12
example	0.312	23
scheme	0.312	16
contract	0.304	9
land	0.304	16
imf	0.244	15
xinjiang	0.219	21
infrastructure	0.217	66
currency	0.212	11
deposit	0.208	7
neighbour	0.207	15
soe	0.207	26
problem	0.206	19
silk	0.194	60
ambition	0.194	13
india	0.186	25
party	0.182	46
soes	0.180	26
city	0.178	33
investor	0.176	18

Figure 1.2 Thesaurus sketch of the top keyword 'OBOR' in the "Sub-corpus of TE on B&R"

Bank), a multilateral development bank that was originally proposed and launched by China and has been perceived as a potential rival to the World Bank and the International Monetary Fund (IMF). Though it is seen as an 'example' and 'scheme' involving 'contract' and 'infrastructure', it is perceived with 'fear'. Some 'problems' are perceived as being related to it, such as 'Xinjiang', 'neighbour' and 'ambition'.

Therefore, the thesaurus sketches of the top keyword 'Belt' in the two sub-corpora reveal again that while the image re-presented by the Chinese government is rather positive, the image perceived by Western media is between neural and negative.

Presentation, re-presentation and perception 19

How is the image of the B&R constructed differently in the perceived discourse: a micro-analysis into concordance lines and semantic prosody of the keywords

With the corpus tool of KWIC, the concordance lines of 'Belt', 'OBOR' and 'BRI' were extracted from the sub-corpus "TE on B&R". A micro-analysis will be done in this section to examine the concordance lines and semantic prosody of the keywords about the B&R. While concordance line is a straightforward concept in corpus linguistics, semantic prosody can be understood as semantic classes of the collocates of a keyword characterised in terms of attitudinal meaning. "When the usage of a word gives an impression of an attitudinal or pragmatic meaning, this is called a semantic prosody" (Sinclair 1999). It is "the spreading of connotational colouring beyond single word boundaries" (Partington 1998: 68). Stubbs (1996) categorised semantic prosody into three types: positive, neutral and negative, which will be used as a framework for analysis in this section.

Labelling of the B&R is perceived with negative semantic prosody

As seen from Concordance Lines Group 1, it is perceived by *The Economist* that the label of the B&R – the 'Silk Road Economic Belt and 21st Century Maritime Silk Road' – as initially proposed by the Chinese government but 'mercifully shortened' by the Chinese media as 'One Belt and One Road', is one of the 'pithy but rather bewildering encapsulations' that are labelled 'confusingly'. Its acronym – 'OBOR' – is 'unlovely' and 'puzzles many Western policymakers'.

Table 1.4 Concordance Lines Group 1

TEdoc#1	With the flair that Chinese leaders share for **pithy but rather bewildering encapsulations**, his vision for the continent is summed up in official jargon as "One Belt, One Road".
TEdoc#6	Chinese officials call that policy "One Belt, One Road", though they often eviscerate its exotic appeal to foreigners by using the **unlovely acronym** OBOR.
TEdoc#6	**Confusingly,** the road refers to ancient maritime routes between China and Europe, while the belt describes the Silk Road's better-known trails overland (see map).
TEdoc#6	OBOR **puzzles** many Western policymakers because it is **amorphous** – it has no official list of member countries, though the rough count is 60 – and because most of the projects that sport the label would probably have been built anyway.
TEdoc#10	Over 60 countries will, for example, supposedly benefit from Mr Xi's nostalgic vision of a revived Silk Road (the "Silk Road Economic Belt and 21st Century Maritime Silk Road", **mercifully shortened to** "One Belt, One Road", or OBOR).
TEdoc#12	The "belt", **confusingly,** is a "New Silk Road": a set of roads, railways and power projects aiming to tie China's western regions more closely to Central Asia and eventually to Europe.
TEdoc#12	The "road" part of the rubric, **equally confusingly,** is a "Maritime Silk Road" intended to link China's landlocked south-west to South-East Asia, the Indian Ocean and beyond.

20 Binhua Wang

Content of the B&R Initiative is perceived with neutral and negative semantic prosody

As is shown in Concordance Lines Group 2, the Belt and Road Initiative is perceived by *The Economist* with neutral and negative semantic prosody. In some cases, the perception is neutral: The BRI "matters" for "big reasons"; it "matters" because "it is important" to the Chinese government led by Mr Xi; it "matters" "because it is a challenge to the United States and its traditional way of thinking about world trade"; it "matters" because it "looks likely to be the toast of Western boardrooms". In other cases, the perception is negative with indication about 'problems'.

As seen from Concordance Lines Group 3, the Belt and Road Initiative is perceived by *The Economist* as being "grandiose" that they (the Chinese government) "boast" about. It is "vague but much-vaunted". It is a "wheeze" that is "much ballyhooed", which means that though it gets much promotion and attention it does

Table 1.5 Concordance Lines Group 2

TEdoc#6	But OBOR **matters** for three big reasons.
TEdoc#6	Next, OBOR **matters** because it is important to Mr Xi.
TEdoc#6	Third, OBOR **matters** because it is a challenge to the United States and its traditional way of thinking about world trade.
TEdoc#20	For years to come, OBOR looks likely to be **the toast of Western boardrooms**, too.
TEdoc#6	Yet while OBOR gathers momentum it is also encountering **problems**.
TEdoc#6	**Problems** have arisen too with OBOR's leadership.

Table 1.6 Concordance Lines Group 3

TEdoc#6	OBOR, they **boast**, is open to all.
TEdoc#14	Chinese officials describe the far western province of Xinjiang as a "core area" in the vast swathe of territory covered by the country's **grandiose** "Belt and Road Initiative" to boost economic ties with Central Asia and regions beyond.
TEdoc#16	At his **much ballyhooed** "Belt and Road Forum", the Chinese leader laid out what was intended to look like a new global economic order: . . .
TEdoc#19	India has also sharply criticised China's broader, pan-Asian Belt and Road Initiative as a **boondoggle** that will trap smaller countries in debt.
TEdoc#23	For China, central Europe is at best a minor element of a larger Eurasian strategy linked to its "One Belt, One Road" infrastructure **wheeze**.
TEdoc#25	China's **vague but much-vaunted** Belt and Road Initiative (BRI) has been providing buzzword fodder for government leaders and official sloganeers since 2013, when the country launched the scheme to extend its political and economic influence abroad by investing in infrastructure and other big projects.

Table 1.7 Concordance Lines Group 4

TEdoc#6	OBOR **is supposed to** extend Chinese commercial influence, reduce the Chinese economy's dependence on investment in infrastructure at home and export a little of China's vast excess capacity in steel and cement.
TEdoc#6	OBOR, officials believe, is **a good way of packaging such a strategy**.
TEdoc#18	The "One Belt, One Road" strategy – the core of Mr Xi's foreign policy – has **made foreign expansion an explicit part** of their mandate.

not deserve the attention it is getting. It is "a boondoggle", which means a plan or project, especially one created by the government, that wastes a lot of time and money.

Concordance Lines Group 4 show that what the Belt and Road Initiative wants to achieve and has achieved is perceived by *The Economist* with suspicion, which can be seen from the semantic prosody of Concordance Line TEdoc#6. Here the BRI is perceived to be proposed and implemented only for China's benefits, including extending its commercial influence, reducing its dependence on investment in infrastructure at home and exporting its excess capacity in steel and cement. According to the perceived discourse, the BRI is "a good way of packaging such a strategy", which aims for "foreign expansion".

Conclusion

It is found through analyses in this chapter that labels of the B&R in Western media's perceived discourse are somewhat different from the Chinese government's presented and re-presented discourse. There is an obvious time lag and discrepancy in labelling of the B&R between China's own re-presentation and Western media's perception. The initial label of it by the Chinese official media at the end of 2013 as 'One Belt, One Road' and its acronym 'OBOR' had dominated the labelling of the B&R in Western media's perceived discourse until the end of 2017 and have even persisted until now, which has caused confusion and misconception about the B&R. A more positive formal re-labelling of the B&R that was later introduced by the National Reform and Development Commission of China in its guidelines about translation of the B&R in Sep 2015 was reflected only after over two years in the perceived discourse of *The Economist*, in mid-2018. Though the guidelines introduced the keyword of 'initiative' to define the name and nature of the B&R in order to stress the openness of the grand scheme and to avoid criticisms over China-centredness in the BRI, such an effort in changing the perception of Western media has not been very successful.

It is also revealed that the image of the B&R as constructed in Western media's perceived discourse is different from the Chinese government's re-presented discourse. As seen from the comparison of the keyword lists between the re-presented discourse and perceived discourse, the overall image of the B&R has changed from positive in re-presentation to neutral and negative in perception. The micro-analysis about the concordance lines and about semantic prosody of the keywords, not only the labelling of the B&R is perceived with negative semantic prosody but also the content of the B&R Initiative is perceived with neutral and negative semantic prosody by Western media.

From the analyses into the re-contextualisation process of the core concepts about the B&R in international communication, we can see the important role of discoursal resources in image building. The original Chinese discourse of the B&R was initially presented with unique Chinese characteristics, which is particularly evident in the encapsulation of 'the Silk Road Economic Belt and 21st-Century Maritime Silk Road' as 'One Belt and One Road' (一带一路). Such unique labelling of the B&R with Chinese characteristics has brought difficulty to the translation or re-presentation process at the initial stage of its international communication, which in turn created confusion in the perceived discourse about the B&R in Western media. Though re-presentation of core concepts about the B&R through institutional translation has had gradual changes towards formalization, especially with the issuance of the guideline document by the China National Development and Reform Commission, such a framing action was passive rather than active, which did not achieved its goal of elaborating the name and nature of the B&R effectively.

While this chapter highlights the importance of recognising the effect of translation as mediation and intervention in international media communication, it must also be pointed out that the discrepancy between presentation, re-presentation and particularly perception about core concepts of the B&R can be partly attributed to different positioning of different agents and partly due to the fact that the Chinese government has not gained the initiative in re-presenting the discourse in English.

Notes

1 Griffiths, J. 'Just What Is This One Belt, One Road Thing Anyway?' Available at: https://edition.cnn.com/2017/05/11/asia/china-one-belt-one-road-explainer/index.html
2 'Will Poor Translation Mislead China's Silk Road Initiative?' Available at: www.xinhuanet.com/english/2015-06/30
3 Sketch Engine. Available at: http://app.sketchengine.eu
4 'About *The Economist*'. Available at: www.economist.com/about-the-economist
5 西部开发司子站 (Website of the Department of Western Development, NDRC). '国家发改委会同外交部、商务部等部门对"一带一路"英文译法进行了规范' (The National Development and Reform Commission together with Ministry of Foreign Affairs and Ministry of Commerce issued regulation guidelines for English translation of the concepts about the Belt and Road). Available at: www.ndrc.gov.cn/gzdt/201509/t20150921_751695.html

References

Al-Hejin, B. (2012) 'Linking critical discourse analysis with translation studies: An example from BBC News', *Journal of Language and Politics* 11(3): 311–335.
Angelelli, C. (2012) 'Introduction: The sociological turn in translation and interpreting studies', *Translation and Interpreting Studies* 7(2): 125–128.
Baker, M. (2006) 'Contextualization in translator- and interpreter-mediated events', *Journal of Pragmatics* 38: 321–337.

Baker, P., et al. (2008) 'A useful methodological synergy? Combining critical discourse analysis and corpus linguistics to examine discourses of refugees and asylum seekers in the UK press', *Discourse & Society* 19(3): 273–305.

Baker, P. and Levon, E. (2015) 'Picking the right cherries? A comparison of corpus-based and qualitative analyses of news articles about masculinity', *Discourse & Communication* 9(2): 221–236.

Bielsa, E. (2009) 'Globalization, political violence and translation: An introduction', in *Globalization, Political Violence and Translation*. E. Bielsa and C. Hughes (eds.), Basingstoke: Palgrave Macmillan. pp. 1–21.

Bielsa, E. and Bassnett, S. (2009) *Translation in Global News*, London and New York: Routledge.

Chilton, P. (2004) *Analysing Political Discourse: Theory and Practice*, London: Routledge.

Hatim, B. and Mason, I. (1997) *The Translator as Communicator*, London: Routledge.

Inghilleri, M. (2003) 'Habitus, field and discourse: Interpreting as a socially situated activity', *Target* 15(2): 243–268.

Munday, J. and Zhang, M. (eds.) (2015) *Target*, Special issue on discourse and translation. *Target* 27(3).

Partington, A. (1998) *Patterns and Meaning: Using Corpora for English Language Research and Teaching*, Amsterdam: John Benjamins.

Pérez-González, L. (2012) 'Translation, interpreting and the genealogy of conflict', *Journal of Language and Politics* 11(2): 169–184.

Schäffner, C. (2004) 'Political discourse analysis from the point of view of translation studies', *Journal of Language and Politics* 3(1): 117–150.

Schäffner, C. (2012) 'Unknown agents in translated political discourse', *Target* 24(1): 103–125.

Sinclair, J. (1999) 'Concordance tasks'. Available at: www.twc.it/happen.html (Accessed: June 2018). The Tuscan Word Centre.

Stubbs, M. (1996) *Text and Corpus Analysis: Computer-Assisted Studies of Language and Culture*, Oxford: Blackwell.

Tymoczko, M. and Gentzler, E. (eds.) (2002) *Translation and Power*, Amherst: University of Massachusetts Press.

Wodak, R. and Fairclough, N. (1997) 'Critical discourse analysis', in *Discourse as Social Interaction*. T. A. van Dijk (ed.), London: Sage. pp. 258–284.

Wolf, M. (ed.) (2006) *Übersetzen – Translating – Traduire: Towards a 'Social Turn'?*, Münster, Hamburg, Berlin, Wien, and London: LIT-Verlag.

2 From linguistic manipulation to discourse reconstruction
A case study of conference interpreting at the World Economic Forum in China

Fei Gao

Introduction

Translation and interpreting studies (T&I) is canonically concerned with the language in use in cross-cultural communications, yet it goes beyond the language proper. Scholarship in T&I predominantly emanates from the languages of source texts (STs) and target texts (TTs), then ascends to higher levels of language functions, discourse and the contexts for the communicative activity of translation/interpreting. This research paradigm in T&I resonates with that of discourse analysis, which "examines patterns of the language across texts and considers the relationship between language and the social and cultural context in which it is used" (Paltridge 2012: 1). Critical discourse analysis (CDA), in particular, approaches texts with an emphasis on the critical examination of institutional, social, political and cultural structures that frame the discourse (Fairclough and Wodak 1997: 55).

There is an increasing body of T&I literature that harnesses the CDA perspective for close examination of linguistic elements in STs and TTs (e.g. Beaton 2007; Beaton-Thome 2013; Schäffner 2012, 2015; Munday 2012; Pan 2015; Zhang and Pan 2015; Wang and Feng 2017; Munday and Zhang 2017; Gu 2018). With the shared recognition that "discourse analysis is holistic, dealing with entire constituents of an act of communication" (Munday and Zhang 2015: 327), these contributions examine STs and TTs contrastively, uncovering translation/interpreting shifts at the language level. For example, Schäffner (2012, 2015) interrogates, with a comparative lens, a plethora of linguistic resources, such as metaphors, interpersonal expressions, EU-specific terminologies, naming choices, formal or informal pronoun selections and turn-taking expressions, all of which are used to point to critical elements of the discourse under investigation.

Nonetheless, there is a conundrum facing T&I researchers. On the one hand, CDA, as an analytical perspective, is devoid of a "guiding theoretical viewpoint that is consistently used within CDA" (Meyer 2001: 18). On the other hand, ample linguistic resources presented in T&I research, if not confusing, could leave scholars spoiled for choices. The "systematic and explicit analysis", as the 'core' for CDA (van Dijk 1997: xxiii) requires T&I scholars to systematically utilise linguistic theories, systems, or frameworks to usefully guide and inform CDA-oriented investigation.

The language of *evaluation*, among others, provides an efficacious departure point for exploring discourse critically in T&I. Evaluation encompasses broad linguistic resources that are used to express personal/interpersonal attitudes, viewpoints and stances (Hunston and Thompson 2000). Therefore, evaluation is "central to communication and central to translation" and exists pervasively in discourse (Munday 2012: 11).

This chapter, hence, intends to make use of evaluative shifts in simultaneous conference interpreting, with an aim at uncovering how interpreters manipulate evaluative resources to reconstruct TT discourse. There are two research questions:

RQ 1: What are the salient patterns of interpreters' reconstruction in the TT discourse?

RQ 2: What linguistic strategies do interpreters use to manipulate STs discursively?

Theoretical frameworks and relevant T&I literature

The purpose of this section is to foreground, situate and justify relevant theories and approaches for the case study. First, the rationale for using SFL tools in CDA studies is offered. Then the concept of evaluation is explained with an emphasis on a linguistic theory – appraisal theory – that systematically theorizes evaluation. Finally, its applications in relevant T&I studies are reviewed.

CDA and SFL

CDA-informed studies tie strongly with systemic functional linguistics (SFL) for its conceptualisations of language in use as an analytical toolkit. CDA, developed from discourse analysis by linguists such as Roger Fowler and Gunther Kress in the 1970s, shares three commonalities with SFL. First, both CDA and SFL position the language in a social context. Second, both acknowledge the reciprocal effects between individual discourse and the context where it takes place. Third, they both approach the analysis of language with an emphasis on the contextually construed meaning. Their common ground is traced back to CDA's origin, where Norman Fairclough's (1989) *Language and Power* based the CDA tenets and basic model largely on SFL systems. Lemke (1997) narrows the gap between textual and social analysis with a social semiotic model (Halliday 1978), which is also a major component of SFL.

The utility of SFL tools in CDA-informed T&I studies has a sound research foundation. T&I study is quintessentially the study of language(s): T&I scholars, with a critical lens, explore the language(s) of speakers and translators/interpreters contrastively. The focus then becomes the investigation of translator/interpreter linguistic choices, the choices made "between near-synonymous lexical items, between ideologically charged naming practices, between different configurations of transitivity, modality or thematic structure" (Munday and Zhang 2015: 326). This selection process can be explained conceptually by the Hallidayan social semiotic with 'meaning potentials' (Halliday 1978, 1994). The analysis of the selected and unselected in a particular context (often politically or ideologically charged) reveals translator/interpreter intervention, agency, or manipulation. CDA with SFL tools, therefore, has been frequently drawn upon by scholars in T&I studies (e.g. Wadensjö 2000; Hatim and Mason 2014; Munday 2012, 2015, 2018). These studies employ linguistic tools afforded by SFL theorisations, identifying and scrutinising the sites of translation/interpreting shifts with a critical prism that point to a myriad of relevant social, cultural, or political facets.

Evaluation and appraisal theory

The linguistic function of evaluation corresponds to SFL's interpersonal meta-function that, in Hallidayan term, enables enacting and negotiating personal and social relationships with others (Halliday and Matthiessen 2014). Evaluation, then, is described as the linguistic mechanism of authorial opinion and is not only a superordinate term but a broad cover concept for expressing "speaker or writer's attitude or stance towards, viewpoints on, or feelings about the entities or propositions that he or she is talking about" (Hunston and Thompson 2000: 5).

The concept of evaluation is studied with varying terminologies with different focal points. Most notable are 'affect' (Leech 1974), 'hedging' (Hyland 1994), 'evidentiality' (Aikhenval'd et al. 2004), 'stance' (Biber and Finegan 1988) and 'evaluation' (Bednarek 2006; Hunston 2013; Hunston and Thompson 2000). Despite varying focuses and uses of terminologies, these concepts share much common ground. This study uses the concept of evaluation due to its wider coverage. Hunston and Thompson (2000: 6) neatly summarise functions of evaluation three points:

(1) to express the speaker's or writer's option, and in doing so to reflect the values system of that person and their community;
(2) to construct and maintain relations between the speaker or writer and hearer or reader;
(3) to organise the discourse.

These functions are captured by a linguistic theory – appraisal theory – a framework developed by Martin and White (2005) from the SFL's interpersonal system. appraisal (short for appraisal theory) focuses on the functional and communicative aspects of language use (Halliday 1978; Halliday and Matthiessen 2014). Stemming from some early works of functional linguists (e.g. Eggins and Slade 1997; Martin 2000) in Australia, research on appraisal theory starts from theorising the attempt to disambiguating texts by positioning readers in certain ways (Bednarek 2006), then evolves from the early focus on attitudinal resources (being positive or negative with amplification or not) (Martin and Rose 2003), adoption of stance through positioning subjects (White 1999) to a more full-fledged system for analysing evaluative resources in three broad categories by Martin and White (2005). Martin (2000: 143) argues that attitudinal sources are not simply "a personal matter" but rather "a truly interpersonal matter", where advancing opinions means eliciting responses of solidarity from the audience. Then the early forms of attitude-oriented frameworks develop into three-pronged appraisal systems accounting for the variations of the inter-subjective stance, and "they operate rhetorically to construct relations of alignment and rapport between the writer/speaker and actual or potential respondents" (Martin and White 2005: 1–2).

Based on linguistic resources that belong to three semantic areas, appraisal theory conceptualises three systems: Attitude, engagement and graduation. Attitude is concerned with ways of feeling. Engagement is concerned with the scalability of the space (contraction and expansion) for introducing and managing other voices and positions. Graduation mainly concerns the gradability of attitudinal meaning (force and focus) (Martin and White 2005). The present study utilises the systems of attitude and graduation for data analysis.

Attitude, as the most basic and early form of evaluation, is prototypically realised through attitudinally loaded adjectives, or "evaluative epithets" (Halliday 1994: 184). The lexicogrammatical resources for the realisation of attitudinal meanings are ample and diverse, and they can be dichotomised into positive and negative polarities (see Table 2.1). Attitude can be further categorised into feelings (affect), moral evaluation of behaviour (judgement) and evaluation of the aesthetic quality of things or processes (appreciation) (Martin and White 2005).

The graduation system is related to the gradability of both attitudinal meanings with the scalable degrees of authorial intensity and the degree of investment in the proposition. As shown in Table 2.2, their semantic values are realised by the scale of intensification and down-toning (Martin and White 2005). There are two semantic categories: focus and force. Focus is dichotomised into prototypicality and non-prototypicality of phenomena, which can be upgraded as being *true* and *genuine* or downgraded as being *sort of* and *kind of*. Force assesses quantitatively or in terms of degrees, the

Table 2.1 Attitude system (adapted from Martin and White 2005)

	Attitude		
	Affect	Judgment	Appreciation
Positive evaluation	happy, joyful, cheerful	balanced, competent, expert	beautiful, worthwhile, balanced
Negative evaluation	upset, sad, fearful	imbalanced, incompetent, uneducated	ugly, worthless, discordant

Table 2.2 Graduation system (adapted from Martin and White 2005)

	Graduation	
	Focus	Force
Intensification	true, genuine, real	very, extremely, most
Down-toning	sort of, kind of, – ish	a few, little, merely

authorial investment or stance by either intensifying the value invested or down-toning it. Numerous linguistic resources of intensifiers and down-toners fall into this category.

Applications of appraisal theory in T&I research

Despite appraisal theory's origin in English monolingual studies, there is an emerging body of T&I studies deploying appraisal theory as a theoretical apparatus. They attest to the feasibility and utility for multi/cross-language investigations. Notably, Munday (2018) proposes a full model of appraisal for T&I scholarship. Among the three systems of appraisal, the attitude system seems to be most appealing to T&I scholars. For example, Pérez-González (2007) utilises the early attitude system of appraisal from Martin's (2000) model, unveiling translation shifts in dubbed conversations from English to Spanish. For the English and Chinese language pair, Zhang's (2009) work on social context and translation of public notices in English and Chinese sheds light on how the attitudinal meanings may shift cross-culturally towards text functions. In a similar vein, Zhang (2013) investigates attitudinal polarities in trans-editing news headlines in which she connects translator mediation and manipulation with stance-taking of news agencies. Munday (2012), with a slant towards attitudinal resources, systematically examines critical points of translator decision-making through applying an appraisal framework to evaluative locutions in ST political speeches and three versions of Spanish TT renditions.

There are a few studies applying engagement or graduation systems in T&I. Among the relatively more parsimonious amount of studies, Rosa (2009, 2013) look into abstract narratorial positioning in Portuguese translations of extracts of Charles Dickens novels. Vandepitte et al. (2011) probe shifts of epistemic modals in two versions of a Dutch translation of Darwin's *On the Origins of Species*. Also with a focus on engagement resources, Qian (2012) investigates speaker's positioning in STs and TTs of the Q&A section of former US Vice President Dick Cheney's speech at Fudan University. In addition to his early studies on attitude systems, Munday (2015) explores the other two strands of appraisal – engagement and graduation – through examining reporting verbs, deictic positioning and intensifiers in STs and TTs of international organizations. He tentatively depicts a distancing trend from the deictic centre and proposes downscaled intensification in terms of engagement values in TTs.

Methodologically instrumental are T&I studies that combine appraisal theory with other approaches and methods. For example, discourse analysis and CDA are interwoven into the analysis of the evaluative discursive resources (e.g. Zhang 2009, 2013; Wang and Feng 2017). The other useful methodological combination is the integration of corpus linguistics to this line of study. For instance, based on a literature-texts dominated Chinese-English corpus, Peng et al. (2012) usefully offer procedures of corpus building, annotation and enquiring with corpus tools, such as the UAM Corpus Tool for tagging and AMParaConc (APPRAISAL Meanings Parallel Concordancer, designed by a computer programmer on their team for the project) for the analytical purposes of appraisal resources. Wang and Feng (2017) efficaciously harness corpus techniques of keywords analysis, in conjunction with appraisal systems, for the investigation of stance-taking in conference interpreting.

Data and method of the case study

Corpus data for this study derive from a panel discussion of the 2016 Summer Davos, organised by the World Economic Forum (WEF). The panel discussion under investigation focuses on "*One Belt, One Road; Many Winners*",[1] a topic germane to economic and political relations between China and other world powers. The video recourses are publicly available online.

To build the English/Chinese interpreting corpus, videos are transcribed orthographically into written texts in English and Chinese. Punctuations (commas and full stops) are assigned to texts based on semantic units and pauses in the ST and TT speeches. The size of the bi-directional corpus is 16,487 words, which is evenly divided between the English → Chinese sub-corpus (8,632 words) and Chinese → English sub-corpus (7,855 words).

Three features of this interpreting corpus are considered in discourse analysis with a critical perspective. First, panelists who are native Chinese and English speakers depend on interpreter renditions for communication; TT evaluative shifts are subsumed into the 'triadic' communication, exerting direct repercussions on subsequent discourse. Second, interpreting is done simultaneously without scripts, since speakers are engaged in spontaneous discussions. Third, the two professional interpreters are Chinese nationals, and they are affiliated with the Chinese government organising the Summer Davos in China.

In terms of the method for the case study, the corpus-based CDA approach is operationalized through using two systems of appraisal theory – attitude and graduation[2] – which are deployed as prior theoretical frameworks for the semantic annotation[3] for corpus data. For this purpose, lexical examples are referenced from Martin and White (2005) for the English language, Peng et al. (2012) for the Chinese language, and Munday (2012) for appraisal shifts in translation/interpreting. Whilst the semantic annotation leverages the high delicacies of appraisal theory for referencing evaluative expressions at a word/phrase level, the analyses primarily utilise two levels of delicacies of attitude (positive evaluation and negative evaluation) and graduation (intensification and down-toning). The main rationale for using two levels is that the higher the levels of delicacy applied, the more researcher subjectivity involved, not least in generating corpus results. Therefore, the quantitative analysis examines the overall evaluative patterns; then the qualitative analysis investigates closely how and why individual evaluative shifts occur in relation to discourse structures and contexts.

Case study analysis

The context: (re)constructing China's economic policy to the world on the WEF platform

Incorporating the economic-political context into discourse analysis is paramount because the situation/context points to critical aspects of discourse. The discussion takes place among key panels of the WEF Annual Meeting, which is a pivotal platform for world political and business leaders to convene, interact and make important decisions. Moreover, discussions are set under the spotlight of world media.

The panel discussion for the present study revolves around the "Belt and Road Initiative" (BRI) policy proposed by Chinese President Xi Jinping in 2013, against the backdrop of complicated geopolitics in the mega-region (Du 2016). On the one hand, China "needs a new, safe, balanced and efficient opening-up strategy" when reaching the top in ODI (overseas direct investment). On the other hand, developed economies like the United States raised the bar of protectionism in the post-crisis era (ibid: 32). The BRI policy aims at improving the connectivity and cooperation among countries, primarily between China and the rest of Eurasia. Meanwhile, as a geopolitical strategy, Western observers claim that it is a move to restructure the dominance and power relations (ibid) in the region that covers the land-based "Silk Road Economic Belt" (SREB) and sea-based "Maritime Silk Road" (MSR) (Ghiasy and Zhou 2017). While China and Beijing are promoting BRI in a highly positive way, the evaluation of the policy outside China is mixed, particularly with the criticism from the West and doubt in neighbouring countries' readiness to cooperate (Du 2016).

Wordings of the topic "One Belt, One Road; Many Winners" construct discursively positive evaluation of the BRI polity. It is created by the Chinese government organiser in the para-text on the meeting venue and on the official website, and it also permeates discourse of STs and TTs. The topical discourse – "many winners" – is framed overtly positively; the quantifying word "many" suggests a rise in degree, and "winners" is an inscribed positive evaluation of attitudinal value.

The list of invited speakers[4] also constitutes the global evaluation of discourse. Speaker representations combine Chinese and Western nationals, including some high-profile speakers, such as the chief of the investment bank of BRI (Jin Liqun, the president of Asian Infrastructure Investment Bank (AIIB), together with Mr Bremmer, an American politician, and Mr Sobotka, director of a European business organisation. The mixed speaker representation is prone to mixed evaluations in the ST discourse, which renders direct bearings on the TT discourse.

Overall evaluative patterns

Figure 2.1 shows the overall pattern of attitude meanings. It is obvious that a positive evaluation of the BRI policy dominates the panel discussion, which is represented in both STs and TTs. Speakers overwhelmingly evaluate BRI policy and related matters with positive evaluations, more than twice as many as negative evaluations. In the corresponding TTs, there is only a marginal dwindling in terms of positive items in the discourse, presumably due to time and cognitive constraints in the simultaneous interpreting process. In sharp contrast, TT negative evaluation decreases drastically by over one-third.

Figure 2.2 presents interpreting shifts in TTs with respect to the graduation category of appraisal. Interpreting shifts of intensification and down-toning are made through interpreters' adding intensifiers/down-toners, omitting them, or changing the original values of them in the co-text of attitudinal values (positive

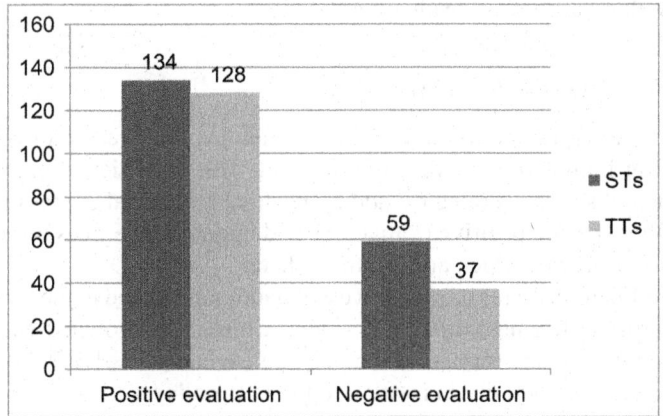

Figure 2.1 Positive/negative evaluations of the attitude system, contrasted by STs and TTs

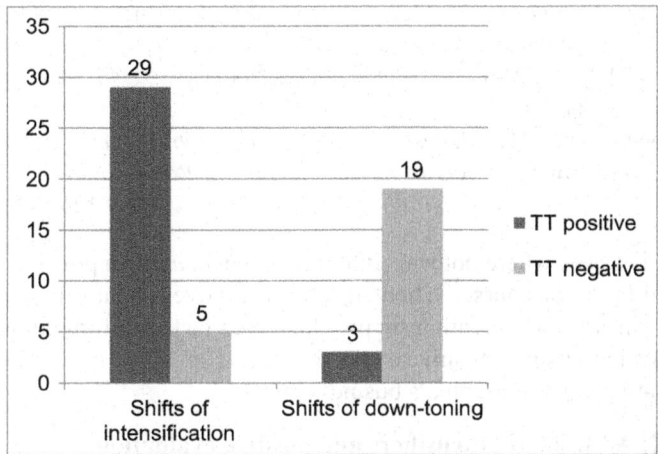

Figure 2.2 Shifts of intensification/down-toning of the graduation system, contrasted by TT positive and TT negative evaluations

or negative). For the positive evaluation, interpreters have a strong tendency to intensify the ST degrees, while the shifts of down-toning are reduced to minimal. Nevertheless, for the negative value, despite occasional cases shifting towards intensification, interpreters are highly likely to downgrade values attached to the negative discourse.

Two discourse features can thus be summarised from the overall evaluative patterns: (i) both Chinese and Western speakers are more positive than negative in their discursive construction regarding the BRI policy; (ii) Chinese interpreters reconstruct the discourse in a more positive manner through manipulating

(a) attitudinal positive/negative evaluative expressions and (b) gradable values attached to these attitudinal evaluations.

Strengthening positive discourse

The Chinese interpreters discursively strengthen positive values of STs through manipulating linguistic resources of appraisal. This is achieved predominantly through three discourse strategies: adding positive attitudinal expressions, inserting intensifiers before positive evaluations and upgrading degrees of positivity in the discourse, three of which are illustrated here.

Example 1 demonstrates how positive evaluations are added to the ST discourse. When a European business director describes Chinese state-owned-enterprises as "going outside", the interpreter adds a positive evaluation "积极地" (*actively*) to modify the business activity in relation to the BRI policy.

Example 1: Addition of positive evaluation

ST (EUROPEAN BUSINESS DIRECTOR): That the big ones, the 170 or 180 biggest SOEs, they are going outside of China and build projects. ("SOEs" refer to Chinese state-owned-enterprises.)

TT: 有最大的170个、180个中国的国企也都**积极地**在"一带一路"方面找到自己的一些工程。

BACK TRANSLATION: *The biggest 170, 180 Chinese enterprises are all **actively** finding their own projects in terms of Belt-and-Road policy.*

(ID = 126; Interpreter 2)[5]

Example 2 is a case where both an additional intensifier and a positive evaluation are inserted in the discourse. When an American government official states that Chinese businesses are "creating supply chains" as factual information, the interpreter adds an intensified positive evaluation "非常好" (*very good*) that strengthens the positive value for China's business moves.

Example 2: Addition of intensifiers and positive evaluation

ST (AMERICAN GOVERNMENT OFFICIAL): Now China's going out and creating supply chains. They will feel much more invested as a country in a much broader area of the world.

TT: 我现在能够看到中国将会有一个**非常好**的供应链。它也愿意在更广泛的世界的范围内进行投资。

BACK TRANSLATION: *I currently can see China will have a **very good** supply chain. It will also invest in broader areas in the world.*

(ID = 81; Interpreter 2)

In Example 3, the Chinese Chief of AIIB comments on the benefits of BRI policy that is "beyond economics", implying other areas could also benefit from it. The interpreter emphasises speaker evaluation "beyond economics" through one intensifier "完全" (*entirely*) and a down-toner "仅仅" (*mere*) enveloping this locution are added, thus, in effect, increasing the degree of the positive evaluation.

Example 3: Increase of degrees for the positive evaluation

ST (CHINESE CHIEF OF AIIB): Because your colleague raised the question. What is the ultimate objective of this? This is a more strategic issue because it's a geopolitical issue. It's beyond economics, but it all boils down to one very simple objective that people of all countries in this world have a good life and live together peacefully. ("[T]his" refers to the BRI policy.)

TT: 因为刚才我们的演讲者，他说我们到底最终的一个目标和目的是什么呢？ 它**完全**超越了**仅仅**是经济的发展。但是最终，它仍然是到了最终的一个目的就是说，所有这个地区人民应该有一个好的生活，并且能够共同一起和平的生存。

BACK TRANSLATION: *Because just now our speaker, he talked about what the ultimate objective was? It goes **entirely** beyond **mere** economics, but ultimately, it arrives at an ultimate objective, that is, all people in this area should give a good life and be able to live together in peace.*

(ID = 265–266; Interpreter 2)

Example 4 is demonstrative of how interpreters discursively increase positive values under time and cognitive constraints in simultaneous interpreting. When a European business director enumerates benefits of BRI policy in a parallel structure where "to the benefit" is repeated three times, the interpreter strategically compresses the long string. This strategy reflects a tendency to avoid repetitions which occur in source texts, either by omitting them or rewording them in simultaneous interpreting (cf. Shlesinger 1991; Toury 1995). Despite the compression, the interpreter employs additionally two strong intensifiers "都是" (*all*) and "巨大" (*huge*) surrounding the positive judgement "利好" (*benefit*). Therefore, the resultant positive value in the TT is strengthened.

Example 4: Increase of degrees for the positive evaluation

ST (EUROPEAN BUSINESS DIRECTOR): And that is **to the benefit** of our countries; that is **to the benefit** of the people that work in our company; that is **to the benefit** of the people that live in the countries that becomes more stable and more integrated into China. ("[T]hat" refers to the BRI policy.)

TT: 这不光对我们公司而言，对我们的国家以及对我们工作的人民而言，对在哈萨克工作的人而言**都是一个巨大的利好**。

BACK TRANSLATION: *Not only for our company, for our country, our working people, for people working in Kazakhstan, it is **for all a huge benefit**.*

(ID = 131; Interpreter 1)

Mitigating negative and 'risky' discourse

Mitigating negative and 'risky' discourse is also a prominent pattern of reconstructing BRI pertinent discourse by the Chinese interpreters. Two strategies are utilised – neutralising negative evaluation and omitting negative expressions or high-risk discourse; both mitigate negative values or 'risky' elements discursively.

In Example 5, the American government official expresses his scepticism towards the BRI policy explicitly with the negative attitudinal expression "a little bit skeptical", which, though with a down-toner, shows his disapproval of the Chinese policy. Then, the interpreter mitigates negative values by replacing the negative chunk with a neutral one "分享一下我的一些想法" (*share some of my thoughts*).

Example 5: Neutralisation of negative evaluation

ST (AMERICAN GOVERNMENT OFFICIAL): I'm not an economist and I am political scientist, and I'm **a little bit skeptical**, at least near term, about some of the economic implications here. So, for example, the fact that, you know, a lot of the banks have been talking about hundreds of billions of dollars, [. . .]

TT: 我并不是一个经济学家，但是我在这里要和大家**分享一下我的一些想法**。现在，很多的银行都在谈有很多的这些钱，[. . .]

BACK TRANSLATION: *I am not an economist, but I here will **share some of my thoughts**. Now, a lot of banks are talking about lots of money,* [. . .]

(ID = 73; Interpreter 1)

Example 6 presents a case with both omitting negative evaluation and neutralising negativity. When a Chinese academic metaphorically compares China to "一个考试成绩不太好的学生" (*a student with not-so-good exam results*), the whole negative chunk is omitted. Moreover, the ST negative evaluation of China's ability in exams "勉强" (*barely enough*) is changed into "able", positively suggesting adequate academic competence for China.

Example 6: Omitting and neutralising negative evaluation

ST (CHINESE ACADEMIC): 这个一带一路啊，打个比方，咱们我们以前，全球是一个班集体，咱们以前中国是一个考试成绩不太好的学生，坐在后排，**勉强**及格。

BACK TRANSLATION: *The BRI policy, for example, we previously, the globe is a class, we, in the past, China was <u>a student with not-so-good exam results</u>, sat at the back and **barely enough** got a pass.*

TT: So, for the One Belt One Road. Just to give you an example, I believe actually, this is actually could be as similar as a whole class, and now we, with our efforts, we will be **able** to get a pass.

(ID = 198; Interpreter 1)

In Example 7, a sentence containing a negative evaluation is omitted. The Chinese academic is using, for allies joined by the BRI policy, the term "共同体" (*union*), borrowed from wordings of the European Union. At the point of time of the 2016 Summer Davos meeting, the European Union was disintegrating due to Brexit. He immediately comments on the use of the term negatively as "不好" (*not good*) and "滥掉" (*cliché*). The interpreter avoids bring in any negative value into the BRI discourse by omitting the entire sentence.

Example 7: Sentence omission of negative evaluation

ST (CHINESE ACADEMIC): 可能，20年、30年以后，一带一路这个倡议如果说是说成功的，未来可能一带一路相关地区，能够跟中国形成一个比较松散、比较有效的，比欧盟可能还要更加的，高效的一个经济的共同体。

BACK TRANSLATION: *Possibly 20 years, 30 years later, if the BRI is successful, in future possibly BRI related regions, can form with China a relatively relaxed, effective, more effective than EU, a more effective economic union.*

TT: I have such kind of idea that after 20 or 30 years, if this initiative is successful, all the regions along the One Belt One Road will form such a, very highly effective and efficient economic and social, region, which is very similar to that of EU. [sentence omission]

(ID = 107–108; Interpreter 2)

Example 8 presents a case of long omissions of 'risky' discourse regarding inappropriate uses of funding that was originally allocated to infrastructure along the Belt-and-Road areas. The American speaker is explicit about the availability of large-sized funding from the investment bank, yet he casts doubts on how such funding is used. In particular, he articulates clearly and concretely that "provincial actors within China" use this funding "for their own domestic purposes" and evaluates such acts as "create inefficiencies" and "never a good thing". This is arguably a high-risk discourse because when the context is considered, misuses of funding by "provincial actors" allude to corruption issues on the part of local governments in China. It is likely that the Chinese interpreter senses the negative connotation and omits the sentence altogether. Therefore, in the interpreted discourse, negativity is significantly diluted and the 'dangerous' information is obliterated.

Example 8: Long omissions of 'risky' discourse containing negative evaluations

ST (AMERICAN GOVERNMENT OFFICIAL): So, for example, the fact that, you know, a lot of the banks have been talking about hundreds of billions of dollars, and it's absolutely not clear how much of that is already in projects, that are kind of, on their books that they were already investing in, they are going to say, sort of, you know, what they are there they meet the One-belt criteria, how much of this is new? It's hard to have projects in this part of the world that are actually investment ready and give you good returns.

TT: 现在，很多的银行都在谈，有很多的这些钱。可是，他们却无法把这些资金来很好地整合并且投入到这些合适的地方来。比如说，他们不能够形成一个合力。[long omissions] 所以，对于我们在这一地区如果想要一些基础设施的工程或者其他的工程，如果要进行融资就**非常**的困难。

BACK TRANSLATION: *Now, there are many banks, talking about lots of such money. But, they did not very well integrate or invest money into these appropriate places. For example, they cannot form a synergy.* [long omissions] *Therefore,*

> *for us in these areas, if we want to have some infrastructure projects or other projects, it is very difficult to invest.*
>
> (ID = 74–76; Interpreter 2)

Discussion

The case study discloses interpreter manipulation in light of appraisal linguistic resources. The reconstruction of the discourse related to the BRI policy in TTs can be summarised by two preeminent patterns: (a) strengthening positive evaluation and (b) mitigating negative evaluation and 'risky' discourse infused with negativity. Both are realised via three strategies deploying linguistic resources in attitude and graduation systems of appraisal: (i) adding positive evaluative expressions or intensifiers for positive values, (ii) upgrading levels of intensification for positive values and (iii) omitting negative and high-risk locutions or even long sentences containing them.

Empirical findings of the present study resonate with previous investigations that reveal interpreter/translator intervention via changing appraisal linguistic resources (e.g. Munday 2012, 2015, 2018; Wang and Feng 2017). Evaluative shifts, in this sense, constitute "sensitive", "value-rich" or "critical" points, where lexical features in STs "are most susceptible to value manipulation" by interpreters/translators (Munday 2012: 41). Meanwhile, reductions in terms of graduation sources found in this study confirm Munday's (2012, 2018) reports on the reduction of intensification. Nonetheless, the additions and increased levels of intensification for positive values offer different evidence in terms of interpreter manipulation. Additionally, interpreting additions/omissions in relation to positive/negative evaluations in the discourse empirically contribute to existing findings.

Conclusion

This study investigates how conference interpreters (at the World Economic Forum) reconstruct discourse through their manipulation of evaluative linguistic resources. A major contribution is methodological, since this study systematically introduces an SFL-oriented linguistic toolkit for examining evaluation – appraisal theory. Meanwhile, this study also illustrates its profitable application with a case study of conference interpreting. The proven utility of this theory attests to Munday's (2018: 192) argument:

> The appraisal-based model provides a very focused and intricate tool for identifying the power behind evaluative words and expressions, and how this fits into an act of communication including, in our case, translator/interpreter intervention.

The integration of appraisal theory into CDA investigation makes the case study more systematic, fine-grained and nuanced in terms of subtle linguistic shifts from STs to TTs. An important implication for T&I researchers may be 'going-interdisciplinary', which enriches methodological inventory of T&I as well as cross-fertilises other fields from which we borrow tools.

Notes

1 Video data are down-loaded from the WEF official website: www.weforum.org/events/
2 This study only focuses on evaluative locutions that belong to the attitude and graduation systems, and those belonging to the engagement system are beyond the remit of this study.
3 There is no space for details of the semantic annotation in this study. Details including an annotation scheme, annotation procedures, and agreement tests are available in Gao (2020).
4 Panelist profiles: Jin Liqun, President, Asian Infrastructure Investment Bank (AIIB); Ian Bremmer, American government official and President, Eurasia Group; Li Daokui, Dean, Schwarzman College, Tsinghua University; Zhang Bingjun, Corporate Chairman, Tianjin TEDA Construction Group Ltd; Benedikt Sobotka, Chief Executive Officer, Eurasian Resources Group Sàrl; Chiang Sheng Yang, Presenter, Phoenix Satellite Television Holdings Limited; Yin Chang, Anchor, Tianjin Radio and Television Station.
5 The parallel corpus data are segmented and aligned at a sentence level. For each sentence, an ID number is assigned for the location of the example in the corpus. The two interpreters working alternatively for this panel are numbered 1 and 2.

References

Aikhenvald, A. Y. (2004) *Evidentiality*, Oxford: Oxford University Press.
Beaton, M. (2007) 'Interpreted ideologies in institutional discourse: The case of the European Parliament', *The Translator* 13(2): 271–296. doi:10.1080/13556509.2007.10799241
Beaton-Thome, M. (2013) 'What's in a word? Your enemy combatant is my refugee: The role of simultaneous interpreters in negotiating the lexis of Guantánamo in the European Parliament', *Journal of Language and Politics* 12(3): 378–399.
Bednarek, M. (2006) *Evaluation in Media Discourse: Analysis of a Newspaper Corpus*, London: Continuum.
Biber, D. and Finegan, E. (1988) 'Adverbial stance types in English', *Discourse Processes* 11(1): 1–34.
Du, M. M. (2016) 'China's "one belt, one road" initiative: Context, focus, institutions, and implications', *The Chinese Journal of Global Governance* 2(1): 30–43.
Eggins, S. and Slade, D. (1997) *Analysing Casual Conversation*, London: Cassell.
Fairclough, N. (1989) *Language and Power*, London and New York: Longman.
Fairclough, N. and Wodak, R. (1997) 'Critical discourse analysis', in *Discourse as Social Interaction*. T. A. van Dijk (ed.), London: Sage. pp. 258–284.
Gao, F. (2020) *Interpreters' Ideological Positioning through the Evaluative Language in Conference Interpreting*. PhD thesis, University of Leeds, Leeds.
Ghiasy, R. and Zhou, J. (2017) 'The Silk road economic belt: How does it interact with Eurasian security dynamics', *Stockholm Institute for Peace Research*. Available at: www.sipri.org/commentary/topical-backgrounder/2017/silk-road-economic-belt
Gu, C. (2018) 'Mediating 'face' in triadic political communication: A CDA analysis of press conference interpreters' discursive (re)construction of Chinese government's image (1998–2017)', *Critical Discourse Studies* 16(2): 201–221. doi:10.1080/17405904.2018.1538890

Halliday, M. A. K. (1978) *Language as Social Semiotic: The Social Interpretation of Language and Meaning*, London: Edward Arnold.
Halliday, M. A. K. (1994) *An Introduction to Functional Grammar*, London: Edward Arnold.
Halliday, M. A. K. and Matthiessen, C. (2014) *An Introduction to Functional Grammar*, New York: Routledge.
Hatim, B. and Mason, I. (2014) *Discourse and the Translator*, London: Routledge.
Hunston, S. (2013) *Corpus Approaches to Evaluation: Phraseology and Evaluation Language*, London: Routledge.
Hunston, S. and Thompson, G. (2000) *Evaluation in Text: Authorial Stance and the Construction of Discourse*, Oxford: University Press.
Hyland, K. (1994) 'Hedging in academic writing and EAF textbooks', *English for Specific Purposes* 13(3): 239–256.
Leech, G. (1974) *Semantics*, Harmondsworth: Penguin Books Ltd.
Lemke, J. (1997) 'Cognition, context, and learning: A social semiotic perspective', in *Situated Cognition: Social, Semiotic, and Psychological Perspectives*. D. Kirshner and J. A. Whitson (eds.), Mahwah, NJ: Erlbaum. pp. 37–56.
Martin, J. (2000) 'Beyond exchange: Appraisal systems in English', in *Evaluation in Text: Authorial Stance and the Construction of Discourse*. S. Hunston and G. Thompson (eds.), Oxford: Oxford University Press. pp. 142–175.
Martin, J. and Rose, D. (2003) *Working with Discourse: Meaning Beyond the Clause*, London: Bloomsbury Publishing.
Martin, J. and White, R. (2005) *The Language of Evaluation: Appraisal in English*, Hampshire: Palgrave Macmillan.
Meyer, M. (2001) 'Between theory, method, and politics: Positioning of the approaches to CDA', in *Methods of Critical Discourse Analysis*. R. Wodak and M. Meyer (eds.), London: Sage. pp. 14–31.
Munday, J. (2012) *Evaluation in Translation: Critical Points of Translator Decision-Making*, New York: Routledge.
Munday, J. (2015) 'Engagement and graduation resources as markers of translator/interpreter positioning', *Target: International Journal of Translation Studies* 27(3): 406–421. doi:10.1075/target.27.3.05mun
Munday, J. (2018) 'A model of appraisal: Spanish interpretations of President Trump's inaugural address 2017', *Perspectives* 26(2): 180–195. doi:10.1080/0907676x.2017.1388415
Munday, J. and Zhang, M. (2015) 'Introduction', *Target: International Journal of Translation Studies* 27(3): 325–334. doi:10.1075/target.27.3.001int
Munday, J. and Zhang, M. (2017) *Discourse Analysis in Translation Studies*, Amsterdam and Philadelphia: John Benjamins Publishing Company.
Paltridge, B. (2012) *Discourse Analysis: An Introduction* (2nd ed.), London: Bloomsbury.
Pan, L. (2015) 'Ideological positioning in news translation: A case study of evaluative resources in reports on China', *Target: International Journal of Translation Studies* 27(2): 215–237. doi:10.1075/target.27.2.03pan
Peng, Xuanwei, Yang, Xiaojun and He, Zhongqing 彭宣维, 杨晓军 and 何中清 (2012) '汉英对应评价意义语料库' (Chinese-English parallel corpus of appraisal meanings), 外语电化教学 (*Computer-Assisted Foreign Language Education*) 5: 3–10.
Pérez-González, L. (2007) 'Appraising dubbed conversation: Systemic functional insights into the construal of naturalness in translated film dialogue', *The Translator* 13(1): 1–38. doi:10.1080/13556509.2007.10799227

Qian, H. (2012) 'Investigating translators' positioning via the appraisal theory: A case study of the Q&A part of a speech delivered by the US Vice President Cheney', *Sino-US English Teaching* 12(9): 1775–1787.

Rosa, A. A. (2009) 'Narrator profile in translation: Work-in-progress for a semiautomatic analysis of narratorial dialogistic and attitudinal positioning in translated fiction', *Linguistica Antverpiensia, New Series: Themes in Translation Studies* (7): 227–248.

Rosa, A. A. (2013) *The Power of Voice in Translated Fiction: Or, Following a Linguistic Track in Translation Studies*. Paper presented at the Tracks and Treks in Translation Studies: Selected Papers from the EST Congress, Leuven, 2010.

Schäffner, C. (2012) 'Unknown agents in translated political discourse', *Target: International Journal of Translation Studies* 24(1): 103–125. doi:10.1075/target.24.1.07sch

Schäffner, C. (2015) 'Speaker positioning in interpreter-mediated press conferences', *Target: International Journal of Translation Studies* 27(3): 422–439.

Shlesinger, M. (1991) 'Interpreter latitude vs. due process: Simultaneous and consecutive interpretation in multilingual trials', in *Empirical Research in Translation and Intercultural Studies*. S. Tikkonen-Condit (ed.), Tübingen: Gunter Narr. pp. 147–155.

Toury, G. (1995) *Descriptive Translation Studies and Beyond*, Amsterdam and Philadelphia: John Benjamins Publishing Company.

Vandepitte, S., Vandenbussche, L. and Algoet, B. (2011) 'Travelling certainties: Darwin's doubts and their Dutch translations', *The Translator* 17(2): 275–299. doi:10.1080/1355 6509.2011.10799490

van Dijk, T. A. (1997) 'What is political discourse analysis?', *Belgian Journal of Linguistics* 11(1): 11–52.

Wadensjö, C. (2000) 'Co-constructing Yeltsin: Explorations of an interpreter-mediated political interview', in *Intercultural Faultlines: Research Models in Translation Studies I: Textual and Cognitive Aspects*. M. Olohan (ed.), London: Routledge. pp. 233–252.

Wang, B. and Feng, D. (2017) 'A corpus-based study of stance-taking as seen from critical points in interpreted political discourse', *Perspectives* 26(2): 246–260. doi:10.1080/090 7676x.2017.1395468

White, P. P. (1999) *Dialogue and Inter-Subjectivity: Reinterpreting the Semantics of Modality and Hedging*. Paper presented at the Dialogue Analysis VII: Working with Dialogue: Selected Papers from the 7th IADA Conference, Birmingham.

Zhang, M. (2009) 'Social context and translation of public notices', *Babel* 55(2): 142–152. doi:10.1075/babel.55.2.03zha

Zhang, M. (2013) 'Stance and mediation in transediting news headlines as paratexts', *Perspectives* 21(3): 396–411.

Zhang, M. and Pan, H. (2015) 'Institutional power in and behind discourse: A case study of SARS notices and their translations used in Macao', *Target: International Journal of Translation Studies* 27(3): 387–405.

3 'The main problems in China–Japan relations lie in <u>**the FACT that**</u> some leaders in Japan keep on visiting the Yasukuni Shrine'

A corpus-based CDA on government interpreters' metadiscursive (re)construction of truth, fact and reality

Chonglong Gu

Introduction

Truth and fact are not an absolute, and instead often constitute a dynamic and continuous process of discursive justification. In other words, what constitutes truth, fact and reality is in many ways mediated through discursive means and is often inextricably linked with power. For Foucault, "truth is a thing of this world" and "each society has its regime of truth, its 'general politics' of truth: that is, the types of discourse which it accepts and makes function as true" (Foucault, in Rabinow 1991). This is because power, knowledge and reality "cannot themselves be established, consolidated nor implemented without the production, accumulation, circulation and functioning of a discourse" (Foucault 1984: 93). This highlights the essentially constructed and discursively mediated nature of the so-called facts and truths we encounter in our daily lives. As such, those in power can often create discourse and, in doing so, enact a version of truth through dominating and controlling this discourse.

The often ideological nature of discourse is evidenced most saliently in the political arena. It can be argued that political language is inherently persuasive in nature, the articulation of which inevitably involves conveying a (desired) version of fact and truth. Perhaps just as Vukovic (2014: 37) rightly puts it, political actors are often "in the business of selling their products", that is, "their policies and their point of view" or their "truth". While a lot has been made of the role of language in the construction of truth, knowledge and sociopolitical reality, for instance, in monolingual critical discourse analysis (CDA), comparatively little attention has focused on the vital role of different agents in shaping reality in bilingual communication (e.g. translation and interpreting).

Despite the relatively recent attention, translation, for example, has been understood as a form of (re)narration in various sociopolitical settings (Baker 2006, 2007, 2008, 2010a, 2010b). That is, rather than simply transferring semantic content from one language to the other, the translators are actively (re)framing and (re)constructing realities in our world (Boukhaffa 2018; Darwish 2006; Dubbati and Abudayeh 2018; Kim 2017a, 2018). In comparison, the role of interpreters in (re)constructing and (re)enacting realities remains significantly underexplored. Some of the few attempts include Beaton-Thome's (2013) study and Gu's (2018b) study. In the former study, it is found that, during the plenary debate from the European Parliament (EP) on the potential resettlement of Guantánamo detainees in European Union (EU) member states, simultaneous interpreters tend to (re)create different versions of reality through different lexical labelling and lexical choices. In the latter corpus-based study, it shows that the government-affiliated interpreters serve to (re)construct a more positive image of the Chinese government being highly efficient, competent and responsive through their proliferated employment of the present perfect (continuous) structures. Although limited in number, these studies suggest that interpreting is in fact a dynamic (re)contextualisation process, where information is inevitably (re)packaged and (re)produced in the sociopolitical, cultural and linguistic context of the TT. This, as such, highlights the potential of interpreter's agency in the mediated communication process. In other words, rather than a completely neutral and value-free enterprise, interpreting in a political and institutional setting is often an ideologically driven activity, where interpreters help contribute to the enactment of different versions of truth, fact and reality.

The televised and interpreter-mediated Premier-Meets-the-Press conferences are an established annual event in mainland China (Gu 2018a). A typical site of ideology, the interpreter-mediated press conferences represent a major *regime of truth*, enabling "one to distinguish true and false statements" and providing "the techniques and procedures accorded value in the acquisition of truth" (Foucault, in Rabinow 1991). That is, featuring the attendance of the Chinese premier (ranked second in the Chinese government), this high-profile discursive event permits the Chinese premier to answer journalists' questions on various interesting and challenging topics (e.g. Sino-Japanese relations, Taiwan, Tibet, China's economic reform and political restructuring, corruption, internet censorship, the US general election, Syria and Crimea) and, in so doing, present and perpetuate Beijing's desired and officially sanctioned version of fact and reality. This version of truth, without doubt, contributes towards the 'Chinese story' (*zhongguo gushi*) Beijing is eager to tell, as pointed out repeatedly in recent years by the latest government administration.

The interpreted nature of the press conferences highlights the interpreters' potential agency in (re)framing truth and fact and in (re)constructing Beijing's discourse and image in the (re)contextualisation process, that is, interpreting. Surely truth value is very much embedded and conveyed in the main propositional content. In this chapter, however, attention is focused on the hitherto largely under-explored category of metadiscourse (e.g. *the fact that, in fact, actually, as a matter of fact, indeed*) in interpreter-mediated political discourse, with a view to establishing the interpreters' mediation of China's discourse and image through metadiscursive devices (focusing in particular on the construction 'the fact that').

To this end, a corpus-based critical discourse analysis (CDA) is carried out on the CE-PolitDisCorp corpus, which contains 20 years of the premier's press conference data (1998–2017) in mainland China. This corpus-based CDA study is of particular interest considering the fact that the interpretation into the global *lingua franca* English represents in many ways China's international voice and is the one that is taken for granted as China's state-sanctioned discourse, quoted verbatim by various media outlets and (re)contextualised on various platforms (Gu 2018a). This is particularly the case given the increasingly mediat(is)ed and re-mediat(is)ed world we live in (Gu 2018b; Gu and Tipton 2020), where the interpreted English discourse constitutes a major starting point in the entire international news production, dissemination and circulation processes. This interdisciplinary study promises to further contribute to translation and interpreting studies (e.g. interpreters' agency), multilingual CDA, the political sciences and Chinese studies (political legitimation through discourse), communication and media studies, and image studies alike.

Metadiscourse: a promising category of knowledge construction and ideological mediation

As various strands of linguistic studies (e.g. critical linguistics, CDA and narrative theory) have attested to, language use is rarely value-free and can essentially be seen as narrative or discourse and a major carrier of power and different ideological beliefs. So far, a wide range of linguistic categories and features (e.g. repetition, modality, nominalisation and passivisation) have been examined within CDA and without as being ideologically salient. However, little attention has focused on the seemingly innocuous category of metadiscourse, and to date, various metadiscursive markers are often treated only as cohesive devices or corresponding to the interactional and interactive aspects of language use.

Literally discourse about discourse, metadiscourse, according to Hyland (2005: 37), is "the cover term for the self-reflective expressions used to negotiate interactional meanings in a text, assisting the writer (or speaker) to express a viewpoint and engage with readers as members of a particular community". It is through metadiscourse that the "propositional content is made coherent, intelligible and persuasive to a particular audience" (Hyland 2005: 39). Examples of such linguistic devices are "needless to say", "obviously", "according to" and "in fact" *etc*. They represent the resources employed by text producers in the organisation of discourse, signalling text producers' attitude and engagement with the audience. Based on the distinction made by Halliday (1973) between the ideational aspects of language use (propositional or informational elements relating to the topic and content) and other non-propositional, interactional and expressive aspects of language use, metadiscourse can be seen as belonging to the latter. That is, they are usually used in a way that refers "not to the substance of their ideas but to themselves, their readers, or their writings" (Williams 2007: 65). Put differently, metadiscourse often does not add propositional information but signals the presence of the writer, as Vande Kopple (1985) similarly argues. Although metadiscourse might not automatically add to the actual proposition, it can indeed be "ideology-bound" and relate "significantly to the distribution of power in a given context" (Mazid 2014: 76).

Thus far, metadiscourse has been relatively well-researched in various monolingual written discourses, with a predominant focus on writing in academic contexts.

These studies include, *inter alia*, students' textbooks (Crismore 1989), doctoral students' dissertations (Bunton 1999), undergraduate textbooks (Hyland 2000) and, more recently, stance nouns in disciplinary writing (Jiang and Hyland 2015). These studies have called into question the long-held belief that (academic) writing is "an objective and impersonal kind of discourse, designed to deal simply with the presentation of facts", showing instead that (academic) writing is "a persuasive endeavour, saturated with the perspectives of" the text producer (Jiang and Hyland 2015: 529). The use of metadiscourse has also been associated with image construction. Notably, in Crismore and Farnsworth (1989) and Hyland (1998), attention has been paid to how a positive image and credible persona can be created on the part of Darwin and CEOs respectively in writing *The Origin of Species* and corporate annual reports through the deployment of metadiscourse.

While a lot has been made of metadiscourse in academic writing and other monolingual written genres, metadiscourse has received little, if any, attention in political discursive articulation. In fact, political language is very much complete with metadiscourse, as a genre featuring the constant interaction, persuasion and negotiation of ideological meanings, the expression of stances and attitudes and the presentation of a certain version of fact, truth and reality. Unsurprisingly, metadiscourse has received even less scholarly attention in (interpreted) bilingual political press conferences, particularly in relation to the interpreters' ideological mediation in the Chinese setting. Unlike the dialogic writer–reader relationship in monolingual written communication, China's political press conferences are essentially triadic and dynamic in nature, featuring the involvement of the interpreter as a third participant. This brings to the fore the potential of metadiscourse as a potentially rich area for interrogating the interpreters' ideological mediation in this political and institutional setting. That is, although truth value is very much embedded and conveyed in the main propositional content and the interpreters' use of metadiscursive devices might not contribute much to the propositional content *per se*, it can be of ideological salience and reveal whether an extra layer of conviction, authoritativeness or factualness might be (re)constructed through interpreting. As such, it is interesting to study the interpreters' mediation of this seemingly innocuous category and see if the truth value of the government's discourse and the image of Beijing might be (re)conditioned in this interpreted political encounter (which is essentially negotiated in nature featuring constant ideological justification).

Corpus-based CDA in exploring interpreters' agency: a useful methodological synergy

This section discusses the theoretical framework and methodology adopted in this study. Conceptualising discourse as essentially "a form of social practice" (Fairclough 1989: 20), critical discourse analysis (CDA) represents an interdisciplinary and problem-oriented approach to the study of discourse used in various sociopolitical and institutional settings. Although often interchangeably used, 'discourse' technically differs from 'language' in that the former is more dynamic a concept that highlights more of the sociopolitical effect and impact of language use. In other words, discourse concerns "what happens when language 'gets done'" and discourse "usefully captures both the meaning and effects of language usage" (Simpson and Mayr 2009: 5). Drawing extensively on various linguistic (e.g. Halliday's systemic functional linguistics) and social theories (e.g. the works of Mikhail Bakhtin and Michel Foucault), the multifarious CDA features different schools or sub-trends (e.g. Fairclough's three-dimensional approach, Wodak's discourse-historical approach (DHA) and van Dijk's socio-cognitive approach).

CDA, however, is united by a shared perspective on doing linguistic, semiotic or discourse analysis (van Dijk 1993a, 1993b). Underpinning all CDA analyses is the dialectical assumption that realities are both reflected in and constantly shaped by discourse. Also, the operative word "critical" here should not be equated with criticism or blaming in a "negative" way (Wodak and Meyer 2009: 2) but concerns the critical attitude to take nothing for granted and take nothing at face value (Gu 2018a: 247) in revealing the (sometimes subtle and non-obvious) enactment of ideologies and power in language at different levels. That is, a central preoccupation of the tradition of CDA is the critical examination of language use, which might potentially serve to reflect ideologies, construct realities and contribute to social inequality and changes in power relations.

In order to gain a deeper understanding of CDA, it is worth contrasting it with the (similarly) sociopolitically and ideologically oriented yet different narrative approach. Despite the overlap, a narrative approach assumes the "entire narrative" as "the unit of analysis" (Baker 2010a: 349) and focuses more on the macro-level structuring and overall organisation of events and experiences as temporally linked and sequentially connected in storytelling within a larger sociopolitical and cultural context (Frank 1998). Some of the main tools of analysis include temporality, relationality, selective appropriation and causal emplotment (Somers and Gibson 1994; Baker 2006). A narrative approach is often considered to lack the toolkits (Sutherland et al. 2013; Atkinson 1997) for more detailed textual analysis. In comparison, a critical discourse analytical approach is more textually oriented and is attentive to the power and ideology enacted in language at a micro-level.

Despite the effectiveness of this largely qualitative approach, CDA is often subject to criticism that practitioners might sometimes cherry-pick information (Widdowson 1995) from a comparatively small data sample and conduct analysis in a way that suits the researchers' own opinions and agendas. This, therefore, challenges the representativeness of the qualitative manual analysis and the validity of the findings. With this in mind, for more systematic analysis, methods of corpus linguistics (CL) have been increasingly employed (*cf.* Hardt-Mautner 1995; Partington 2004) to significantly reduce researcher bias. Triangulating between the typically qualitative (CDA) and quantitative (CL), this mixed-methods approach constitutes a "useful methodological synergy" (Baker et al. 2008). Thus far, this corpus-based CDA approach has been extensively applied in examining monolingual discursive communication.

Interestingly, since the "cultural turn" (Bassnett and Lefevere 1990: 1) in translation and interpreting studies (TIS), although there is an increasing number of studies that adopt the mostly qualitative CDA in investigating the intricate interplay of power and ideologies enacted in translation (cf. Hatim and Mason 1990; Kang 2007; Munday 2007; Zhang 2013) and more recently interpreting (cf. Beaton 2007; Beaton-Thome 2013; Gu 2018a), a systematic application of a corpus-based CDA approach in TIS is particularly rare. The few examples of its application in translation studies so far include Kim's (2013, 2017b) studies. The former has focused on American and South Korean news discourses on North Korea mediated through translation, whereas the latter study has investigated Newsweek discourses on China and their translations in Korean. Similarly, Li's (2019) corpus-based study explores how China is represented in the translations of two Korean news outlets.

The empirical application of the corpus-based CDA approach in interpreting is exemplified in Li's (2016), Wang and Feng's (2018) and Gu's (2018b, 2019) studies, all using corpus data in China's political context. In Li's (2016) study, he examines the translators and interpreters' role in mediating appraisal resources when rendering China's political discourse (Chinese–English). In Wang and Feng's (2018) study, the authors have focused on the interpreters' differentiated treatment of the value-laden item 问题 (*wenti*) as an important critical point which can reveal their stance-taking in interpreting. Lastly, Gu's (2018b) corpus-based CDA study explores the press conference interpreters' mediation of Chinese government's discourse on its past actions and achievements and their (re)construction of Beijing's image, whereas his (2019) study examines the interpreters' mediation of China's discourse on 'people' and how a stronger consent has been (re)manufactured in English as a result.

Therefore, it seems interesting to see how this mixed-methods approach can be applied with some systematicity in exploring the government-affiliated interpreters' further mediation of China's version of fact, truth and reality through metadiscourse. In executing the methodology, considering the aims and nature of this study, the corpus-based analysis does not limit itself to any CDA subtrends but entails meticulous and critical comparisons between the STs and TTs, focusing on the ideologically salient "shifts" (Toury 1995) that occur in interpreting at different levels.

Data, corpus linguistics software and procedures for analysis

For the purpose of this study, the Chinese-English Political Discourses Corpus (CE-PolitDisCorp) developed by the author for the investigation of interpreting and (interpreted) political discourse is used. The CE-PolitDisCorp consists of 20 years' transcribed bilingual premier's press conference data in China (1998–2017), covering three latest administrations: Zhu Rongji (1998–2002), Wen Jiabao (2003–2012) and Li Keqiang (2013–2017). The press conference sessions are consecutively interpreted by experienced interpreters. These interpreters are communist party members and civil servants affiliated with China's Ministry of Foreign Affairs (FMPRC) and more specifically The Department of Translation and Interpretation. As such, they can be seen as members of the upper echelon of China's ruling elite (Gu 2018a). Directionally, apart from the Chinese and foreign journalists' questions posed in Chinese or English (and their respective interpretations in the other language), the bulk of the data involves the Chinese premier's answers in Chinese and then their English interpretations. As such, the bilingual data was separated into subcorpus A (premier's answers in Chinese) and subcorpus B (English interpretations) for comparative analysis between the ST and TT.

The data was transcribed verbatim from video clips available on the government's official websites as well as from such video-sharing websites as YouTube and Youku. The data transcription and preparation (e.g. segmentation for Chinese) processes were highly time consuming and labour intensive, involving considerable human efforts. The fully prepared data was processed using AntConc, a corpus linguistics software developed by Laurence Anthony which features various tools and functions (e.g. concordancing tool, frequency list, N-Gram and Kwic sort). In terms of the procedures, eligible items are first established in both subcorpora for an overall idea as to how metadiscourse is mediated by the interpreters. In addition, individual items in English are investigated and retrospectively compared with their Chinese counterparts to identify possible shifts. Illustrative examples are then provided to show the workings of the interpreters' possible agency at a micro-level.

Data analysis

For an understanding of the interpreters' discursive (re)construction at different levels, attention is first focused on their mediation of various items overall before examining the more specific metadiscursive items and expressions. Essentially hybrid in nature, metadiscourse is a fuzzy concept difficult to pin down and can contain various linguistic realisations. Metadiscourse, therefore, constitutes an open category (Hyland 2005: 27). For an overall idea of how fact, truth and reality are mediated by the interpreters, only the metadiscursive items and expressions semantically related to fact, truth and reality are established in the Chinese and English sub-corpora. That is, while common metadiscourse markers such as *in other words, thirdly, unfortunately, for example, might, in addition, namely, to some extent, as a result* might serve certain (interactive and interactional) functions in communication, they are potentially less interesting to explore from the perspective of ideology and are thus excluded in this study.

The eligible items are identified using AntConc's N-Grams (clusters) tool as well as by carefully looking through the corpus data. The identification of eligible items also draws on Hyland's (2005) taxonomy, which contains a relatively comprehensive list of metadiscourse markers. The established items in both subcorpora and their respective frequencies are detailed in Table 3.1.

Statistically, there are 161 instances of relevant items in the Chinese sub-corpus yet 392 instances of their counterparts in the English sub-corpus, accounting for a noticeable 143.5% increase. The interpreters' increased (re)production of items (semantically related to truth, fact and reality) has rendered the premier's English

Table 3.1 Established items and expressions in both sub-corpora

Chinese subcorpus	English subcorpus
事实 (14); 事实上 (4); 的确 (13); 确实 (58); 真理 (6); 真实 (2); 实在 (2); 实际 (16); 实际上 (22); 现实 (4); 其实 (20)	*fact(s)* (15); *as a matter of fact* (18); *in fact* (9); *(the/this) fact that* (20); *factual* (1); *truth* (17); *true* (51); *truly* (12); *reality* (9); *really* (26); *real* (35); *actually* (153); *actual* (5); *indeed* (21)
161 instances in total	**392 instances in total**

discourse considerably more emphatic and persuasive, suggesting at least rhetorically that what is conveyed is unquestionably true and real. This, therefore, adds an additional layer of factualness to the TT and (re)creates a stronger overall image of Beijing being fact-based, convincing and authoritative in its English discourse.

General illustrations of interpreters' metadiscursive mediation

To illustrate this overall trend, a few detailed examples are provided here before proceeding to more systematic analysis of the metadiscursive structure 'the fact that'. These illustrative examples highlight the interpreters' repeated additions of metadiscourse markers (semantically related to fact, truth and reality) in English. Without doubt, such ideologically salient additions (e.g. *in fact, as a matter of fact, the truth is, actually*) serve to further strengthen the Chinese ST and make it more emphatic and convincing. This, discursively, leads to an additional level of commitment to the propositions' truth value.

Example 1 (2004)

ST: 日中两国关系存在的主要问题是日本的有些领导人多次参拜供有甲级战犯亡灵的靖国神社，极大地伤害了中国人民的感情和亚洲人民的感情。在中国受害的不是一两个家庭，死亡的就有二千多万。

GLOSS: The main problem that exists in Japan-China bilateral ties is some Japanese leaders' repeated visiting of the Yasukuni shrine housing Class-A war criminals, which tremendously hurts Chinese people's feelings and Asian people's feelings. In China, the victims are not just one or two families. The dead were over 20 million.

TT: Now the main problems in China-Japan relations lie in the fact that some leaders in Japan keep on visiting the Yasukuni Shrine many times, which enshrined Class-A war criminals. This has hurt the pride of the Chinese people and people in other Asian countries. <u>In fact</u>, in China those who suffered from the Japanese war of aggression were by no means just individual families. More than 20 million people died as a result of Japanese aggression.

In this example, the seemingly innocuous "in fact" is added by the interpreter, further foregrounding (Fairclough 1995) the objective "fact" that the Japanese invasion brought untold sufferings to over 20 million ordinary Chinese people. Such negative (re)presentation points to the unjust and unjustifiable nature of the Japanese leaders' repeated visits to the Yasukuni shrine (which are responsible for the difficulties in Chinese–Japanese relations).

Example 2 (2000)

ST: 我看不出这个反腐败的问题跟一个党执政，多党轮流执政有什么太大的关系[...]关键是法制，尤其要坚决地执法，中国在这方面已经取得了很大的成绩。

GLOSS: I don't see this anti-corruption issue having anything significant to do with one-party rule or multi-party rule [. . .] the key is the rule of law, especially to strictly enforce the law. China has in this respect achieved great results.

TT: I do not see a very significant link or clear logic between fighting corruption on the one hand and exercising one-party rule or multi-party rule [. . .] in my view the key is for us to work to build our legal system and also to exercise very strict law enforcement in our country. So <u>in fact</u>, we have already made significant result and accomplishment.

In this example, the journalist hinted that the one-party rule is the cause of China's widespread corruption. However, it is refuted in the Chinese premier's answer that one-party or multi-party rule is almost irrelevant. Instead, the important thing is the rule of law. Interestingly, the emphatic metadiscourse marker "in fact" is added by the interpreter in the TT, thus further foregrounding and (re)framing China's achievements made in the enforcement of law as "fact" that is irrefutable and praiseworthy.

Example 3 (2012)

ST: 群众许多批评的意见值得我们深思，而政府重视和决定的许多重大问题，经常是从群众拍砖里头得到的。

GLOSS: A lot of the public's critical views are worthy of our deep reflections and many major issues the government pays attention to and decides upon are often derived from the public's brickbats.

TT: I believe that the government must seriously reflect on the critical views that the people have made. <u>As a matter of fact</u>, the government has often found food for thought from those critical comments and views made by the public while taking decisions on major issues.

Example 4 (2015)

ST: 至于中国现在的物价总水平比较低，但并不是中国向世界输出了通缩。你说叫输出者，我们是被通缩。

GLOSS: Regarding China's current level of overall consumer prices being relatively low, it, however, is not China who has exported deflation to the world. You said (China) is called an exporter. We are being deflated.

TT: Recently, consumer prices in China have been quite low, but China is not exporting deflation to other parts of the world. <u>The truth is</u> we have been on the receiving end of deflation.

Example 5 (2007)

ST: 推动经济社会发展，改善人民生活，需要不断地增加经济总量，但是这种总量的增加是不能以过度地消耗资源能源和污染环境为代价的。

GLOSS: Promoting economic and social development and improving people's livelihood require the continuous growth of the overall economic size. Yet this increase in overall size cannot come at the price of the excessive consumption of resources and energy and pollution of the environment.

TT: <u>Actually</u>, to promote our social progress and improve people's livelihood, it is important to grow the economy on one hand, but at the same time, our economic growth must not come at the expense of resource and energy depletion or environmental pollution.

Similarly, in Examples 3, 4 and 5, metadiscourse markers "as a matter of fact", "the truth is" and "actually" have been respectively added by the interpreters. Discursively and rhetorically, these serve to (re)frame the premiers' discourse in a more persuasive, convincing and emphatic manner. This has also (re)presented a positive image that the government speaks in a factual and truthful way in front of the international audience.

Notably, some of the metadiscourse markers semantically related to fact, truth and reality, as pointed out in these examples (e.g. *actually*), are subsumed under the category of boosters in Hyland and Tse's (2004) taxonomy, which function to "emphasise force or writer's certainty in proposition" (ibid: 169). Such repeated additions by the government-affiliated interpreters are particularly salient, considering the observation that interpreters tend to omit certain "peripheral elements" (such as boosters) in the highly demanding interpreting process (Bartłomiejczyk 2010: 185). Using this as a useful departure point, more detailed attention is focused on the particular structure 'this/the fact that' in the corpus data.

Interpreters' metadiscursive mediation using "this/the fact that"

Attention is now focused on "this/the fact that", a noun complement structure featuring what is variously designated as a shell noun (Schmid 2000), stance noun (Jiang and Hyland 2015) or metadiscursive noun (Jiang and Hyland 2017, 2018). Metadiscursive nouns are defined as nouns that refer to the organisation of the discourse or the readers' understanding of it (Jiang and Hyland 2018). As illustrated in Jiang and Hyland's (2015) analysis focusing on academic writing, metadiscursive nouns in noun complement structures (e.g. *the reality that, the fact that*) tend to front-load attitudinal meanings, presupposing what follows as reality and fact. The use of these structures is highly relevant to engagement and is indicative of authorial stance and voice, serving to render (academic) writing more convincing. Despite its obvious merits, the definition of the metadiscursive noun structure is relatively restrictive (reader-writer relationship), and its scope of application seems to have focused largely on written communication in academic context so far. Looking beyond its interactive and interactional uses, the noun complement structure featuring metadiscursive noun can potentially be fruitful and of ideological salience in (interpreted) discursive communication in political and institutional settings.

Facts, *per definitionem*, refer to things that are true. According to the Cambridge Dictionary, fact is "something that is known to have happened or to exist, especially something for which proof exists, or about which there is information" or, according to the Oxford Dictionary, "a thing that is known or proved to be true". Since political discourse is essentially about presenting a certain version of fact and truth, a focus on the "this/the fact that" construction is potentially more interesting to explore in investigating the interpreters' ideological mediation than such structures as "the hope that", "the plan that" or "the information that". That is, the semantic and attitudinal meaning is explicitly indicated through the foregoing noun *fact*, which seemingly predetermines the truth value of the statement or proposition to follow. A systematic corpus-based analysis of this particular structure also promises to shed light on what is considered by the government and interpreters as "fact" over the course of 20 years.

To this end, "fact that" was searched in the English sub-corpus as a way to retrieve other possible variants such as 'this fact that'. It is shown that there are 20 concordance lines in the data, averaging slightly over one concordance line each year (Figure 3.1). Some of the concordance lines are: "I was more reassured by <u>the fact that</u> these policies resulted in the increase of fiscal revenue by 196 billion yuan last year" (2001); "There is only one China in the world. Although the mainland and Taiwan have not been reunified, <u>the fact that</u> there is only one China has never

high, but here I'd like to call your attention to this	fact, that in China we have 500 extremely large or mega state-owned enterprises,	1998
ease of the fiscal deficit, but you have to mind the	fact that all the deficits have been used to support infrastructure projects. We are	2001
ssured. But certainly, I was more reassured by the	fact that these policies resulted in the increase of fiscal revenue by 196 billion yua	2001
of headache. I don't know if you are aware of the	fact that the amount of soya bean that the United States exports to China is as mu	2002
main problems in China-Japan relations lie in the	fact that some leaders in Japan keep on visiting the Yasukuni Shrine many times,	2004
I think a very important contributing factor is the	fact that we have always upheld unity of the Party and safeguarded social and po	2004
nainland and Taiwan have not been reunified, the	fact that there is only one China has never changed, not even in the slightest way.	2005
s and deceptive. We need to stay alert against the	fact that they are now intensifying their efforts to pursue the secessionist activitie	2006
ith the Japanese people. They have to do with the	fact that the leader of Japan continues to visit the shrine where the class-A war cr	2006
eautiful next year. A: As for your question on the	fact that the Chinese government did not meet the goal in environmental protecti	2007
nismatch of investment and consumption and the	fact that our current economic growth relies too heavily on investment and expor	2007
ood job in addressing those challenges lies in the	fact that whether we can do a good job in conserving energy, reducing discharge	2007
lacao. A: People are all very concerned about the	fact that whether China will be able to attain the goal of 8% GDP growth for this y	2009
tryside and take a look for yourself, you'll see the	fact that no matter how much investment you may make in the countryside that v	2009
ur question the other way around. That is the true	fact that Tibet's peace and stability and Tibet's continuous progress have proven t	2009
t you described in your question accords with the	fact that there has been a large inflow of foreign capital into China every year. But	2010
saving on the part of some major economies, the	fact that some financial institutions have been blindly pursuing their own profits,	2010
ng the trip in 2011, I was deeply impressed by the	fact that Hong Kong was brimming with vitality under "One country two systems'	2013
ormance in the past several years in particular the	fact that we sustained a medium-high growth of the economy last year in spite of	2017
gh growth of the economy last year in spite of the	fact that both the world economic and global trade growth hit a seven year low sl	2017

Figure 3.1 Screenshot of concordance lines featuring *this/the fact that*

changed, not even in the slightest way" (2005); "We need to stay alert against the fact that they [Taiwan] are now intensifying their efforts to pursue the secessionist activities aimed at the so-called Taiwan independence" (2006); and [the difficulties in China–Japan relationship] "have to do with the fact that the leader of Japan continues to visit the shrine where the class-A war criminals are worshiped on various occasions" (2006).

To explore the interpreters' level of mediation, meticulous comparative analyses were carried out between the isolated concordance lines and their Chinese originals on a one-to-one basis. If concepts relating to "fact" and its near synonyms are explicitly mentioned in the Chinese STs, they can be deemed direct triggers responsible for the interpreters' use of the noun complement structure in the English TTs. Otherwise, any additions of the construction untriggered by the STs can be deemed signs of the interpreters' agency. Comparative analyses suggest that, out of the 20 instances of "this/the fact that", only one instance (in 2005) is at least partially triggered by the Chinese ST ("一个中国的现实" or literally "the reality that there is only one China"). Put differently, the interpreters have added the metadiscursive structure "this/the fact that" in 19 of the 20 instances (95%). As such, the interpreters' repeated additions of the structure enable them to front-load attitude meanings, thus bringing to the fore the "factualness" of the statements to follow and (re)configure Beijing's version of reality. Discursively, this helps make the Chinese premier's already authoritative remarks appear even more convincing, trustworthy and rhetorically forceful overall.

For more insights into exactly what are metadiscursively (re)packaged and (re)presented as solid and indisputable "fact" in English, further (comparative) CDA analysis was carried out. It shows that the interpreters' repeated additions of the structure can be placed within three major categories in terms of discursive function: (1) general argument and justification, (2) positive *self*-presentation and (3) negative *other*-presentation. These along with illustrative examples are discussed next.

General argument and justification

First and foremost, the interpreters' repeated additions of "the fact that" serve to boost the government's argument and justificatory discourse in a general manner (e.g. defending China's positions and policies, denying others' claims, and reassuring the public). This is illustrated noticeably in Examples 6 and 7.

Example 6 (2009)

ST: 中国13亿人口有9亿农民，如果你到农村去看，我以为在那里有多少的投资都不算多。中国的市场无论从人口和面积来看，都比欧美的市场更大。

GLOSS: China has a population of 1.3 billion including 0.9 billion farmers. If you go to the countryside and have a look there, I think over there however much you invest is not enough. China's market, whether from the perspective of population or size, is bigger than Europe and the United States.

TT: Among the 1.3 billion people we have in this country, about 900 million are farmers. If you go to the countryside and take a look for yourself, you'll see <u>the fact that</u> no matter how much investment you may make in the countryside that will not be enough. China's market potentials are far larger than European countries or the United States, given the population it has and given its size.

In this example, the Chinese premier responds to the journalist's question on how the government is confident that it will achieve a high GDP growth rate of 8% amidst the global financial crisis. In his answer, the premier highlights that there is a huge rural population in the countryside and thus great market potential for investment. When (re)packaged into English, the interpreter has added the meta-discursive expression "the fact that". This conveys a sense that there are great market potentials and ample room for China's economic development at a high speed, given that China's countryside has a huge population and is in need of investment (which is an objective fact). Rhetorically and discursively, this makes the premier's words appear even more fact-based, reassuring and compelling in English, thus seemingly giving the argument more weight in front of a global audience.

Example 7 (2010)

ST: 其实你说的情况和每年大量的外资进入中国并不完全符合。

GLOSS: Actually, the situation you've mentioned and (the situation) that each year a large amount of foreign capital enters into China do not completely match.

TT: I don't think the situation that you described in your question accords with <u>the fact that</u> there has been a large inflow of foreign capital into China every year.

In this example, the Chinese premier calls into question the journalist's description, arguing that it contradicts the current situation that there is a large inflow of foreign capital into China each year. Notably, the emphatic "the fact that" is added by the interpreter. This adds further validity and factualness to the premier's discourse in English, making it more convincing that the journalist's utterance is not in line with the actual "fact".

Positive *self*-presentation

Close critical comparisons between the STs and TTs suggest that the interpreters' proliferated additions of "this/the fact that" also lead to positive *self*-presentation and negative *other*-presentation, a scenario described in van Dijk's ideological square. According to van Dijk (1993a, 1993b, 1997), for various ideological and legitimating purposes, sociopolitical actors (e.g. politicians) tend to emphasise positive elements about *Us* (self) and negative elements about *Them* (other) in order to gain advantages (dominance, power *etc.*).

Discursively, the interpreters' repeated additions of the seemingly innocuous metadiscursive structure have (re)framed reality, further foregrounding positive things as "facts" in an emphatic manner (usually achievements thanks to the Chinese government). This is evidenced in Examples 8–10.

Example 8 (2004)

ST: 上个世纪 80年代末、90年代初，在中国发生了一场严重的政治风波。苏联解体，东欧剧变，在这个关系党和国家命运的严重的时刻，党中央紧紧依靠全党同志和全国人民，坚持十一届三中全会以来的路线不动摇，成功地稳住了中国改革开放的大局，捍卫了中国特色的社会主义事业。15年过去了，中国的改革开放和社会主义现代化建设取得了巨大的成就，这是有目共睹的。取得这样重大的成就，一个重要的原因就是我们坚持维护全党的团结和统一，维护社会政治的稳定。

GLOSS: Last century, at the end of the 1980s and in the beginning of the 1990s, in China occurred a serious political turbulence. The Soviet Union disintegrated and Eastern Europe underwent drastic transformations. At this critical moment bearing on the party and the country's fate, the Party Central Committee closely relied on the whole party comrades and all the Chinese people, unswervingly adhered to the lines adopted since the Third Plenary Session of the 11th Party Central Committee, successfully stabilised the big picture of China's reform and opening-up, and defended the cause of socialism with Chinese characteristics. 15 years on, China's reform and opening-up and socialist modernisation drive made tremendous achievements. This is evident to all eyes. Having made such tremendous achievements, one important reason is that we stuck to the maintenance of unity and solidarity of the whole party and the maintenance of social and political stability.

TT: At the end of the 1980s and in the beginning of the 1990s, China faced a very serious political turbulence. At that time, the Soviet Union disintegrated and drastic changes took place in Eastern Europe. So at that critical moment what hung in the balance was the future of our Party and the future of our country. At that time, the Party Central Committee closely rallied the whole Party and all the Chinese people together. We adhered to the lines and policies adopted since the Third Plenary Session of the 11th Party Central Committee, and we successfully stabilised the general situation of reform and opening up in China and safeguarded the cause of building socialism with Chinese characteristics. Fifteen years have passed. During this time, tremendous achievements were made in China's reform, opening up and socialist modernisation. These achievements are self-evident to all. I think a very important contributing factor is <u>the fact that</u> we have always upheld unity of the Party and safeguarded social and political stability in this country.

In this example, the Associated Press journalist poses a highly sensitive, if not taboo, question regarding the crushed student protest in Beijing in 1989 in a face-threatening way. In response, the premier discursively justifies the government's decision to crack down on the protest movement at a "critical" moment when the future of the Party and China was hanging "in the balance". Through uniting "the whole party and all the Chinese people together", the outcome of the Reform and Opening-up was "successfully stabilised" and the "cause of building socialism with Chinese characteristics" was defended. Now 15 years on, the achievements made in China's economic reform and modernisation are "tremendous" and "self-evident to all".

Interestingly, in English, upholding "unity of the Party" and safeguarding "social and political stability" by the government are explicitly (re)framed as solid "fact" responsible for China's accomplishments. Whilst the interpreter's employment of the metadiscursive structure "the fact that" might serve certain syntactic functions, its use is highly salient in such political communication. Discursively and rhetorically, the addition further facilitates the government's positive *self*-portrayal, effectively turning the otherwise face-threatening topic into a glorification of the government as the restorer of China's stability and guardian of China's national interests. This therefore leads to further legitimisation of the crackdown, which presumably was for the greater good of the country. Interestingly, the interpreted version was quoted verbatim and (re)contextualised in a CNN article (Figure 3.2), thus giving the interpreting product further international exposure beyond the *hic-et-nunc* confines of the conference hall.

Another two examples relating to the interpreters' metadiscursive (re)construction and positive *self*-representation of their institutional employer are discussed next.

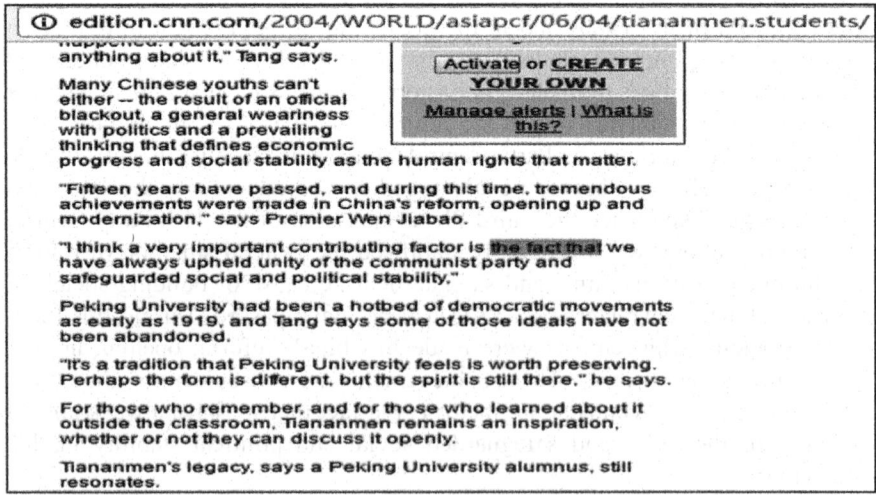

Figure 3.2 Screenshot of the interpreted discourse (re)contextualised on the CNN website

Example 9 (2009)

ST: 你所提的问题，恰恰相反，西藏的安定和西藏继续的进步，说明我们政策的正确。

GLOSS: The question you've raised. . . . Quite the contrary, Tibet's stability and Tibet's continued progress indicate that our policies are right.

TT: Actually I believe that we need to put your question the other way around. That is <u>the true fact that</u> Tibet's peace and stability and Tibet's continuous progress have proven that the policies we have adopted are right.

In response to the *Financial Times* journalist's potentially challenging question on whether there exist serious problems with China's policies in Tibet as well as other Tibetan parts of China, the premier defends China's policies, emphasising that Tibet's stability and progress have proven that Beijing's policies are right. Interestingly, the metadiscursive structure "the true fact that" is added by the interpreter in English. By pre-modifying the achievements, that is, Tibet's stability and progress, as "true fact", the interpreter has positioned with Beijing and foregrounded (Fairclough 1995) the positive elements further in English. This adds an additional layer of factualness and persuasiveness to the original Chinese discourse that the government's policies on Tibet are successful rather than problematic.

Example 10 (2013)

ST: 我访港的时候深感一国两制下的香港充满活力。

GLOSS: I, when visiting Hong Kong, deeply felt that Hong Kong was full of vitality under One Country, Two Systems.

TT: During the trip in 2011, I was deeply impressed by <u>the fact that</u> Hong Kong was brimming with vitality under One Country, Two Systems.

This extract from the 2013 conference constitutes another case in point concerning the interpreters' positive *self*-representation of their institutional employer. Clearly, the already positive discourse of Hong Kong being prosperous and dynamic in Chinese is further strengthened through the interpreter's employment of the metadiscursive structure "the fact that". As such, by (re)configuring this as undeniable 'fact', Hong Kong's impressive achievements are effectively (re)framed as the direct result of the central government's successful administration under the "One Country Two Systems" formula since the 1997 handover from British rule. Once again, the metadiscursively (re)framed discourse featuring 'the fact that' was later taken for granted and appeared on various websites such as C-SPAN (USA) as an official record of the premier's words. The same extract was also quoted verbatim and (re)contextualised in an article on the *China Daily* newspaper website (cf. Figure 3.3).

Negative *other*-presentation

In addition to strengthening China's discourse of positive *self*-presentation, the metadiscursive construction "the fact that" is also strategically employed by the interpreters in the negative (re)framing of the ideological *other* in a more

Figure 3.3 Screenshot of the interpreted discourse (re)contextualised on the *China Daily* website

convincing and factual manner (e.g. the assignment of blame). This is illustrated in the following examples.

Examples 11 (2004)

ST: 现在日中两国关系存在的主要问题是日本的有些领导人多次参拜供有甲级战犯亡灵的靖国神社，极大地伤害了中国人民的感情和亚洲人民的感情。

GLOSS: Now the major issue that exists in Japan-China relations is that some leaders in Japan have on numerous occasions visited the Yasukuni Shrine, where class-A war criminals' dead bodies are enshrined. This has greatly hurt the feelings of the Chinese people and the feelings of people in Asia.

TT: Now the main problems in China-Japan relations lie in <u>the fact that</u> some leaders in Japan keep on visiting the Yasukuni Shrine many times, which enshrined Class-A war criminals. This has hurt the pride of the Chinese people and people in other Asian countries.

In this example, the Chinese premier makes his position explicitly clear regarding the root cause behind the current difficulties in China–Japan ties. Evidently, the ideologically salient "the fact that" is added in the English interpretation. Such metadiscursive (re)configuration by the interpreter highlights that it is an irrefutable fact that the Japanese side is solely to blame for the difficult bilateral relations. This, without doubt, shows the interpreter's alignment with their institutional employer. More importantly, the addition leads to further *othering* of the Japanese side, discursively (re)creating a more pronounced dichotomy between the positive *Us* and the negative *Them* (van Dijk 1993a, 1993b, 1997). Notably, the interpreter-mediated *othering* discourse featuring the metadiscursive expression was later invoked verbatim and published on the English version of the Chinese government website (www.gov.cn/) as official record without further changes (cf. Figure 3.4).

The following example from the 2006 conference is another good case in point, illustrating how the interpreter has served to foster a heightened version of external reality using metadiscourse. In this example, the Chinese premier answers questions on China's position on Taiwan at a time when the tensions between mainland China and Taiwan became a focal point.

Example 12 (2006)

ST: 台湾当局领导人[. . .]公然挑衅一个中国的原则，严重破坏两岸的和平稳定[. . .]值得警惕的是，他们正在加紧台独分裂活动，推行以法理台独为目标的宪法改造工程。

GLOSS: The leader of the Taiwan authorities [. . .] openly confronted the One-China principle and seriously undermined peace and stability across the Taiwan Straits. [. . .] It is worth staying alert that they are now intensifying efforts to conduct secessionist activities aimed at Taiwan independence, pushing for the constitutional re-engineering project with the goal of *de jure* Taiwan independence.

TT: The leader of the Taiwan authorities [. . .] recently provocated the one-China principle and seriously undermined peace and stability in the Taiwan Straits. [. . .] We need to stay alert against the fact that they are now intensifying their efforts to pursue the secessionist activities aimed at the *so-called* Taiwan independence. They are also going all out to pursue their goal of *so-called de jure* Taiwan independence through the *so-called* constitutional re-engineering.

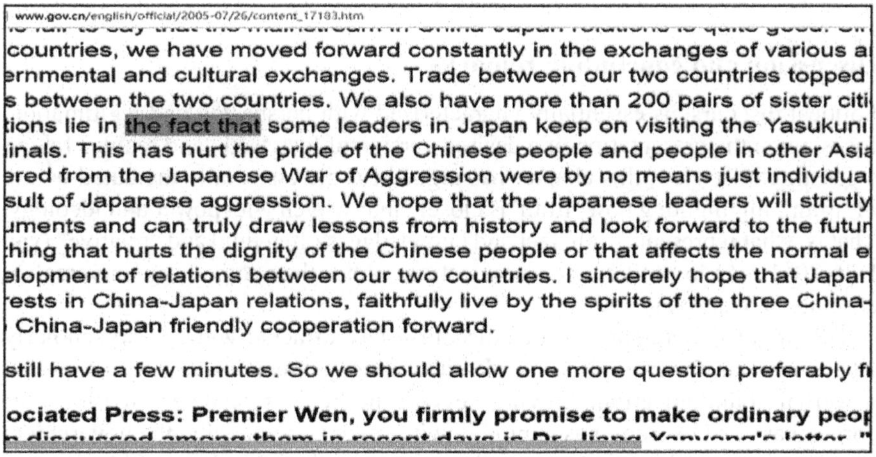
www.gov.cn/english/official/2005-07/26/content_17183.htm

countries, we have moved forward constantly in the exchanges of various a
ernmental and cultural exchanges. Trade between our two countries topped
s between the two countries. We also have more than 200 pairs of sister citi
tions lie in the fact that some leaders in Japan keep on visiting the Yasukuni
inals. This has hurt the pride of the Chinese people and people in other Asi
ered from the Japanese War of Aggression were by no means just individua
sult of Japanese aggression. We hope that the Japanese leaders will strictl
uments and can truly draw lessons from history and look forward to the futu
thing that hurts the dignity of the Chinese people or that affects the normal e
elopment of relations between our two countries. I sincerely hope that Japa
ests in China-Japan relations, faithfully live by the spirits of the three China-
China-Japan friendly cooperation forward.

still have a few minutes. So we should allow one more question preferably f

ociated Press: Premier Wen, you firmly promise to make ordinary peo

Figure 3.4 Screenshot of the interpreted discourse appearing on the official Chinese government website (English)

In this example, the premier made his position explicitly clear that the secessionist forces in Taiwan are pursing Taiwan independence, warning that this move is dangerous and deceptive in nature and has "seriously undermined peace and stability in the Taiwan Straits". Interestingly, "the fact that" is added by the interpreter in the English interpretation. This addition is salient and emphatic, laying bare the "fact" that the "secessionist" activities the Taiwan leader pursues are real and worrying. This therefore adds a heightened sense of urgency. Notably, the unfavourable image of the Taiwanese leader is further strengthened through the interpreter's repeated use of the attitudinal epithet (Halliday 1985) "so-called". This leads to the further *othering* of the independence-related activities as illegitimate, groundless, wrong or perhaps even farcical. Such active mediation illustrates the interpreter's disapproval of the very idea, thereby signalling a strong level of institutional alignment *vis-à-vis* Beijing's official stance. Relationally, assigning blame to the *other* in such an emphatic manner has also served to (re)construct a more positive image of the *self* being just and justified.

To sum up, moving beyond written discourse, the metadiscursive structure "this/the fact that" was explored from the perspective of ideology in interpreter-mediated political discursive communication. Statistically, it is found that the interpreters tend to proliferate the use of the structure in English overall. Considering the essentially categorical and non-negotiable semantic meaning of "fact", such pre-modification sets the tone for the propositional information that comes afterwards. Apart from merely indicating the interpreters' ideological stances and institutional identity, their additions of the metadiscursive construction strengthen Beijing's justificatory discourse in general. Discursively, it contributes to positive *self*-presentation and negative *other*-presentation, leading to the polarised (re)presentations of *us* (Chinese government) and *them* (e.g. Japan and pro-Taiwan independence forces). Discursively and rhetorically, such (re)configuration of reality serves to portray a significantly more favourable image of Beijing being truthful, trustworthy, fact-based and just in English.

Discussion and concluding remarks

Political discourse is essentially characterised with persuasion and legitimation, focusing on the presentation of a desired version of fact, truth, and reality. Taking a constructivist view, this chapter has argued for the essentially mediated nature of 'truth', highlighting how 'truth' is closely interwoven with power and ideology. That is, what represents truth, fact and knowledge is often fluid and "relative" (van Dijk 2011: 45) in political communication, rather than something universalist, absolute and hard-and-fast.

The linguistic category of metadiscourse has attracted widespread scholarly attention so far, for example, in academic writing, yet remains largely unexplored in verbal communication. Moving beyond the field of academic writing, this corpus-based CDA study has explored, with some systematicity, the government interpreters' metadiscursive (re)framing of fact, truth and reality at China's press conferences, drawing on 20 years' corpus data. A macro-level comparison of the established metadiscursive markers (semantically relating to truth, fact, and reality) between both sub-corpora points towards the government interpreters' (over) production of relevant metadiscursive items in English (a noticeable 143.5% increase). Cumulatively, the interpreters' repeated additions of these metadiscourse markers serve to further strengthen China's discourse, thus rendering the premiers' already authoritative utterances even more emphatic, persuasive and convincing. That is, although there might not be fundamental changes to the propositional content *per se*, such (re)framing serves to add an additional layer of persuasiveness and authority to Beijing's discourse and (re)creates a more positive image of the Chinese government being truthful, factual and trustworthy overall.

To explore how Beijing's discourse is mediated metadiscursively at a micro-level, specific attention was focused on the metadiscursive expression "this/the fact that". The pre-modification featuring the head noun "fact" (categorical and non-negotiable in semantic meaning) sets the tone for the propositional content to follow. This, therefore, presupposes the ensuing information as seemingly indisputable truth and fact with little room for negotiation. Apart from an overall strengthening of Beijing's argument and justificatory discourse, the interpreters' repeated additions of the noun complement structure "this/the fact that" lead to a heightened sense of positive *self*-presentation and negative *other*-presentation in English. In other words, such metadiscursive (re)framing fosters further legitimation and justification of the government's decisions and policies and glorification of its achievements and, meanwhile, leads to a negative presentation of the ideological *other* (that is, Japan and the Taiwan leaders, for example, are to blame for certain undesirable situations). This, therefore, effectively contributes to the dichotomy between *Us* and *Them* (van Dijk 1993a, 1993b, 1997) in discourse.

As such, the seemingly innocuous category of metadiscourse has proven a very interesting site of linguistic engineering and constitutes one of the "critical points" in establishing the interpreters' subjectivity and evaluative stance in the decision-making processes (Munday 2012). Such active (re)framing by the interpreters, as (re)assigners of truth value, signals their agency on different levels. First and foremost, it reflects their evaluations of the sociopolitical realities, thus pointing to their institutional alignment with Beijing's official positions and their in-group identity as key members of the Chinese government. Also, their mediation highlights their crucial role as agents of knowledge in fostering truism and perpetuating a desired version of fact and reality through discursive means. Such (re)construction arguably enforces a sort of "ideological closure" (Hartley 1982: 63) regarding what is undeniable "fact" and "truth", thereby precluding and further stifling other voices of disagreement partly through the proliferated use of metadiscursive devices.

As exemplified previously, in view of the increasingly globalised and (re)mediat(is)ed world (Gu 2018b; Gu 2020; Gu and Tipton 2020) we live in, such metadiscursive (re)construction by the government interpreters seems to be of additional discursive salience and can potentially carry far-reaching ramifications and trigger a chain of events internationally. That is, given the high-profile and outward-facing nature of the press conferences, the interpreted English discourse often represents China's official positions and gets headlined in newspapers (e.g. the *Guardian*), quoted verbatim on international news networks (e.g. CNN and BBC), (re)contextualised on social media platforms (e.g. Facebook, Twitter, and Instagram) and extensively invoked in official government records and academic works as the state-sanctioned version of Beijing's voice. To conclude, essentially interdisciplinary in nature, this corpus-based CDA study demonstrates that the interpreter-mediated press conferences are a major discursive event and a core mechanism in producing knowledge and circulating truth and fact beyond a country's national borders. Traditionally tending to be evanescent and die in the air (Cencini and Aston 2002: 47), the interpreter-mediated product in the political arena is now often heavily relied upon and thus (semi)perpetuated and enshrined as a vital source of sociopolitical knowledge and a powerful shaper of realities, thanks to modern technological advances.

References

Atkinson, P. (1997) 'Narrative turn or blind alley?', *Qualitative Health Research* 7(3): 325–344.
Baker, M. (2006) *Translation and Conflict*, Manchester: St Jerome Publishing.
Baker, M. (2007) 'Reframing conflict in translation', *Social Semiotics* 17(2): 151–169.
Baker, M. (2008) 'Ethics of renarration', *Cultus* 1(1): 10–33.
Baker, M. (2010a) 'Narratives of terrorism and security: 'Accurate' translations, suspicious frames', *Critical Studies on Terrorism* 3(3): 347–364.
Baker, M. (2010b) 'Interpreters and translators in the war zone: Narrated and narrators', *The Translator* 16(2): 197–222.
Baker, P., Gabrielatos, C., KhosraviNik, M., Krzyzanowski, M., McEnery, T. and Wodak, R. (2008) 'A useful methodological synergy? Combining critical discourse analysis and corpus linguistics to examine discourses of refugees and asylum seekers in the UK press', *Discourse & Society* 19(3): 273–306.
Bartłomiejczyk, M. (2010) 'Effects of short intensive practice on interpreter trainees' performance', in *Why Translation Studies Matters*. D. Gile, G. Hansen and N. K. Pokorn (eds.), Amsterdam and Philadelphia: John Benjamins. pp. 183–194.
Bassnett, S. and Lefevere, A. (1990) *Translation, History and Culture*, London and New York: Pinter Publisher.
Beaton, M. (2007) 'Interpreted ideologies in institutional discourse: The case of the European Parliament', *The Translator* 13(2): 271–296.
Beaton-Thome, M. (2013) 'What's in a word? Your e*nemy combatant* is my r*efugee*: The role of simultaneous interpreters in negotiating the lexis of Guantánamo in the European Parliament', *Journal of Language and Politics* 12(3): 378–399.
Boukhaffa, A. (2018) 'Narrative (re)framing in translating modern Orientalism: A study of the Arabic translation of Lewis's *The crisis of Islam: Holy war and unholy terror*', *The Translator* 24(2): 166–182.
Bunton, D. (1999) 'The use of higher level Metatext in PhD Theses', *English for Specific Purposes* 18(Supplement): 41–56.
Cencini, M. and Aston, G. (2002) 'Resurrecting the Corp(Us/Se): Towards an encoding standard for interpreting data', in *Interpreting in the 21st Century*. G. Garzone and M. Viezzi (eds.), Amsterdam and Philadelphia: John Benjamins. pp. 47–62.
Crismore, A. (1989) *Talking with Readers: Meta-Discourse as Rhetorical Act*, New York: Peter Lang.

Crismore, A. and Farnsworth, R. (1989) 'Mr. Darwin and his readers: Exploring interpersonal metadiscourse as a dimension of ethos', *Rhetoric Review* 8(1): 91–112.

Darwish, A. (2006) 'Translating the news reframing constructed realities', *Translation Watch Quarterly* 2(1): 52–94.

Dubbati, B. and Abudayeh, H. (2018) 'The translator as an activist: Reframing conflict in the Arabic translation of Sacco's Footnotes in Gaza', *The Translator* 24(2): 147–165.

Fairclough, N. (1989) *Language and Power*, London: Longman.

Fairclough, N. (1995) *Discourse and Social Change*, Cambridge: Polity Press.

Foucault, M. (1984) 'Truth and power', in *The Foucault Reader: An Introduction to Foucault's Thought*. P. Rabinow (ed.), London: Penguin. pp. 51–75.

Frank, A. (1998) 'Just listening: Narrative and deep illness', *Families, Systems and Health* 16: 197–212.

Gu, C. (2018a) 'Towards a re-definition of government interpreters' agency against a backdrop of sociopolitical and cultural evolution: A case of premier's press conferences in China', in *Redefining Translation and Interpretation in Cultural Evolution*. O. I. Seel (ed.), Hershey: PA IGI Global. pp. 238–257.

Gu, C. (2018b) 'Forging a glorious past via the "present perfect": A corpus-based CDA analysis of China's past accomplishments discourse mediat(is)ed at China's interpreted political press conferences', *Discourse, Context & Media* 24: 137–149.

Gu, C. (2019) '(Re)manufacturing consent in English: A corpus-based critical discourse analysis of government interpreters' mediation of China's discourse on PEOPLE at televised political press conferences', *Target: International Journal of Translation Studies* 31(3): 465–499.

Gu, C. (2020) 'Concordancing China's friend, foe and frenemy: A corpus-based CDA of geopolitical actors (re)presented at China's interpreter-mediated political press conferences', in *Corpus-based Approaches to Grammar, Media and Health Discourses*. Yang B., and Li W (eds.), Singapore: Springer. pp. 197–232.

Gu, C. and Tipton, R. (2020) '(Re-)voicing Beijing's discourse through self-referentiality: A corpus-based CDA analysis of government interpreters' discursive mediation at China's political press conferences (1998-2017)', *Perspectives* 28(3): 406–423

Halliday, M. A. K. (1973) *Explorations in the Functions of Language Explorations in Language Study*, London: Edward Arnold.

Halliday, M. A. K. (1985) *An Introduction to Functional Grammar*, London: Arnold.

Hardt-Mautner, G. (1995) 'Only Connect', *Critical Discourse Analysis and Corpus Linguistics*. UCREL Technical Papers 6. University of Lancaster, Lancaster.

Hartley, J. (1982) *Understanding News*, London: Methuen.

Hatim, B. and Mason, I. (1990) *Discourse and the Translator*, London: Longman.

Hyland, K. (1998) 'Exploring corporate rhetoric: Metadiscourse in the CEO's letter', *The Journal of Business Communication* 35(2): 224–245.

Hyland, K. (2000) *Disciplinary Discourses: Social Interactions in Academic Writing*, London: Longman.

Hyland, K. (2005) *Metadiscourse: Exploring Interaction in Writing*, London and New York: Continuum.

Hyland, K. and Tse, P. (2004) 'Metadiscourse in academic writing: A reappraisal', *Applied Linguistics* 25(2): 156–177.

Jiang, F. and Hyland, K. (2015) '"The fact that": Stance nouns in disciplinary writing', *Discourse Studies* 17(5): 529–550.

Jiang, F. and Hyland, K. (2017) 'Metadiscursive nouns: Interaction and cohesion in abstract moves', *English for Specific Purposes* 46: 1–14.

Jiang, F. and Hyland, K. (2018) 'Nouns and academic interactions: A neglected feature of metadiscourse', *Applied Linguistics* 39(4): 508–531.

Kang, J. (2007) 'Recontextualization of news discourse: A case study of translation of news discourse on North Korea', *The Translator* 13(2): 219–242.

Kim, K. H. (2013) *Mediating American and South Korean News Discourses about North Korea through Translation: A Corpus-Based Critical Discourse Analysis*, Unpublished Ph.D. Thesis. University of Manchester, Manchester.

Kim, K. H. (2017a) 'Reframing the victims of WWII through translation: *So far from the Bamboo Grove* and Yoko Iyagi', *Target* 29(1): 87–109.

Kim, K. H. (2017b) 'Newsweek discourses on China and their Korean translations: A corpus-based approach', *Discourse, Context & Media* 15: 34–44.

Kim, K. H. (2018) 'Retranslation as a socially engaged activity: The case of the Rape of Nanking', *Perspectives* 26(3): 391–404.

Li, T. (2016) *Re-Shaping Appraisal Stance towards Self and Others in Chinese-English Translation of Political Discourse: A Corpus-Based Discourse Analysis Approach*. Unpublished Ph.D. Thesis, Shanghai Jiao Tong University, Shanghai.

Li, T. (2019) 'Representing China in translations of two Korean news outlets: A corpus-based discourse analysis approach', in *Corpus-Based Translation and Interpreting Studies in Chinese Contexts: Present and Future*. K. Hu and K. H. Kim (eds.), Cham: Springer. pp. 183–220.

Mazid, B. M. (2014) *CDA and PDA Made Simple: Language, Ideology and Power in Politics and Media*, Newcastle upon Tyne: Cambridge Scholars Publishing.

Munday, J. (2007) 'Translation and ideology: A textual approach', *The Translator* 13(2): 195–217.

Munday, J. (2012) *Evaluation in Translation: Critical Points of Translator Decision-Making*, London and New York: Routledge.

Partington, A. (2004) 'Corpora and discourse: A most congruous beast', in *Corpora and Discourse*. A. Partington, J. Morley and L. Haarman (eds.), Bern: Peter Lang. pp. 11–20.

Rabinow, P. (1991) *The Foucault Reader: An Introduction to Foucault's Thought*, New York: Penguin Books.

Schmid, H. (2000) *English Abstract Nouns as Conceptual Shells from Corpus to Cognition*, Berlin and New York: Mouton.

Simpson, P. and Mayr, A. (2009) *Language and Power: A Resource Book for Students*, London: Routledge.

Somers, M. R. and Gibson, G. D. (1994) 'Reclaiming the epistemological "other": Narrative and the social constitution of identity', in *Social Theory and the Politics of Identity*. C. Calhoun (ed.), Oxford and Cambridge: Blackwell. pp. 37–99.

Sutherland, O., Breen, A. V. and Lewis, S. P. (2013) 'Discursive narrative analysis: A study of online autobiographical accounts of self-injury', *The Qualitative Report* 18(48): 1–17.

Toury, G. (1995) *Descriptive Translation Studies- and Beyond*, Amsterdam and Philadelphia: John Benjamins.

Vande Kopple, W. J. (1985) 'Some exploratory discourse on metadiscourse', *College Composition and Communication* 36: 82–93.

van Dijk, T. A. (1993a) 'Editor's foreword to critical discourse analysis', *Discourse and Society* 4(2): 131–132.

van Dijk, T. A. (1993b) 'Principles of critical discourse analysis', *Discourse and Society* 4(2): 249–283.

van Dijk, T. A. (1997) 'What is political discourse analysis?', in *Political Linguistics*. J. Blommaert and G. Bulcaen (eds.), Amsterdam: John Benjamins. pp. 11–52.

van Dijk, T. A. (2011) 'Discourse, knowledge, power and politics: Towards critical epistemic discourse analysis', in *Critical Discourse Studies in Context and Cognition*. C. Hart (ed.), Amsterdam: John Benjamins. pp. 27–64.

Vukovic, M. (2014) 'Strong epistemic modality in parliamentary discourse', *Open Linguistics* 1(1): 37–52.

Wang, B. and Feng, D. (2018) 'A corpus-based study of stance-taking as seen from critical points in interpreted political discourse', *Perspectives* 26(2): 246–260.

Widdowson, H. G. (1995) 'Discourse analysis: A critical review', *Language and Literature* 4(3): 157–172.

Williams, J. (2007) *Style: Ten Lessons in Clarity and Grace*, New York: Pearson-Longman.

Wodak, R. and Meyer, M. (2009) 'Critical discourse analysis: History, agenda, theory, and methodology', in *Methods for Critical Discourse Analysis*. R. Wodak and M. Meyer (eds.), London: Sage. pp. 1–33.

Zhang, M. (2013) 'Stance and mediation in transediting news headlines as paratexts', *Perspectives: Studies in Translatology* 21(3): 396–411.

4 Competing narratives and military interpreters' choices

A case study on China–US disaster-relief joint military exercise

Qianhua Ouyang and Qiliang Xu

Introduction

Choices of language resources that carry evaluation are omnipresent in communication, including translation and interpreting (Munday 2012: 11). Previous research on translators' choices probes not only into the linguistic and cognitive aspects of translation and interpreting (T&I) but also to the social and cultural aspects, which relates to the purported "sociological turn" of T&I studies (e.g. Angelelli 2012; Pöchhacker 2009). Research on choices as the result of cognitive restraints focuses on the use of strategies to mitigate high cognitive loads. In other words, interpreters follow certain "laws" in their adoption of strategies (Gile 2009: 211) for problem solving and task-facilitating purposes (e.g. Bartlomiejczyk 2006; Chang and Schallert 2007; Liu 2009). Choices motivated by socio-cultural and political factors, on the other hand, reflect interpreters' more 'active' role as sociological and ideological mediators (e.g. Inghilleri 2004; Tryuk 2010; Lü and Li 2012). For instance, discourse-analytical approaches to interpreters' role in community settings suggest that interpreters are not literally performing linguistic conversion but often take an active or even intrusive role in the triadic communication (e.g. Wadensjö 1998: 112–113; Angermeyer 2009; Wang 2018).

Interpreted political events are perhaps the setting where most "discursive transformations, recontextualizations and retranslations" are found (Zheng and Ren 2017). Interpreters in discursive political events, such as political meetings and press conferences, sometimes make deliberate choices to alleviate or strengthen political or ideological tensions, alter value systems and reiterate a nation's stance-taking (e.g. Schäffner 2012; Munday 2012, 2018; Guo 2015b; Wang and Feng 2018).

Interpreters' choices in military events, a highly political and ideological setting, also deserve close examination. However, due to relatively scant and limited forms of documentation (Inghilleri 2015), product-oriented research on the role and choices of interpreters in the military setting is at best sporadic if not absent. With the author's experience as part of the language service to a China–US joint military exercise, this research has access to the authentic data of the midterm consultation conference of the aforementioned event. This chapter attempts to use a discourse-analytical approach to examine episodes of interpreting in the aforementioned event to unveil how context in military events may influence interpreters' choices. Context in this research is scrutinized via the lens of narrative theory. Different layers of narratives are brought as a more omnipresent context of the interpreting process.

The chapter starts with a short review of relevant literature on military interpreting and interpreters' choices, followed by elaborations on an analytical framework enlightened by narrative theory. The framework is then used to explore contextual elements of the China–US joint military exercise and how different layers of context influence interpreters' choices. The chapter concludes with a summary and implications.

Literature review

Military interpreting: a field of sensitivity

Military/conflict zone interpreting is situated in complex context. Language can be utilized as a fundamental political tool in military settings, especially when there is asymmetry of power or social hierarchy (Rafael 2007; Footitt and Kelly 2012: 7). In violent conflicts, interpreting is not only a mediating activity but is sometimes used as a "weapon" for the purpose of counterinsurgency (Rafael 2012). In other words, disorder or violence may disrupt the established norms of interpreting, which otherwise give way to alternative approaches for more desirable results. Under such circumstances, interpreters are not only cross-linguistic experts but also serve as an "important strategic resource" (Guo 2015a).

Previous research on military interpreting look primarily at three issues – the instability of interpreters' identity and positionality in war; the role of institutional affliations in the expression of interpreters' agency; and the protection of interpreters' security. Research on these factors discloses the underlying political, ideological and social concerns of this activity (Inghilleri 2015). Discursive research that investigates military interpreters' roles suggests multiple identities far beyond language service providers. Interpreters are sometimes endowed with the power to re-interpret the original according to their stances and motivations (e.g. Palmer 2007; Inghilleri 2005, 2010; Baker 2007; Sanatifar and Daghigh 2018). More interestingly, some interpreters in military settings are not professionally trained or employed and hence are positioned within the social/institutional frame of the military-political field, which results in a more volatile situation for interpreting activity (Guo 2015a; Inghilleri 2010). In other words, military interpreters' roles are in general instable in that they are subject to manipulation.

Interpreters' choices at "critical points"

"Critical points" is a concept proposed by Munday (2012) in the analysis of translators' and interpreters' decision-making process. Derived from the appraisal theory in systemic-functional linguistics, the concept seeks to identify translators' subjective intervention in the translating activity represented in the translated text. "Critical points" in translation refer to those points and lexical features in a text that in translation are most susceptible to value manipulation; those points that most frequently show a shift in translation, and those that generate the most interpretative and evaluative potential; those that may be most revealing of the translator's values.

(Munday 2012: 41)

The cultural or ideological manipulation in translation and interpreting mostly occurs at "critical points", where lexical shifts can often be observed. Intentional word choices can be made in interpretations to consolidate a particular political or ideological stance to deliver values that correspond with the interpreter's. As Munday (2012: 40) suggests, "a more pervasive question, more pressing for the understanding of the micro-level process of translation or interpreting, is the uncovering of values inserted into the text by the translator, perhaps surreptitiously and not consciously". For instance, Munday's (2012, 2018) detailed discussions on US presidents' inaugural addresses reveal 'translation shifts' at critical points where interpreters intervene. Wang and Feng (2018) also point out that the investigation of critical points in interpreting may unveil a nation's stance towards political issues. Hence, it is believed that in interpreter-mediated settings where political, ideological, cultural or value-imbued comments are conveyed, interpreters may confront stance-taking and more 'active' linguistic choices.

Analytical framework

The chapter argues in the opening sections that military interpreting unfolds in complex context and postulates high level of sensitivity. It is hence necessary to define context and operationalize this concept as an analytical tool to canvas the complexity of military events and explain interpreters' choices at critical points.

Context is a term coined by anthropologist Bronisław K. Malinowski and developed to its full extent by systemic functional linguistics (SFL). In the conception of SFL, text or discourse is always accompanied by other texts, namely the context. Context does not stop at the surrounding texts but "goes beyond what is said and written: it includes other non-verbal goings-on – the total environment in which a text unfolds" (Halliday and Hasan 1989: 5). The stratum of context in SFL has two layers, context of situation and context of culture. The former is "the immediate environment in which a text is actually functioning" (Halliday 1994: 46). The latter refers to the total socio-cultural background against which a text has to be interpreted. It is "the institutional and ideological background that gives value to the text and constrains its interpretation" (Halliday and Hasan 1989: 49). T&I studies is reaching a greater consensus that study of discursive events has to be situated in its environment (Hatim and Mason 1990, 1997a, 1997b; Munday and Zhang 2015; Zhang and Munday 2018). It is generally agreed that understanding of translational activities has to start at social context and situational context and looks at how language both acts upon and is constrained by this social context.

This research uses narrative theory as the explanatory tool to explicate the context of military events. The reason for choosing narrative theory to substantiate

Military interpreters' choices 67

contextual analysis is twofold. First, narrative is an important component of context. The general tenet is that narrative is a meta-code that "underpins all modes of communication", including translation (Baker 2006: 9). Fisher (1987: 193) even argues that "narration is the context for interpreting and assessing all communication". Second, narrative theory as an explanatory tool has been widely used to analyse translational activities with inherent conflict. Baker, for example, argues that translation and interpreting participate in shaping the way in which conflict unfolds (Baker 2006: 2). It is also discovered that translators and interpreters act as both the narrated and narrators in military settings, and their roles cannot be understood in isolation from the narrative of the military event (Baker 2010). If military interpreters' decision making does hinge upon the narration of the particular military event, a narrative account can yield fruitful results.

Baker presents a four-layer typology of narrative, namely, ontological narratives, public narratives, conceptual narratives and meta-narratives. This research employs the latter three to explicate the situational and socio-cultural context of military events. Public narratives are "stories elaborated by and circulating among social and institutional formations larger than individual, such as . . . [a] religious or educational institution, the media and the nation" (ibid: 33). Conceptual narratives are "concepts and explanations" constructed by social researchers that are penetrating and are powerful in "shaping public narratives during a specific period of history" (Baker 2006: 39). Meta-narrative is one of "the epic dramas of our time". Accounts of "Capitalism vs. Communism, the Individual vs. Society, Barbarism/Nature vs. Civility" are the resounding meta-narrative of this era (ibid: 44).

Figure 4.1 encapsulates the analytical framework of this research. The socio-cultural context of the particular military event to be analysed is instantiated through meta-narratives, conceptual narratives and public narratives on China–US relations. Public narratives on the military event are translated as the

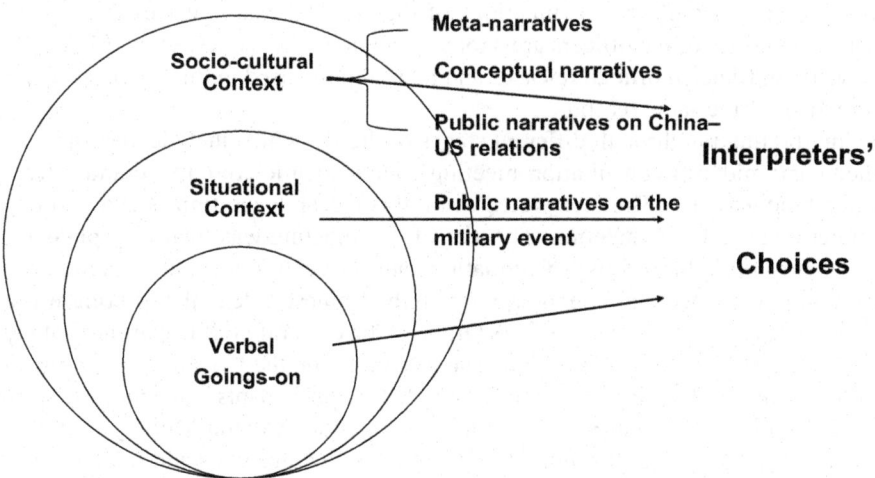

Figure 4.1 Analytical framework of the narratives

situational context. The chapter assumes that both contexts and verbal goings-on of the event can activate interpreter choices. Research on ideology of China and US is reviewed for a snapshot of meta-narratives and conceptual narratives. Related reports of mainstream media and government portals are surveyed for a summary of public narratives on China–US relations and the military event. Corpus-based discourse analysis is then carried out to probe into the triggers of interpreters' choices.

Narratives

As discussed in the previous section, narratives prospected in this research are meta- and conceptual narratives on China and the United States, public narratives on China–US relations or military relations in particular, and public narratives on the joint exercise (JE). This section starts with an introduction to the interpreted military event and then a summary of each layer of narratives.

The event

The military event analysed is an edition of the China–US Joint Humanitarian Assistance and Disaster Relief Exercise. Although the People's Liberation Army (PLA) of China carries out frequent bilateral and multilateral joint exercise and training in various domains, the Joint Humanitarian Assistance and Disaster Relief Exercise is the only regular bilateral JE between China and the United States. In this JE, the US Army and the PLA provide humanitarian assistance and disaster relief (HADR) to a third affected state (imagined) through a multinational coordination centre in an effort to better coordinate responses to disasters.

One of the authors was part of the language service to the JE, offering translational support to the liaison officers of the event. As a result, the author has access to the recordings of various meetings of the JE. The exact year of the JE and names and titles of the officers are anonymized upon the request of the PLA units concerned. Links to official releases and news reports used in this chapter are not provided for the same reason.

Interpreting ran through different stages of the JE, which included preparatory meetings, midterm consultation meetings, an academic conference and a live-troop field exercise. The interpreted event this research scrutinizes is a two-day midterm consultation meeting. The aim of this meeting was finalizing plans for the live troop field exercise. Negotiations and in-depth discussions were hence common in the meeting. The interpreter on the Chinese side to the meeting was a staff officer from the Foreign Affairs Office of the General Staff Department of the PLA Central Military Commission. The interpreter on the US side was a civilian officer of the US Pacific Command (USPACOM). Participants in the meeting were officers from the General Staff Department of the PLA Central Military Commission, a regional Theatre Command of PLA, two PLA hospitals and officers from USPACOM. The midterm consultation meeting took place in the United States, while the final live troop field exercise took place in a city in China.

Overarching meta- and conceptual narratives

Meta-narrative is defined as narratives 'in which we are embedded as contemporary actors in history" (Baker 2006: 44). The United States and China fall into multiple pairs of dichotomy in terms of meta-narratives. The following is a short list that covers dichotomic differences between the two countries in terms of social and economic systems and personal values:

- Socialism vs. capitalism: China being the largest socialist country in the world, the United States the largest capitalist country.
- South vs. North: China being the largest developing country, the United States the largest developed country.
- Collectivism vs. individualism: Chinese people looking more at how their deeds affect the whole, Americans more at themselves.
- Rule of people vs. Rule of Law: China having its alternative to the Western conception of the rule of law.

(Chew 2005; Han et al. 2011; Qin 2011)

Conceptual narratives, as introduced in the previous section, are concepts and explanations that shape public minds and narratives. For China–US relations, one of the overarching concepts in recent years has been the *Thucydides trap*. The general argument of this concept is that when a rising country causes fear in an established power, the tension may escalate towards war. The concept got its name from Thucydides, the Greek philosopher who argues that the rise of Athens instilled fear in Sparta and hence caused the war (Allison 2017). Although raising more controversies than positive responses, the conceptual narrative of the Thucydides trap has its audience across the academia and media. Suggesting that there are tensions between China and United States is at least theoretically true as China is now the world's second largest economy and an increasingly active player in global governance (Zhang 2016; Kennedy 2018). Therefore, the Thucydides trap has become a popular conceptual tool in studying US relations. For instance, about 200 research papers can be found through *Google Scholar Search* discussing China–US relations through the lens of the Thucydides trap. Harvard University even has a special initiative on US–China relations named after Allison's book. For the media, this concept, being highly sensational, has helped to coin many headline stories on China–US relations. A quick search on any major search engine yields a long list of results.

Public narratives on China–US relations

Public narratives are "stories elaborated by and circulating among social and institutional formations larger than the individual" (Baker 2006: 39). Government and the media are typical institutional producers of public narratives. This chapter mainly looks at reports from government portals and mainstream media a year prior to the JE. The former represents official narratives and the latter mass media narratives.

The Chinese government portals screened are the Ministry of Foreign Affairs (MFA) and the Ministry of Defense (MoD) (English version) and their US counterparts, the Department of State (DoS) and the Department of Defense (DoD). Articles surveyed are hard news, annual reports on bilateral relations and regular press conference wrap-ups. These news genres are more factual and less biased. Selected news agencies and mainstream media of the United States are the Associated Press, Reuters and the *Washington Post*. Selected mainstream media of China are the *People's Daily* and the *Global Times*, two state media of China, and the *South China Morning Post*, a local media of Hong Kong. A simple search was carried out on the government and media portals via keywords like "China US relations", "China and US", "China, US, military", etc. Search results were manually screened for relevance. The survey aims at locating individual reports on China–US relations that can represent public narratives on this topic.

Located articles or public narratives do reflect the ups and downs of China–US relations. There are articles narrating stability or even the progress of bilateral relations. But quantitatively more significant are negative stories on issues like trade imbalance, differentiated opinions on rule of trade and human rights, etc. Events on national security being frequently reported are also more negative than neutral, which include South China Sea disputes, East China Sea issues and intellectual property rights concerns of military technology.

Echoes between public the conceptual narratives can be captured easily. Both public narratives from mainstream media and government portals are to a certain extent shadowed by the conceptual narratives of the Thucydides trap, that is, competitive relations between the two countries. News headlines on China–US relations often see wordings such as 'US-China rivalry', 'power rivalry', 'collision', 'fight', 'competition' and 'dispute'. Reports in Chinese language use dodgy terms like "新型大国关系" (new type of relation between major countries), "中美关系新定位" (new positioning of China–US relations) and "中美关系十字路口" (crossroads of China–US relations), etc. These headline wordings imply a competing relation between China and the United States.

A glimpse at headlines on China–US military relations from Chinese and US national security portals reveals a similar picture (Table 4.1). The left column of Table 4.1 lists headlines from the MoD website, saturated with attitude-carrying

Table 4.1 Headlines on MoD and DoD portals

Ministry of Defense (China) portal	*Department of Defense (US) portal*
• China <u>refutes</u> U.S. allegation of . . . • China <u>strongly opposes</u> U.S. • China <u>blasts</u> new U.S. . . . • Military <u>rebuts</u> U.S. report . . . • China <u>urges</u> U.S. to be rational	• U.S. <u>Must</u> Act Now to Maintain Military Technological Advantage . . . • U.S. advantages <u>eroding</u> . . . • China a <u>Rising Threat</u> to National Security . . . • U.S. <u>Protests</u> Chinese Interference With . . . . . .

verbs such as "refutes", "opposes", "blasts", "rebuts", etc. Headlines from the DoD website, on the other hand, use verbs with negative connotations and strong modal verbs. And the content is mostly about China threatening the leading position of the United States in military power and technology. It can hence be observed that the official narratives are imaging the two nations as military competitors or even opponents.

Public narratives on the event

Quite opposite to the imaging of China–US military relation in general, reports on the JE are factual and positive.

The MoD released seven reports in Chinese and four reports in English on the JE. News headlines of the four English reports are as follows:

> *China, U.S. militaries wrap up joint disaster relief drill*
> *China, U.S. begin joint disaster relief drill*
> *U.S.-China humanitarian assistance and disaster relief exercise in progress*
> *China-U.S. holds HADR Expert Discussion before disaster relief exercise*

These four titles, providing factual information of "who and what", contrast substantially with those attitude-sated headlines in Table 4.1.

Not many news articles can be found on the selected mainstream media in China. The few search results are reposts of official releases of the MoD. Mainstream media narratives on the JE hence kept the same tone as the official narrative.

One official release on the JE was found on the US DoD portal. The title of the release is "U.S., Chinese Troops Attend Disaster Management Exchange". A close reading of the release sees a positive evaluation of the exchange as an "invaluable" opportunity of building understanding and trust. The news release from the Associated Press is titled "China, US militaries stage joint humanitarian relief drill", assuming the same factual tone as the official narrative. The news headline from Reuters, – "China, U.S. look past tension with joint relief drill"–, is rather positive. The wording "look past tension" suggests that the JE opens up opportunities for positive development.

Summary: competing narratives

This section discusses meta- and conceptual narratives on China and the United States and surveys reports from government and mainstream media portals for public narratives on bilateral (military) relations and the JE. It is found that meta-, conceptual and public narratives on bilateral relations epitomize the two countries as competitors. Public narratives on the JE, on the other hand, are in general positive. This contrast can be inferred as inconsistency between socio-cultural context and situational context of the interpreted event, that is, the JE. As this research argues earlier that both contexts and verbal goings-on can activate interpreter choices, the next section will look at how this inconsistency in different strata of context influences interpreter's choices.

Choices of interpreters: intertextual analysis and discussion

The corpus

The two-day midterm consultation conference consisted of plenary sessions and parallel group discussions. Group discussions were among military professionals from fields such as engineering and medical relief. These small-scale meetings were not supported by interpreting service. Plenary sessions gathered all the participating officers of the two armies and one interpreter from each side. Each interpreter interpreted for his or her own side during ceremonial addresses, briefings and presentations. The interpreters worked on 20–30 minutes shifts in both language directions during question and answer sessions. The plenary sessions lasted altogether for 4.5 hours. All speakers and interpreters were recorded and transcribed verbatim. A 48,000+ word corpus of aligned source and interpreted texts was built for intertextual analysis.

General pattern of interpreters' choices

As introduced in the previous section, the mission of the JE is carrying out coordinated responses in disaster relief. And the aim of the midterm consultation meeting is to finalize plans for the live troop field exercise. The two parties in the meeting were keen to identify procedural gaps and understand the know-how and institutional construct of their counterpart for efficient and collaborative responses. Cooperation, coordination and reaching consensus are hence the general themes of the JE, which can be proven by the public narratives on the event. These elements construct the situational context of the event. All interlocutors, including the interpreters, are hence expected to make concerted efforts to reach the communicative goal.

The corpus shows that the participating officers did meet this expectation: opening remarks are friendly, praising the glorious history and capacity of their counterpart; briefings and presentations are informative, sharing the two armies' past experiences on disaster relief; and Q&A sessions are highly interactive. Choices of the interpreters in general also meet the communicative goal and fit the context of situation of the meeting. Interpreters of both armies chose to render information in an accurate and complete way. Moreover, they proactively chose to play an expert role, bridging communicative gaps between the two armies. This role is demonstrated by quite frequent choices of elaborating acronyms, explaining technical terms and adding information. Number of occurrences of the three types of choices is provided in Table 4.2.

Table 4.2 Expert role of interpreters and its instantiations

Type of instantiation	*Number*
Elaboration of acronyms	69
Explanation of technical terms	27
Addition of information	32

The following examples demonstrate interpreters' choices through intertextual analysis. Source text or interpretation in the Chinese language is followed by literal translation (LT) in English.

Examples 1 and 2 are instances of explaining technical terms. Example 1 is also an example of elaborating an acronym. In this example, there's the first mentioning of two proper names, "DCO" and "FEMA". The USPACOM officer assumed that his counterparts knew what the acronyms stand for and didn't offer the full names. The interpreter offered the translation of the acronyms in its full, – "Defense Coordinating Officer" and "Federal Emergence Management Agency". The interpreter even remarked at the end of the segment that "When FEMA is used again, you know it is Federal Emergency Management Agency", trying to reinforce the connection between the acronym and the full name. Also, in this example, the interpreter explained that "FEMA regions" means "FEMA regional command". This helps the PLA audiences to understand the function of this regional organization, hence explicating the term "FEMA region".

In Example 2, the interpreter explained that "presidential declaration" means "presidential declaration of emergency state". The logic between presidential declaration and sending federal assistance is hence made more explicit.

Example 1

USPACOM OFFICER (UO): So what I will do for a couple of minutes is try to explain how DCO support FEMA on the mainland in United states, where there are ten FEMA regions.

USPACOM INTERPRETER (UI): 接下来我想用几分钟向各位介绍一下我们的国防协调官，如何支援美国联邦应急反应署。在整个美国的辖区，美国联邦反应署有十个指挥部。接下来再用到 FEMA 的时候呢，大家就知道这是美国联邦反应署。

(LT: Next, I want to use a few minutes to introduce to you how our Defense Coordinating Officer supports the Federal Emergency Management Agency. In the United States we have ten Federal Emergency Management Agency regional commands. When FEMA is used again, you know it is Federal Emergency Management Agency.)

Example 2 (place name anonymized)

UO: The state of X would run out of its resources both civilian and with the national guard. The government of X would ask for a presidential declaration in order to have federal assist response to that disaster.

UI: 我们州的民兵，还有国防的国民兵都已经耗尽应付之力的时候，X州的州长呢，他会要求总统宣布紧急状态，这样呢才能要求联邦派下支援的一些能力。

(LT: If our civilian guard and our national guard have exhausted our means. The governor of the state of X would ask for the presidential declaration of emergency state in order to have federal government offer assistance.)

Examples 3 and example 4 are instances of addition of information. In Example 3, USPACOM officers were introducing qualifications for DCO. The speaker himself is a DCO and hence made those remarks. In this example, the interpreter added two pieces of information. The first addition is the requirement of military rank, that is, a candidate for DCO has to be a colonel-level officer. The second addition is a clarification that the function of the DCO is responding to disasters.

In Example 4, the PLA office was introducing the disaster relief mechanism of a past earthquake in China. The speaker used an exophoric reference like "such a mechanism" and a fuzzy subject, "we". The original message is not clear. For example, one may assume that "we" refers to PLA. If the mechanism were established by PLA, it would surely involve regional military leaders. Then the following clause, "relevant leaders of the X military region joined the mechanism of the province", is logically confusing. To make the message clearer, the interpreter made two additions. First, he clarified the exophoric reference by naming it specifically as an "emergency disaster response mechanism". Second, the interpreter made it clear that the mechanism was established by "X provincial government and party committee". The roles of army, government and party are made clear with this addition of information.

Example 3

UO: I am an army aviator by trade. I am a OH50 Scout Pilot. That's not to say that being an army aviator makes an expert in disaster. Any army officers whether it is infantry, aviation can be qualified as a DCO.

UI: 我是陆航飞行员，是OH50侦察机飞行员。那么并不是说，因为我是一个陆航的飞行员，那就说就能够资格吗，并不是这样，其他<u>任何的上校这一级别的军官</u>，不管他是步兵或者空军，他都可以作为我们就是<u>灾难响应方面</u>的 DCO.

(LT: I am an army aviator by trade, an OH50 Scout Pilot. That's not to say it is because I am an army aviator that I am qualified. No. <u>Any colonel level officer</u>, infantry, aviation, can be the <u>disaster responding</u> DCO.)

Example 4 (place names anonymized)

PLA OFFICER (PO): 我们在X省也建立了<u>这样一个组织机构</u>，当地X军区的领导也参加了省里的联合指挥机构。

(LT: <u>We</u> set up <u>such a mechanism</u> in X province as well. Relevant leaders of the X military region joined the mechanism of the province.)

PLA INTERPRETER (PI): On the provincial level, the <u>X provincial government and party committee</u> established the <u>emergency disaster response mechanism</u> and the relevant leaders of the X military regions joined the command as participants.

In these four examples, two interpreters explicate or add information that they deemed as useful or relevant. The communicative effect, as one can observe from the intertextual data and analysis, is positive. We suggest that both explicating and

Military interpreters' choices 75

adding of information are conscious choices of the interpreters rather than results of their interpreting style. This is because, on the one hand, neither explicating nor adding of information is commonly seen as a strategy of interpreting, considering the high cognitive load as discussed in the introduction section. On the other hand, interpretations in the midterm meeting are in general succinct and faithful.

Then what activated these choices? First of all, military interpreters were able to make such choices because they were competent to do so. Both interpreters were staff or civilian officers of their army. In other words, they were insiders. Knowledge of the construct and practices of their own army were the prerequisite of making these choices. But what's more interesting is the motivation behind such choices. This research suggests that it is the context of situation, that is, the cooperative nature of the event and collaborative spirits of all participants, that motivated the interpreters to strive for the best communicative effect possible. They made efforts to play an expert role, bridging the knowledge gap between the two sides through explicating and adding of information.

Interpreter's choice at critical points

Although interpreters' choices in general were activated by the immediate context of situation, there were moments when choices were triggered by a complex constellation of contexts, or more specifically, layers of narratives. If a certain moment entails discrepancies between verbal goings-on and layers of narratives, it is taken as critical points in this research. Critical points in our case, though rare in number, bespeak values of military interpreters and the ideology of the groups to which they belong. Following are two examples of this. Both examples are from the question and answer sessions of the meeting. PLA and USPACOM interpreters worked on shifts during these sessions and interpreted for both sides. The interpreter in both of the examples was the PLA interpreter.

Example 5 is from a Q&A round on guiding principles for sending troops. The US officer answered the question first and remarked that the US Army send troops based on two principles, capability and vicinity. The United States would send capable troops from the mainland or the nearest overseas military base to the affected area. The following example is excerpted from the answer of the PLA officer, who spoke after his US counterpart.

Example 5: Topic: principle of vicinity in sending troops

- PO: 其实在这一点上咱们应该是有接近的做法，如果按照这个情况里给的，这个，我们都在这个地区内有部队能 12 小时内提供支援，如果说我们在这个地区内有这样的部队，我们也是首先使用这样的部队。因为中国军队在参加救援的时候，它强调一个原则叫就近原则，也是要第一时间能够来处置这个灾害带来的后果。
- (LT: Actually, we have a similar practice. According to the incident, we have units in the region that can respond in 12 hours. I mean if we have this kind of unit. We will send it first. Because when the PLA participate in relief,

we emphasize a principle of vicinity, that is to say we are able to respond to the disaster at the earliest time possible.)
PLA *interpreter interrupted the speaker and whispered to him in Chinese*
PI: *"它这个就是在国内？ (It is in the mainland?)"*, PO responding: *"国内国外只要有这个救援条件的话 (mainland or overseas if it has the capacity)"*
(*interpreter hesitating, speaker taking over and speaking directly to US officer in English*)
PO: For example, if our mission ships just through this sea, we can change the mission, change its mission if the ship can complete the task.
UO: OK, so you can divert them from the mission.
PO: For example, if our medical ship just go to other country, through this island, we can change it if they can complete the task.

This example sees the only disruption of interpreting in the meeting. The interpreter interrupted the PLA officer and asked for clarification. The officer made a quick response to the interpreter. Yet the interpreter was still hesitating. The officer then took over and spoke to his counterpart directly in not so good English.

Interrupting the speaker, the interpreter's superior both in function and military rank, was definitely a high-stakes choice for the interpreter. Then, why did he make this choice? One could hardly assume that the interpreter was having difficulty in understanding what the speaker was literally saying, given the fact that the speaker was speaking in the interpreter's A language and has been quite logical. One possible explanation is that the information from the verbal input contradicts with the background knowledge of the interpreter. The question from the interpreter, "*It is in the mainland?*", reveals his judgement that the PLA officer was perhaps making a mistake. The interpreter's confusion might be: How could China send troops from places other than Chinese territory?

Then, where did the judgement and confusion come from? One reason is the simple fact that China did not have an overseas military base at the time of the meeting. But this confusion can be better explained through a narrative that might override the interpreter's information processing and decision-making: China upholds an "independent foreign policy of peace". An important part of it is the country's own "territorial integrity" and "non-interference with the internal affairs of other countries".[1]

The United States, on the other hand, has been positioning itself as the world police. This self-positioning was disagreed with by Chinese academia and media. The retention of more than 100 overseas military bases has been narrated in China as evidence of the United States' hegemonic control over other countries. As the US officer was saying that they would send troops from the nearest overseas military base, it was quite possible that these remarks activated the aforementioned narrative about overseas military bases.

From that perspective, it is easier to empathize with the interpreter's confusion. Conceptual and public narratives have been dichotomizing China and United States in their foreign policy, or more specifically, on the issue of overseas military bases. Therefore, it makes sense that the interpreter could not understand why the PLA officer said "we have similar practices". It also explained the interpreter's choice of interrupting the speaker and asking for confirmation.

In Example 6, the two parties were discussing a scenario where the host country has been devastated and lost most of its security capacity. The question was: Can the relief troop carry weapons and provide security for itself?

Example 6: Topic: provider of security support

PO: 根据奥斯洛的那个准则，别的国家来的救灾部队的安全由当地政府来提供，但是如果当地政府已经失去了它的功能了，就是它不能提供这种保护的时候，到时候如果我们跟受援国之间有协议，你们可以派出适当的部队，来保护自己救援人员的安全。
(PI's interpreting accurate and faithful, literal translation omitted)

PI: According to the *Oslo Agreement* (sic Guideline), the host country is supposed to provide security to the troops. But in case the host country won't be able to provide those security, the PLA and US should make an agreement with the host country like we can send troops and provide the security by ourselves.

UO: Yeah, we would have to make that agreement, but we would have part of the agreement with the host nation that they have to secure us, because the original request was to provide humanitarian support and this is not humanitarian support. And if the country can't provide us with that support, we would have limited our capability to deploy.

PI: 所以美军他会和受灾国还是要签订协议，因为这个前提是人道主义救援，所以协议的一部分是一定要要求受灾国提供安全保障。如果受灾国没办法提供相应的安全保障，对我们的救灾能力会限制很多。

(LT: So, the US army will still have to sign an agreement with the host country. As the premise is providing humanitarian support, part of the agreement must be that the host country provide security. If the host country can't provide security support, our relief capability will be limited.)

In this example, the PLA interpreter misinterpreted the US officer's remarks. Before analysing this segment, it is necessary to first look at the PLA officer's answer, the co-text. The PLA officer started with acknowledging stipulations in the *Oslo Guidelines*[2] that security has to be provided by the host country. However, the officer then suggested that the two countries can sign an agreement that override the *Guidelines*.

The US officer was actually voicing a different view in a polite way, disguising his attitude in the subjunctive mood "would". His overall message was: even if the agreement were to be signed (though not really a right choice), the content would be to reassure that the host country would provide security to the troops. If the host country couldn't provide security support, the US army would have to reconsider their plan of troop deployment.

The interpretation from the PLA interpreter tells a different story. First, the possibility of the signing of the agreement is upgraded to "US will still have to sign an agreement". Second, by saying "part of the agreement must be that the host country provide security", it is suggested that the other agreements can be reached as well. Third, "our relief capability will be limited" is different from "limit our capability to deploy". The latter raises concerns over whether the US army will send troops or not. The former, however, confirms the deployment of US troops. The only concern is that their performance will be affected if insufficient security is provided.

The narrative that caused this mis-translation is perhaps the meta-narrative of China's alternative understanding of rule of law. In this alternative understanding, rule of law does not exclude the negotiating power of social norms, cultural norms and moral imperatives (Chew 2005). Therefore, the ideology or meta-narrative behind the two army officers' remarks were different. And it's quite possible that the interpreter had the similar conception of rule of law as the PLA officer. He agreed with the PLA officer's proposal that an alternative agreement on security support can be signed with the host country. This then leads to his misunderstanding and misinterpreting of the US officer's remarks.

Conclusion

With a corpus of the interpreted text of the China–US disaster-relief joint military exercise, the present study discusses military interpreters' choices and decision-making mechanism situated in a political, social and ideological context that hinges much upon public, conceptual and meta-narratives. It is found that the interpreters make sense against certain frames or schema, which in most cases are activated by immediate verbal input with reference to the closest context and narratives. Interpreters in the JE played a facilitating expert role, demonstrated by frequent choices of elaborating acronyms, explaining technical terms and adding information. This role positioning and general pattern of choices are determined by the cooperative nature of the event. However, when the verbal input competes with the broader conceptual and meta-narratives, the interpreters may refer to the latter in their decision-making, which is performed mostly below level of consciousness and turns out to be a disruption of communication or misinterpretation (see Examples 5–6).

Despite some interesting qualitative findings, this study is subject to certain limitations. Discussions about the results of intertextual analysis are largely based on dialectical reasoning, which cannot be freed from authors' subjective decisions. If the interpreters were accessed for interviews, it would be possible to triangulate the data to validify the abovementioned findings. Ethnographic research involving practicing military interpreters can be the next step of research.

Though limited in many ways, this research has implications for military interpreters' role and the norms of military interpreting. It finds that interpreting in military settings is influenced not only by institutional affiliations or stances the interpreters take but also by the narratives that (dis)accord with the interpreters' conception towards the verbal goings-on at critical points. In this light, military interpreters' role can be reframed as more of a narrative elaborator than a political, social or ideological mediator. This sheds light on the training of military interpreting professionals, who should be "strategic resources", that is, experts up to the standard of a well-trained military personnel and interpreter (Hou and Han 2012). The cultivation of such professionals is key to national security, given the increasing number of cross-border military exchanges in recent years. Moreover, this research also echoes previous research that interpreters should be empowered in military events, as their roles go far beyond that of a linguistic conduit.

Notes

1 see Ministry of Foreign Affairs of China portal, retrieved from <www.fmprc.gov.cn/mfa_eng/wjdt_665385/>.
2 The *Oslo Guidelines* is a UN document that serves as a basic framework for the use of foreign military defence assets in international disaster relief. To protect the sovereignty of the country where the disaster has struck, foreign rescuing troops cannot carry weapons to the affected country.

References

Allison, G. (2017) *Destined for War: Can America and China Escape Thucydides's Trap?*, California: Houghton Mifflin Harcourt.
Angelelli, C. (2012) 'Introduction: The sociological turn in translation and interpreting studies', *Translation and Interpreting Studies* 7(2): 125–128.
Angermeyer, P. S. (2009) 'Translation style and participant roles in court interpreting', *Journal of Sociolinguistics* 13(1): 3–28.
Baker, M. (2006) *Translation and Conflict: A Narrative Account*, London and New York: Routledge.
Baker, M. (2007) 'Reframing conflict in translation', *Social Semiotics* 17: 151–169.
Baker, M. (2010) 'Interpreters and translators in the war zone', *The Translator* 16(2): 197–222.
Bartlomiejczyk, M. (2006) 'Strategies of simultaneous interpreting and directionality', *Interpreting* 8(2): 149–174.
Chang, C.-C. and Schallert, D. L. (2007) 'The impact of directionality on Chinese/English simultaneous interpreting', *Interpreting* 9(2): 137–176.
Chew, P. K. (2005) 'The rule of law: China's skepticism and the rule of people', *Ohio State Journal of Dispute Resolution* 20(9): 43–48.
Fisher, W. R. (1987) *Human Communication as Narration: Toward a Philosophy of Reason, Value, and Action*, Columbia: University of South Carolina Press.
Footitt, H. and Kelly, M. (2012) *Languages and the Military: Alliances, Occupation and Peace Building*, Basingstoke: Palgrave Macmillan.
Gile, D. (2009) *Basic Concepts and Models for Interpreter and Translator Training* (Rev ed.), Philadelphia: John Benjamins.
Guo, T. (2015a) 'Interpreting for the enemy: Chinese interpreters in the Second Sino-Japanese War (1931–1945)', *Translation Studies* 8(1): 1–15.
Guo, Y. J. (2015b) 'The interpreter's political awareness as a non-cognitive constraint in political interviews: A perspective of experiential meaning', *Babel* 61(4): 573–588.

Halliday, M. A. K. (1994) *An Introduction to Functional Grammar*, London: Arnold.
Halliday, M. A. K. and Hasan, R. (1989) *Language, Context, and Text: Aspects of Language in a Social-Semiotic Perspective*, Oxford: Oxford University Press.
Han, Ruixia, et al. 韩瑞霞等 (2011) '差异中的同一: 中美文化价值观比较 – 基于一项对美国民众的大型国际调研' (Unity in difference: A comparison of the value between China and USA), 上海交通大学学报 (*Journal of Shanghai Jiaotong University*) 19(6): 49–55.
Hatim, B. and Mason, I. (1990) *Discourse and the Translator*, London: Longman.
Hatim, B. and Mason, I. (1997a) *The Translator as Communicator*, London and New York: Routledge.
Hatim, B. and Mason, I. (1997b) *Communication across Cultures: Translation Theory and Contrastive Text Linguistics*, Devon: University of Exeter Press.
Hou, Jianwei and Han, Ziman 侯建伟, 韩子满 (2012) '论新形势下的军事翻译与军事翻译人才的培养' (Military translation and military translator training in the new era), 高等教育研究学报 (*Journal of Higher Education Research*) 35(2): 12–14, 20.
Inghilleri, M. (2004) 'Habitus, field and discourse: Interpreting as a socially situated activity', *Target* 15(2): 243–268.
Inghilleri, M. (2005) 'Mediating zones of uncertainty: Interpreter agency, the interpreting habitus and political asylum adjudication', *The Translator* 11(1): 69–85.
Inghilleri, M. (2010) '"You don't make war without knowing why": The decision to interpret in Iraq', *The Translator* 16(2): 175–196.
Inghilleri, M. (2015) 'Military Interpreting', in *Encyclopedia of Interpreting Studies*. F. Pöchhacker (ed.), New York: Routledge. pp. 260–261.
Kennedy, S. (ed.) (2018) *Global Governance and China: The Dragon's Learning Curve*, New York: Routledge.
Liu, M. (2009) 'How do experts interpret? Implications from research in interpreting studies and cognitive science', in *Efforts and Models in Interpreting & Translation Research: A Tribute to Daniel Gile*. G. Hansen, A. Chesterman and H. Gerzymisch-Arbogast (eds.), Amsterdam: John Benjamins. pp. 159–177.
Lü, S. and Li, S. (2012) 'The role shift of the interpreter to a cultural mediator: From the perspective of cultural orientations and contexting', *Babel* 58(2): 145–163.
Munday, J. (2012) *Evaluation in Translation: Critical Points of Translator Decision-Making*, London and New York: Routledge.
Munday, J. (2018) 'A model of appraisal: Spanish interpretations of President Trump's inaugural address 2017', *Perspectives* 26(2): 1–16.
Munday, J. and Zhang, M. F. (2015) 'Introduction', *Target* 27(3): 325–334.
Palmer, J. (2007) 'Interpreting and translation for western media in Iraq', in *Translating and Interpreting Conflict*. M. Salama-Carr (ed.), Amsterdam and New York: Rodopi. pp. 13–28.
Pöchhacker, F. (2009) 'The turns of interpreting studies', in *Efforts and Models in Interpreting & Translation Research: A Tribute to Daniel Gile*. G. Hansen, A. Chesterman and H. Gerzymisch-Arbogast (eds.), Amsterdam: John Benjamins. pp. 22–46.
Qin, Zaidong 秦在东 (2011) '中美意识形态社会管理机制之比较' (A comparison of ideological and social governance mechanism between China and USA), 华中人文论丛 (*Huazhong Humanity Forum*), 2(1): 5–15.
Rafael, V. L. (2007) 'Translation in wartime', *Public Culture* 19(2): 239–246.
Rafael, V. L. (2012) 'Translation and the US empire', *The Translator* 18(1): 1–22.
Sanatifar, M. S. and Daghigh, A. J. (2018) 'Translation as renarration: A case of Iran's nuclear program as circulated in the Western and Iranian media', *Asia Pacific Translation and Intercultural Studies* 5(1): 1–18.

Schäffner, C. (2012) 'Unknown agents in translated political discourse', *Target* 24(1): 103–125.

Tryuk, M. (2010) 'Interpreting in Nazi concentration camps during World War II', *Interpreting* 12(2): 125–145.

Wadensjö, C. (1998) *Interpreting as Interaction*, London: Longman.

Wang, B. H. and Feng, D. Z. (2018) 'A corpus-based study of stance-taking as seen from critical points in interpreted political discourse', *Perspectives* 26(2): 246–260.

Wang, J. H. (2018) '"I only interpret the content and ask practical questions when necessary": Interpreters' perceptions of their explicit coordination and personal pronoun choice in telephone interpreting', *Perspectives*: 1–18.

Zhang, M. F. and Munday, J. (2018) 'Innovation in discourse analytic approaches to translation studies', *Perspectives: Studies in Translation Theory and Practice* 26(2): 159–165.

Zhang, Yuyan 张宇燕 (2016) '全球治理的中国视角' (Global governance: China's perspective), 世界经济与政治 (*World Economics and Politics*) 2016(9): 4–9.

Zheng, L. Q. and Ren, W. (2017) 'Interpreting as an influencing factor on news reports: A study of interpreted Chinese political discourse recontextualized in English news', *Perspectives* 26(5): 1–17.

Part II
Linking linguistic analysis with socio-cultural interpretation

5 Functions of the pronoun 'we' in the English translations of Chinese government reports

Hailing Yu and Canzhong Wu

Introduction

Personal pronouns, though traditionally classified as merely 'functional words', can have significant practical implications in translation (García and Lanza 2018; Yu and Wu 2017). In the case of the language pair English–Chinese, there are typological differences in the use of personal pronouns. Chinese tends to use fewer personal pronouns, as they are often omitted when the speaker assumes that the audience can get the necessary information from the context (Halliday and McDonald 2004; Lv 1999; Wang 2002). Therefore, quantitively speaking, English translations of Chinese texts usually have more personal pronouns (Wang and Hu 2010; Huang 2008; Zhao 1996) as a result of explicitation (Baker 1993; Olohan and Baker 2000). But there are few studies describing in detail what particular pronouns are added in the process of translation and what roles such added pronouns are playing in the translated text.

Given that the choice of personal pronouns in Chinese to English translation is usually contextually motivated (Yu and Wu 2017), this chapter aims to investigate the use and functions of the first-person plural 'we' in the English translations of the Annual Work Report (AWR) of the Chinese government. Specifically, it will look at: (1) The distribution of the Chinese first-person plural pronoun 'wŏmen' in the Chinese AWRs from the year 2000 to 2019 and the English pronoun 'we' in the corresponding translations and (2) the interpersonal and experiential functions of clauses containing 'we' in the English translations. The theoretical framework is systemic functional linguistics (SFL). In terms of methodology, the study adopts a two-pronged approach combining low-level automatic analysis and high-level manual analysis. In the automatic analysis, the distribution and collocation of 'wŏmen' and 'we' in the AWRs are explored by singling out all the clauses containing 'wŏmen' and 'we'. The clauses obtained through this automatic analysis are then analysed from the interpersonal and experiential perspectives. The automatic analysis is carried out in SysConc, and the manual analysis is mainly conducted in SysFan. The findings are twofold. As for the diachronic distribution, 'we' in the English translations displays much higher frequencies (from 7 to 27 times) than 'wŏmen' in the Chinese AWRs. This means that 'we' is usually added in the process of translation. As for the functions of 'we', it has been found that, interpersonally, 'we' is always used in positive declarative clauses, followed by median- and high-value modal verbs such as *will*, *should*, *must* and *need to*. Experientially, 'we' is mainly presented as the agent in material processes, with the emphasis more on transforming existing entities rather than on creating new ones.

The structure of the chapter is as follows. The second section presents the data and methodology. The third section concerns the distribution of 'wǒmen' in the original Chinese AWRs and 'we' in the English translations in the 20-year span. The fourth and fifth sections are analyses of the interpersonal and experiential functions of clauses containing 'we' in the English translations of AWR, and the final section concludes the whole study.

Data and methodology

Data: the Chinese AWR

Each year in March, the Chinese premier, on behalf of the State Council, delivers the government's Annual Work Report to deputies of the National People's Congress (NPC). According to China's legislation system, the NPC is the largest institution of power where people exercise their right in governing the country. The premier of the State Council is required to deliver a work report to the representatives attending the congress, who then judge whether the government has fully fulfilled its responsibility in the past year. As the NPC usually takes place not long after the Spring Festival, the traditional Chinese New Year, another purpose of the AWR is to provide a feasible work plan for the ongoing (new) year. Starting from 1954, the AWR is now a highly formulated discourse with relatively stable topics, schema, and style.

The data for this study is a diachronic parallel corpus of the Chinese AWRs and their English translations published from 2000 to 2019. Both the Chinese and English versions of the AWRs were obtained through the official website of Xinhua Net, China's biggest state-run press agency responsible for publishing government documents. Both the Chinese and English AWRs are divided into two sections: a review of the work done in the past year and a plan for the work to be done in the ongoing year. Of the available reports, those in the years 2001, 2006, 2011, 2016 and 2019 are considered of special interest in this study. The years 2001, 2006, 2011 and 2016 are the beginning years of the tenth, eleventh, twelfth, and thirteenth Five-Year-Plans, and the AWRs were delivered by three premiers: Zhu Rongji (2001), Wen Jiabao (2006, 2011) and Li Keqiang (2016). The AWR in 2019 is the latest one issued by the Chinese government and is therefore also worth detailed analysis.

Methodology

This study combines low-level automatic analysis and high-level manual analysis. For the automatic analysis, SysConc, developed by Wu (2000), has been adopted. SysConc is a concordance tool for corpus analysis. It focuses on the lexical level and is powerful in investigating word frequencies and associations. It can produce frequency lists, collocational patterns and concordances and has been successfully applied to many studies (Herke-Couchman and Wu 2004; Herke-Couchman 2006; Wu and Fang 2006; Yu and Wu 2017).

In our analysis, we used SysConc to obtain the frequencies of 'wǒmen' in the Chinese AWRs and 'we' in the English translations. The clauses containing 'we' (2,166 in total) were then extracted to be further analysed manually in SysFan, also developed by Wu (2000). SysFan is powerful in conducting analysis at the clausal level, in terms of the experiential, interpersonal and textual metafunctions (Yu and Wu 2016; Yu 2017). In this study, clauses containing 'we' were analysed both in the interpersonal and experiential systems with built-in options of SysFan, clause by clause. Analysis results were summarized automatically, and clauses exhibiting a certain feature could be retrieved. Each clause in the data was double checked by both authors of the chapter, and independent scholars familiar with Chinese and English as well as SFL were asked to look through the data analysis to ensure accuracy.

Distribution of 'wǒmen' and 'we'

The distribution of 'wǒmen' in the Chinese government reports and 'we' in the English translations in the years 2000 to 2019 is presented in Table 5.1. The percentages of 'wǒmen' and 'we' are obtained by dividing the numbers of each pronoun by the numbers of words in each year's report in total, and the ratio is obtained by comparing the percentages of 'wǒmen' and 'we' in each year.

As is shown in Table 5.1, 'we' in the English translations displays much higher frequencies than 'wǒmen' in the original Chinese reports. While the occurrences of 'wǒmen' in the Chinese reports range from 20 to 41, the numbers of 'we' in the English translations are between 125 and 515. This is reflected in the ratio of the percentage of 'we' in the English translations to that of 'wǒmen' in the Chinese reports, which varies from 7 to 27. That is to say, the use of 'we' in the English translations is 6 to 26 times higher than the use of 'wǒmen' in the Chinese reports. The tendency remains stable across the 20 years in spite of occasional fluctuations, resulting in a total number of 613 'wǒmen' in the Chinese reports and 7,731 'we' in the English translations.

The discrepancy between the source and target texts in the use of the first-person plural is often contributed to the typological difference between English and Chinese. In Chinese, subjects tend to be omitted in the texts, especially when they are recoverable from the co-text or context (Halliday and McDonald 2004; Lv 1999; Wang 2002). By contrast, subject omission is restricted in English, and pronouns are frequently used as references to entities involved/mentioned in the communication and as substitutes for proper nouns. This explanation for the addition of 'we' in the English translations of the AWRs seems plausible when the distribution of the same pronoun in the 2000–2019 State of the Union addresses is used as a comparison, as shown in Figure 5.1.

Table 5.1 Diachronic distribution of 'wǒmen' and 'we'

Year	Speaker	Chinese			English			Ratio
		No. of words in total	No. of 'wǒmen'	Pct. of 'wǒmen'	No. of words in total	No. of 'we'	Pct. of 'we'	
2000	Zhu	15,563	22	0.14%	12,059	125	1.04%	7
2001	Zhu	15,764	20	0.13%	12,010	283	2.36%	19
2002	Zhu	15,437	21	0.14%	11,802	251	2.13%	16
2003	Zhu	23,502	38	0.16%	17,202	319	1.85%	11
2004	Wen	16,906	35	0.21%	12,881	311	2.41%	12
2005	Wen	18,407	33	0.18%	11,518	294	2.55%	14
2006	Wen	20,693	30	0.14%	15,400	396	2.57%	18
2007	Wen	20,148	30	0.15%	15,972	415	2.60%	17
2008	Wen	24,124	34	0.14%	18,889	476	2.52%	18
2009	Wen	19,749	30	0.15%	14,933	483	3.23%	21
2010	Wen	20,387	41	0.20%	14,297	497	3.48%	17
2011	Wen	19,788	38	0.19%	15,062	460	3.05%	16
2012	Wen	18,292	33	0.18%	13,733	458	3.34%	18
2013	Wen	15,308	35	0.23%	11,388	267	2.34%	10
2014	Li	16,020	30	0.19%	12,606	388	3.08%	16
2015	Li	18,080	40	0.22%	15,713	419	2.67%	12
2016	Li	19,586	30	0.15%	16,866	421	2.50%	16
2017	Li	19,275	25	0.13%	16,081	515	3.20%	25
2018	Li	20,596	21	0.10%	17,044	472	2.77%	27
2019	Li	20,186	27	0.13%	16,796	481	2.86%	21
Total		377,811	613	0.16%	292,252	7,731	2.65%	–

While the use of 'we' in the English translations of the AWRs can be seen as a sign of conforming to the convention of English political discourses, this is hardly the whole picture. Firstly, there is an uneven distribution of 'we' across the whole report. 'We' tends to cluster in the plan section (the second third of the report). This is different from the generally even distribution of 'we' in the State of the Union address. For instance, the concordance plot results for the 2016 English translation of the AWR and the Obama address in the same year (Figure 5.2) show that 'we' is mainly used in the beginning and middle of Obama's address, whereas it begins to increase significantly after the first third of the English translation of AWR. In fact, the majority of 'we's appear in the plan rather than the review section of the AWRs. In the 2016 English translation of AWR, there are 40 'we's in the review section, and the number soars to 365 in the plan section.

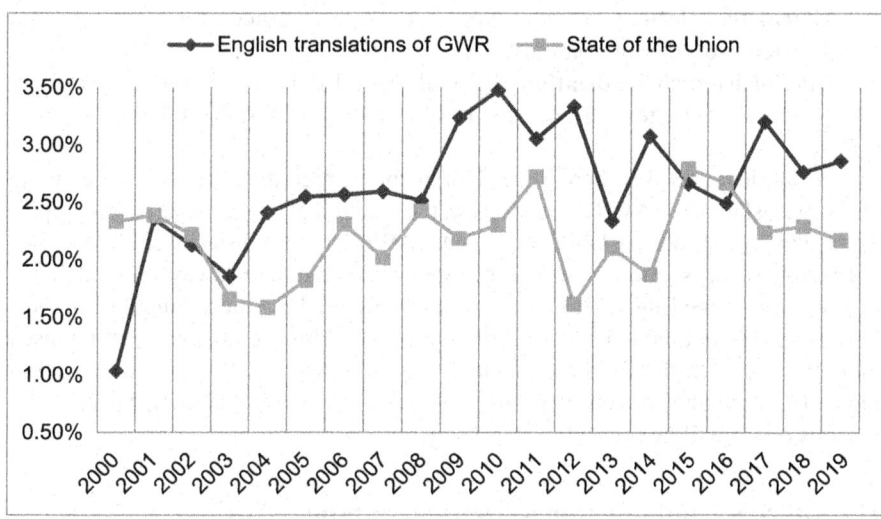

Figure 5.1 'We' in English translations of AWR and State of the Union addresses

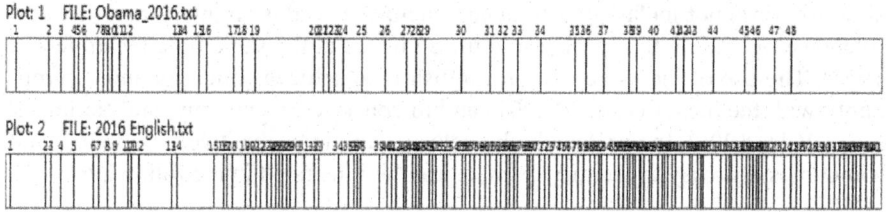

Figure 5.2 Concordance plot of 'we' in the 2016 English AWR and Obama address

Secondly, even in the plan section, there are cases where the original Chinese clauses are translated into English without using the pronoun 'we'. For instance, a number of passive structures are found in the plan section of the AWR in 2013, where 'we' is used less frequently in comparison with the translations of other years.

> **Chinese AWR**: 要加大对社会养老服务体系和儿童福利机构建设的支持力度。
> **Literal translation**: should increase support for social services for the elderly and child welfare agencies.
> **Official English translation**: Greater support *should be* given to developing child welfare agencies and the system of social services for the elderly.

This can be contrasted with another example taken from the plan section of the 2011 AWR, where the pronoun 'we' is added in the English translation.

> **Chinese AWR**: 将新型农村社会养老保险试点范围扩大到全国 40% 的县
> **Literal translation**: put new type of old-age insurance for rural residents extend to 40% of counties.
> **Official English translation**: <u>We</u> will extend the pilot project for the new type of old-age insurance for rural residents to 40% of counties.

Such examples show that there is freedom in choice regarding the use of 'we' in the English translations of AWR. That is to say, the addition of 'we' is not always compulsory in the process of translating the Chinese AWRs into English (Yu and Wu 2018).

The following sections will explore the interpersonal and experiential functions of 'we' in the English translations of AWRs and how these functions of 'we' contribute to establishing a certain image of the Chinese government. Clauses containing 'we' in the English translations in the years 2001, 2006, 2011, 2016 and 2019 are analysed from the interpersonal and experiential perspectives. The analysis result will be presented and discussed.

The interpersonal function of clauses containing 'we'

Seen from an interpersonal perspective, the choice to use the pronoun 'we' is itself significant. 'We' can be either exclusive or 'inclusive' (Duszak 2002). While exclusive 'we' does not include the audience, inclusive 'we' is an interactant personal reference, including the speaker and the audience at the same time (Matthiessen 1995). The use of inclusive 'we' in English is to achieve solidarity and communality with the hearer (Hyland 2001) and to construct a 'chummy' and 'intimate' tone (Wales 1996). In our data, both exclusive and inclusive 'we's are found, and sometimes it is easy to identify them, as can be illustrated in the following.

> Exclusive 'we': We must stay true to the vision of people-centered development and do everything within our capacity to meet people's basic needs.
> (2019_P_45)

> Inclusive 'we': We, the Chinese people of all ethnic groups, guided by Xi Jinping Thought on Socialism with Chinese Characteristics for a New Era, forged ahead and overcame difficulties.
> (2019_R_1)

Most of the time, however, it is difficult to identify the exact nature of 'we', as is common in political discourse. Whether exclusive or inclusive, 'we' always refers to the Chinese government. This is why we believe the analysis of clauses containing 'we' is important in exploring the government's image projection.

According to SFL, interpersonally the clause is organized as an interactive event involving the speaker and the audience. The speaker uses language to enact personal and social relationships. In the act of speaking, the speaker adopts for her/himself a particular speech role, and in so doing assigns to the listener a complementary role that he or she wishes him to adopt in his turn (Halliday and

Matthiessen 2014). The interpersonal function of clauses containing 'we' will be explored in terms of mood type, polarity and modality.

Polarity and mood type

In SFL, polarity refers to the opposition between positive (*It is. Do that!*) and negative (*It isn't. Don't do that!*). Choosing either one indicates the speaker's belief concerning the yes or no of the proposition or proposal. Two mood types, indicative and imperative, are recognized in SFL, with indicative further subdivided into declarative and interrogative. Typically, a declarative clause functions to provide information, an interrogative clause to ask for information, and an imperative clause to ask for goods or services.

As for the clauses containing 'we' in the English translations of AWR, it will not be surprising to see that all of them are declarative, and they are overwhelmingly positive. Out of the 2,116 clauses analysed, only 13 are negative in terms of polarity. Some examples are presented in the following.

(1) ST: 贯彻寄希望于台湾人民的方针决不改变
    TT: We *will never* change the principle of placing our hopes on the people of Taiwan.
(2) ST: 绝不能让物价上涨影响低收入群众的正常生活
    TT: We *cannot* allow price rises to affect the normal lives of low-income people.
(3) ST: 对我国发展的影响不可低估
    TT: We *should not* underestimate the impact all of this will have on China's development.
(4) ST: 事不避难、义不逃责
    TT: We *must never* sidestep difficulties or shirk obligations.

It can be seen that negative polarity (expressed by '不') in the source text clauses is generally maintained in the English translations (with an added pronoun 'we'). Moreover, negative polarity is used in combination with modal auxiliaries, such as *will*, *can* and *should*, in the English translations. Although negative in polarity, such expressions function to demonstrate the determination of the speaker in taking actions in the future and his strong appealing to the audience at the same time.

Modality

Different from polarity, modality is neither yes nor no. It creates various intermediate degrees between the categorical extremes of unqualified positive and negative. Modality can be categorized according to the functions of the clause as a proposition or proposal. Modality in propositions is termed as modalisation and is about how probable or frequently the information is valid. Modality in proposals, termed as modulation, is about the obligation and inclination of the interlocutors. Modality can be realized in the form of modal auxiliaries, modal adverbs or separate clauses.

Moreover, the value of modality can be graded as low, median or high according to the strength of the assessment. Interpersonally, the more certain the speaker is about the proposition, the more likely he is expecting assent from the hearer, and the higher the value of obligation, the more likely the speaker is expecting the hearer to respond (Croft 1994). A combination of type and value is exhibited in any modal expression, such as those illustrated in Table 5.2.

Of the 2,116 clauses containing 'we', 86 are embedded clauses such as "[A]ll the measures *we took* have proven to be entirely correct". These embedded clauses do not realise a move in the exchange (Halliday and Matthiessen 2014) and are therefore excluded in the interpersonal analysis. The remaining 2,030 clauses are analysed in the interpersonal system of SysFan. Among these clauses, clauses where modality is used dominate, taking up 84% (1,701 clauses), and the remaining 16% (329) of clauses express tense (past, present and future). The type, value and most frequently adopted expressions of modality are presented in Table 5.3.

Table 5.2 Modality type and value in English

Modality type		Modality value		
		Low	Median	High
Modalisation	Probability	can/could/may/might possibly, I guess . . .	will/would probably, I think . . .	must/should certainly, I know . . .
	Usuality	can/could/may/might sometimes . . .	will/would usually . . .	must/should always
Modulation	Obligation	can/could/may/might it's permissible . . .	should/had better, it's desirable . . .	must/have to/ought to it's necessary . . .
	Inclination	willing to . . .	will/would like to . . .	must/have to . . .

Table 5.3 Modality used in clauses containing 'we'

Modality type		Modality value		
		Low (1%)	Median (74%)	High (25%)
Modalisation (0.3%)		–	–	we're confident that . . . we're convinced that . . .
Modulation (99.7%)	inclination (72%)	can	will	–
	obligation (28%)	–	should	must, have/need to

There are only a few clauses where modalisation is adopted, mainly to express the speaker's estimation of the probability of future events. What distinguishes these clauses are (1) most of the expressions are grammatical metaphor, where a clause with relational or mental process such as '*we are confident/convinced*' is used to function as a modal auxiliary (*must*) or adverb (*definitely*), and (2) their corresponding source text clauses all contain the pronoun 'wŏmen' (我们). That is to say, 'we' in these clauses are not added. Some of the clauses and their corresponding source text are presented in the following.

(1) ST: 我们坚信，经过中华儿女的不懈奋斗，祖国统一大业必将早日完成。
   TT: *We are confident* that with the unremitting efforts of all Chinese people, the great cause of national reunification will surely be accomplished at an early date.
(2) ST: 我们坚信，香港、澳门一定能够保持长期繁荣稳定。
   TT: *We firmly believe* that Hong Kong and Macao will remain prosperous and stable for a long time to come.
(3) ST: 我们坚信，只要海内外中华儿女继续共同努力奋斗，祖国和平统一大业一定能够实现！
   TT: *We are convinced* that as long as all Chinese people at home and abroad work together, the great cause of peaceful reunification of the motherland will be realized.
(4) ST: 展望今后五年，我们充满必胜信心。如期实现全面建成小康社会目标 . . .
   TT: Looking ahead to the next five years, *we are fully confident* that we will finish building a moderately prosperous society in all respects within the set timeframe.
(5) ST: 我们坚信，香港、澳门一定能与祖国内地同发展共进步、一定能保持长期繁荣稳定
   TT: *We are convinced* that Hong Kong and Macao will maintain long-term prosperity and stability.
(6) ST: 我们坚信，香港、澳门一定能与祖国内地同发展共进步、一定能保持长期繁荣稳定
   TT: *We have every confidence* that Hong Kong and Macao will develop and thrive together with the mainland and maintain long-term.

All these expressions indicate high probability, demonstrating the speaker's strong belief in the happening of these events in the future. Interestingly, such expressions tend to appear in clauses that concern Hong Kong, Macao and national reunification and appear at the end of the report. They function to reassure the audience of the strong will of the Chinese people as a whole to reunite and maintain stability.

Modal expressions of inclination and obligation are usually used in proposals. Inclination expresses the speaker's willingness or volition to do something (*wants to*), and obligation expresses the speaker's command for the audience to carry out an action (*is wanted to*). In the clauses under analysis, inclination

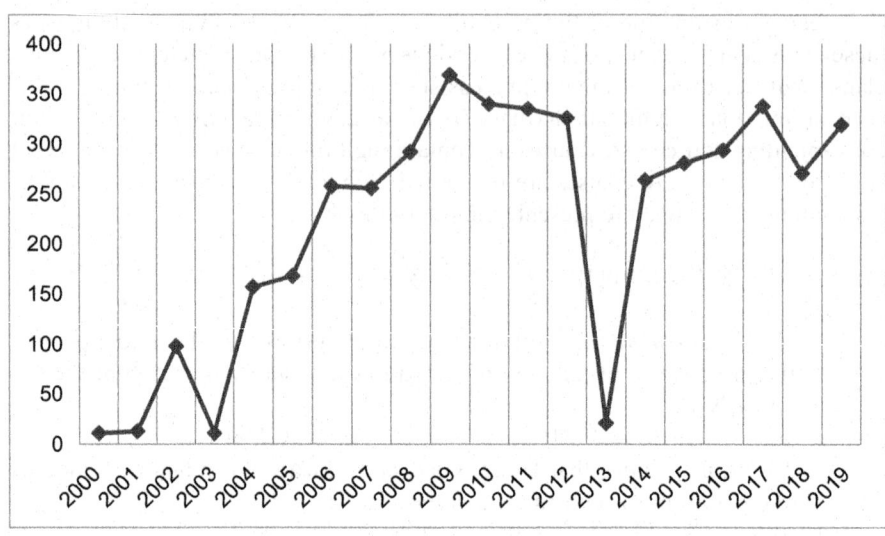

Figure 5.3 Occurrences of '*we will*' in each year's English translation of the AWR

is mainly expressed through the modal auxiliary 'will', which is of median value. 'Will' is notoriously difficult to analyse as it is often hard to determine whether 'will' expresses future tense or modality (see Sarkar 1998 on the conflict between future tense and modality). In our analysis, we identify clauses where 'will' clearly expresses future tense (which are only a few), and in cases where uncertainty arises, 'will' is analysed as modality. This is defendable in that there are significant fluctuations of 'we will' in the reports of different years (Figure 5.3).

As can be seen in Figure 5.3, the numbers of clauses containing '*we will*' range from only 11 in 2000 to 369 in 2009. Given that the section of a plan for the future development is an indispensable part of all the reports, we believe that in the English translations of AWR, modal auxiliaries typically also function as indications of futurity. Some of the clauses containing modal expressions of inclination and obligation are presented as follows.

We *will* continue to improve production safety.

(2006_P_238)

We *will* effectively conserve resources and protect the environment.

(2011_P_25)

We *will* pursue a more proactive fiscal policy.

(2016_P_66)

We *should* establish more equitable and sustainable social security systems.

(2016_P_32)

We *must* establish laws and mechanisms for ensuring that wages are paid on time.

(2006_P_27)

We *need to* protect the environment while pursuing development.

(2016_P_16)

We *need to* create 50 million plus new urban jobs.

(2016_P_34)

As '*we will*' is used in the plan section of the English translations of the AWR, it can be interpreted as expressing the meaning 'this is our plan and this is what we intend to do in the new year'. It should also be noted that most of the pronoun 'we's in these clauses are added in the process of translation.

As can be seen from Table 5.3, apart from the modal auxiliary 'will' that expresses inclination, modal auxiliaries expressing obligation are also used (around 500 in total), whereby the speaker requests or commands the audience to carry out a certain action. The median-value modal auxiliary 'should' is used around 60 times, taking up 13% of all of the clauses containing obligation. By comparison, high-value modal auxiliaries 'must' and 'have/need to' appear more than 400 times, taking up the remaining 87%. There is no low-value obligation modal expression in the clauses under analysis. Although this can be interpreted as a sign of the speaker's (premier's) assumed authority in demanding, a careful examination reveals that clauses where 'should', 'must', 'have/need to' appear are usually about topics of great concern for the public, such as air pollution, unemployment and income distribution. The use of these modal auxiliaries therefore functions to indicate that the government takes as its responsibility to deal with the issues affecting people's daily life and is determined to protect their well-being.

The experiential function of clauses containing 'we'

According to SFL, we can use language to construe our outer and inner experience of the world. This is the experiential metafunction of language. The experiential metafunction can be explored from two complementary perspectives, agency and transitivity. In this section, we will look at the agentive and transitive roles of 'we' in the English translations of AWR.

Agentive roles of 'we'

The linguistic construal of our experience of the world is realized through choices of two core components: the *process*, and the *participant(s)* involved in the processes. The system of agency highlights the causal origin of the action. The process can be either represented as self-engendering, in which case there is *medium* only, or as engendered from outside, in which case there is another participant functioning as the *agent*. If the process is self-engendering with only the medium, the clause is middle. If the process is caused by an outside agent, the clause is effective.

In the English translations of AWR, 'we' appears in both middle and effective clauses, serving either as the medium or the agent. But middle and effective clauses are not evenly distributed. The majority of the clauses containing 'we' are effective (1885, taking up 89%), and middle-voice clauses take up only 11%. Some of the middle-voice clauses are presented in the following.

> We *opened* wider to the outside world.
>
> (2001_R_2)

> Meanwhile, we *adhered to* the principle of "doing two jobs at once and attaching equal importance to each".
>
> (2001_R_12)

> We *did a good job* providing employment for urban residents newly entering the workforce, college graduates and demobilized soldiers.
>
> (2006_R_23)

> We *played* an important and constructive role in international affairs.
>
> (2011_R_2)

> We energetically *participated* in the reform of global economic governance and the development of mechanisms for regional cooperation.
>
> (2011_R_37)

> We *pressed ahead* with the reform of the household registration system.
>
> (2016_R_21)

> We *responded* effectively to natural disasters and emergencies.
>
> (2016_R_28)

> We *moved ahead* with the demonstration initiative to ensure food safety.
>
> (2016_R_30)

In the middle clause "we opened wider to the outside world", 'we' is the medium, as the process of opening is presented as taking place by itself. Interestingly, most of the middle-voice clauses appear in the review section of the reports. That is to say, while reviewing the achievements of the last year, the report not only uses fewer 'we's, but also tends to put 'we' in a less active role. In a previous study (Yu and Wu 2018), we interpret this as an indication of modesty when talking about achievements: The government does not take credit for itself.

As most of the clauses containing 'we' are effective in nature, let's now look at some of the effective-voice clauses.

> We need to *put water conservation high on our work agenda*.
>
> (2001_P_47)

> We will *further open the service sector* to foreign competition.
>
> (2006_P_189)

> We will *make government more open*.
>
> (2006_P_346)

We will *keep financing from all sources at an appropriate level.*

(2011_P_62)

We cannot *allow price rises to affect the normal lives of low-income people.*

(2011_P_81)

We must never *allow economic indicators to slide out of the appropriate range.*

(2019_P_40)

We will *let market entities, especially small and micro businesses, feel the weight of their burden being meaningfully lightened.*

(2019_P_61)

To this end, we will *keep grain output stable.*

(2019_P_177)

We will *keep central and local governments motivated.*

(2019_P_366)

In contrast to the middle-voice clause, the effective clause "we will further open the service sector to foreign competition" presents 'we' as the agent, the external cause of the process of 'opening'. Also different from middle-voice clauses is that effective clauses usually appear in the plan section of the reports. This helps to present the government (and sometimes Chinese people as well) as active in carry outing out the plan for a new year. While putting 'we' as medium presents the government as modest, the use of 'we' as agent presents the government as capable and responsible.

In order to investigate the process types of these effective clauses and the participant roles of 'we', further analysis of the effective clauses containing 'we' is carried out according to the system of transitivity.

Transitive roles of 'we'

While the system of agency generalizes across the various domains of experience, the system of transitivity is particularistic. It diversifies our experience into different process types, with the major ones being the process of doing and happening (material process), the process of sensing (mental process), and the process of being and having (relational process). Apart from these three major process types, there are also three minor process types, the verbal, behavioural and existential processes. These will not be discussed here, as no examples of such processes have been found in our data.

Some examples of these major process types are provided in the following.

Material process

ST: 实现城镇新增就业5000万人以上
TT: We need to *create* 50 million plus new urban jobs.

(2016_P_34)

Relational process

ST: *我们对国家的锦绣前程充满信心*
TT: We *are* even more *confident* in the splendid future of our country.

(2011_P_374)

Mental process

ST: *我们坚信，香港、澳门一定能够保持长期繁荣稳定。*
TT: *We firmly believe* that Hong Kong and Macao will remain prosperous and stable for a long time to come.

(2006_P_290)

As is shown in these examples, while most clauses with material processes have an added 'we' as the actor, 'we' serving as carrier or senser in the relational and mental processes is usually a literal translation of the original 'wǒmen' in the source text. Analysis of the effective clauses containing 'we' in the English translations of AWR indicates that material process dominates (96%), and there are also a few relational processes (around 3%) and very few mental processes (around 1%).

Material process

Material process typically involves an *actor*, the participant who carries out the action, and a *goal*, the participant towards which the action extends. According to the nature of the outcome affecting the actor or the goal, material process can be further classified into 'creative' and 'transformative'. In a creative material clause, the actor or goal is construed as being brought into existence as the process unfolds. The outcome is the coming into existence of the actor or the goal. The outcome is thus this participant itself, and there is no separate element in the clause representing the outcome. In a 'transformative' clause, a pre-existing actor or goal is construed as being transformed as the process unfolds. The outcome is the change of some aspect of an already existing actor or goal. For instance, while 'she painted a portrait of the artist' is 'creative' since the outcome is the creation of the portrait, 'she painted the house red' is 'transformative' since the outcome is the transformation of the colour of the house (Halliday and Matthiessen 2014).

Table 5.4 Clauses of material process

Creative clauses		202 (10%)
Transformative clauses		1,803 (90%)
	elaborating	1,369 (76%)
	enhancing	333 (18%)
	extending	101 (6%)
		2005

Analysis of the more than 2,000 material clauses reveals that creative clauses make up around 10% of all the clauses containing 'we', and the remaining 90% clauses are transformative in nature (Table 5.4). The most frequently used verbs in the creative clauses are *establish, launch, build*, and *create*. Some of the typical clauses are presented as follows.

> We will quickly *establish* a system for monitoring income distribution.
>
> (2011_P_230)

> We should *establish* more equitable and sustainable social security systems.
>
> (2016_P_32)

> We *launched* 178 major projects that save energy and water and comprehensively utilize resources.
>
> (2006_R_11)

> In transportation, we need to *build* highways, railways, ports, channels, airports and pipelines.
>
> (2001_P_50)

> We will work hard to *build* a clean government and combat corruption.
>
> (2006_P_348)

> We will promptly *create* a mechanism for ecological compensation.
>
> (2006_P_97)

> We need to *create* 50 million plus new urban jobs.
>
> (2016_P_34)

In these clauses, 'we' is the actor who *establishes, launches, builds* and *creates*. The goal that comes into existence as a result of the process of establishing, launching, building and creating is usually abstract systems, projects or the environment, though concrete things in the material world, such as highways or houses, are also built or created.

The more than 1,800 transformative clauses containing 'we' can be further divided into elaborating, enhancing and extending according to the outcome of the transformation. Elaborating transformative clauses represent qualitative change, that is to say, some quality of the actor or goal, such as size, shape, amount or make-up, changes as an outcome of the process. Enhancing transformative clauses represent circumstantial outcomes, especially the change of location. Extending transformative clauses mainly represent change of possession, and the commonly used verbs are *give, present, provide, send* and so on. Of the three types of transformative clauses, elaborating dominates in the clauses containing 'we' (76%), which is followed by enhancing (18%) and extending (6%, Table 5.4).

Some of the typical elaborating transformative clauses containing 'we' in the English translations of the AWR are presented as follows.

> We *improved* vocational training and employment services.
>
> (2011_R_40)

We will work to *improve* rural living environments in light of local conditions.

(2019_P_188)

We vigorously *developed* clean energy.

(2011_R_25)

We will *develop* defense-related science, technology, and industries.

(2016_P_348)

We will *strengthen* the protection of cultural and natural heritage sites.

(2006_P_147)

We will *reform* the civil servant pay system.

(2006_P_29)

We will *reform* the operating mechanisms of vocational colleges.

(2019_P_78)

We strongly *promoted* the development of the circular economy.

(2011_R_29)

We will *promote* the dynamic development of renewable energy.

(2019_P_228)

We will *increase* funding for agriculture, rural areas, and farmers.

(2011_P_111)

We will *increase* cross-Straits exchanges between people of all walks of life.

(2011_P_365)

We *deepened* the reform and opening up of the insurance industry.

(2011_R_35)

We will strongly *support* social programs in literature, art, radio and television, film, mass media, and publishing.

(2006_P_146)

We will *support* popular activities which promote cultural and ethical progress.

(2016_P_295)

As these examples demonstrate, the most frequently used verbs in the elaborating transformative clauses are *improve, strengthen, promote, reform, increase,* and *support*. The actor that performs the activities of improving, strengthening, promoting, reforming, increasing and supporting is 'we' in all these clauses.

Apart from elaborating clauses, there are also more than 300 enhancing transformative clauses, which represent the circumstantial change of the actor or the goal. Typical examples are as follows.

We will *accelerate* implementation of the free trade zone strategy.

(2016_P_231)

We will *adhere to* the path of urbanization with Chinese characteristics.

(2011_P_160)

We will closely *follow* national development strategies.

(2019_P_158)

We continued to *move* forward with structural reform.

(2016_R_9)

We *moved* ahead with the demonstration initiative to ensure food safety.

(2016_R_30)

We will energetically yet prudently *press ahead* with reform of national defense and the military.

(2011_P_352)

In these examples, while 'we' accelerate(d) the forward movement of the goal (the transformation, implementation and establishment) in some cases, 'we' serves as the participant that undergoes the movement in clauses where the process is realized through verbs such as *adhere to, follow, move ahead/forward,* and *press ahead*.

In comparison with elaborating and enhancing clauses, extending clauses are much fewer (around 100), and they usually represent the change of possession of the goal. Typical clauses in the data are as follows.

We must *give* priority to raising the people's living standards.

(2001_P_11)

We will *give* more aid to ethnic groups with small populations.

(2006_P_121)

We will also continue to *provide* free textbooks to students from poor families.

(2006_P_133)

We will *provide* incentives to research institutes, universities, scientists and engineers.

(2011_P_207)

Last year, we *achieved* significant results in all our work.

(2011_P_49)

We will definitely *achieve* the targets for economic and social development in 2016.

(2016_P_60)

In these clauses, 'we' *give, provide* something (concreate or abstract) to a beneficiary, and 'we' also *achieve* something.

Taking all the analysis results of material process into consideration, it can be seen that the choice of process type is itself meaningful. While from time to time 'we' create something new, 'we' improve, strengthen and reform things already existing most of the time. That is to say, as a government, 'we' develop mainly on the basis of what we already have, not on constantly creating new things. Even when transforming what is already there, the focus is on bringing qualitative change rather than changing the location or possession of things.

Relational and mental processes

Apart from the material process, relational and mental processes also appear in clauses containing 'we'.

> Looking back, we *are* proud of our extraordinary, glorious achievements . . .
> (2011_P_373)

> and looking forward, we *are* even more confident in the splendid future of our country.
> (2011_P_374)

> We *have* the unshakable will and the ability needed to prevail over difficulties and challenges of any kind.
> (2019_P_8)

> We *have* every confidence that Hong Kong and Macao will develop and thrive together with the mainland.
> (2019_P_388)

> We *are* convinced that Hong Kong and Macao will maintain long-term prosperity and stability.
> (2016_P_354)

> We firmly *believe* that Hong Kong and Macao will remain prosperous and stable for a long time to come.
> (2006_P_290)

In the relational process, 'we' is described as having a certain attribute (proud, confident) or possessing a certain quality (will, ability and confidence) that is desirable in achieve the outlined goals. The few mental processes use verbs such as *realize* and *believe* to describe the inner activities of 'we'. It is also interesting to note that relational and mental processes tend to appear at the end of the reports, when issues related to Hong Kong, Macao and Taiwan are discussed.

Circumstance of manner

More often than not, between the participant 'we' and the processes in which 'we' is involved (material, relational or mental), there are adverbs serving as circumstances of manner. Such circumstantial elements construe the way in which the process is actualized. Some examples are as follows.

We *vigorously* developed clean energy.

(2011_R_25)

We will *fully* revitalize old industrial bases such as northeast China.

(2011_P_154)

We will *energetically yet prudently* press ahead with reform of national defense and the military.

(2011_P_352)

We will *energetically yet steadily* develop the market for bonds and futures.

(2006_P_168)

We responded *effectively* to natural disasters and emergencies.

(2016_R_28)

We worked *tirelessly* to ensure everyone has access to old-age care, medical treatment, and housing.

(2011_R_46)

Apart from these most frequently adopted adverbs, *vigorously*, *fully*, *energetically*, *effectively* and *tirelessly*, words like *actively*, *steadfastly*, *successfully* and *unswervingly* are also used many times in clauses containing 'we'. In addition to specifying the manner in which the activities were/will be carried out, such circumstantial elements also embody positive interpersonal evaluations (Halliday and Matthiessen 2014). That is to say, they help to build a positive image of the Chinese government represented in the text as 'we'.

Conclusion

Combining automatic and manual analysis, this study investigated the diachronic distribution of 'wǒmen' and 'we' in the Chinese and English AWRs across 20 years and the interpersonal and experiential functions of clauses containing 'we' in the 2001, 2006, 2011, 2016 and 2019 English translations. It has been found that 'we' is used much more frequently in all the English translations than 'wǒmen' is used in the original Chinese work reports, in spite of some fluctuations in the ratio of 'we' to 'wǒmen'. In terms of the interpersonal function, nearly all the clauses are positive, and median- and high-value modulation (will/should/must/need to) is frequently used, indicating a sense of volition and obligation. In terms of the experiential function, 'we' is predominantly presented as the agent, carrying out mainly material processes which lay more stress on transforming existing entities rather than creating new things.

As has been pointed out, 'we' is usually added in the process of translation, as there are far fewer clauses containing 'wǒmen' in the Chinese AWRs. By investigating the interpersonal and experiential functions of clauses containing the added 'we', it is hoped that a better understanding of the government's projection of its own image on the international stage can be obtained, especially since the translation of the AWRs is under strict governmental supervision. Our study also supports enlarging the database and taking a diachronic view in analysis, as the translation is usually the result of teamwork, and there will be fluctuations in the use of certain words. For instance, a previous study of the 2013 English AWR (Meng and Yu 2016) shows that '*we should*' dominates, and very few '*will*'s are used. It is therefore stated that 'we should' constitutes a unique lexicogrammatical feature of the AWR (ibid, 208). Viewed diachronically, however, one can see that this is an exception rather than convention, as '*we will*' apparently dominates in the AWRs in most of the other years.

Acknowledgement

This work is funded by [Social Science Fund of China] under grant number [20VYJ012].

References

Baker, M. (1993) 'Corpus linguistics and translation studies: Implications and applications', In *Text and Technology: In Honour of John Sinclair*. M. Baker, G. Francis and E. Tognini-Bonelli (eds.), Amsterdam and Philadelphia: John Benjamins. pp. 233–250.

Croft, W. (1994) 'Speech act classification, language typology and cognition', in *Foundations of Speech Act Theory: Philosophical and Linguistic Perspectives*. S. L. Tsohatzidis (ed.), London: Routledge. pp. 460–477.

Duszak, A. (2002) *Us and Others: Social Identities across Languages, Discourses and Cultures*, Amsterdam: John Benjamins.

García, N. R. and Lanza, M. D. C. G. (2018) 'Translation description for assessment and post-editing: The case of personal pronouns in translated Spanish', *Target* 30(1): 112–136.

Halliday, M. A. K. and Matthiessen, C. M. I. M. (2014) *Halliday's Introduction to Functional Grammar*, London: Routledge.

Halliday, M. A. K. and McDonald, E. (2004) 'Metafunctional profile of the grammar of Chinese', in *Language Typology: A Functional Perspective*. A. Caffarel, J. R. Martin and C. M. I. M. Matthiessen (eds.), Amsterdam: John Benjamins. pp. 305–396.

Herke-Couchman, M. (2006) *SFL, Corpus and the Consumer: An Exploration of Theoretical and Technological Potential*. PhD thesis, Department of Linguistics, Macquarie University, Sydney.

Herke-Couchman, M. and Wu, C. (2004) *Stylistic Features as Meaning Representation: Text as Phase Portrait*. Proceedings of AAAI Fall Symposium. Available at: www.aaai.org/Papers/Symposia/Fall/2004/FS-04-07/FS04-07-009.pdf

Huang, Libo 黄立波 (2008) '英汉翻译中人称代词主语的显化 – 基于语料库的考察' (Explicitation of personal pronoun subjects in English-Chinese translation: A corpus-based investigation), 外语教学与研究 (*Foreign Language Teaching and Research*) 40: 454–459.

Hyland, K. (2001) 'Bringing in the reader addressee features in academic articles', *Written Communication* 18(4): 549–574.

Lv, Shuxiang 吕叔湘 (1999) 现代汉语八百词 (*Eight Hundred Words of Modern Chinese*), Beijing: Commercial Press.

Matthiessen, C. M. I. M. (1995) *Lexicogrammatical Cartography: English Systems*, Tokyo: International Language Sciences Publishers.
Meng, C. and Yu, Y. (2016) '"We should . . ." versus "we will . . .": How do the governments report their work in "one country two systems"? A corpus-driven critical discourse analysis of government work reports in Greater China', *Text & Talk* 36: 199–219.
Olohan, M. and Baker, M. (2000) 'Reporting that in translated English: Evidence for subconscious processes of explicitation?', *Across Languages and Cultures* 1(2): 141–158.
Sarkar, A. (1998) 'The conflict between future tense and modality: The case of will in English', *University of Pennsylvania Working Papers in Linguistics* 5(2): 91–117.
Wales, K. (1996) *Personal Pronouns in Present-Day English*, Cambridge: Cambridge University Press.
Wang, Kefei and Hu, Xianyao 王克非 胡显耀 (2010) '汉语文学翻译中人称代词的显化和变异' (The explicitation and deviation of personal pronouns in Chinese literary translation), *Foreign Languages in China* 7(1): 16–21.
Wang, Li 王力 (2002) 王力选集 (*Selected Works of Wang Li*), Jilin: Northeast Normal University Press.
Wu, C. (2000) *Modelling Linguistic Resources: A Systemic Functional Approach*. PhD thesis, Department of Linguistics, Macquarie University, Sydney.
Wu, C. and Fang, J. (2006) *The Social Semiotics of University Introductions in Australia and China*. 33rd International Systemic Functional Congress, São Paulo, Brazil.
Yu, H. (2017) 'How should Huineng speak? Text complexity in translations of the *Platform Sutra*', *New Voices in Translation Studies* 16(1): 1–22.
Yu, H. and Wu, C. (2016) 'Recreating the image of Chan master Huineng: Roles of mood and modality', *Functional Linguistics* 3(1): 1–20.
Yu, H. and Wu, C. (2017) 'Recreating the image of Chan master Huineng: The role of personal pronouns', *Target* 29(4): 64–86.
Yu, H. and Wu, C. (2018) 'Images of the Chinese government projected in its work reports: Transformation through translation', *Lingua* 214: 74–87.
Zhao, Shikai (1996) 'The contrastive study of English and Chinese personal pronouns: A preliminary pragmatic analysis', in 英汉语言文化对比研究 (*Contrastive Studies on English and Chinese Language and Culture*). R. Li. 李瑞华 (ed.), Shanghai: Shanghai Foreign Language Education Press. pp. 185–199.

6 Interpreting as institutional gatekeeping

A critical discourse analysis of interpreted questions at the Chinese foreign minister's press conferences

Xin Li and Ranran Zhang

Introduction

Government press conferences (GPC) addressed to the international media play a significant role in the communication of a country's national policies and stances to the international media, yet the crucial role of interpreters in these political-diplomatic communicative events has not received enough attention in academia. With China in recent years stepping up efforts to establish its GPC system as a means of proactive public diplomacy, there is a growing body of literature (Ouyang 2010; Wang 2012; Sun 2013; Wang and Feng 2018; Fu 2018; Gu 2018; Liao and Pan 2018; Li 2018) discussing the role of GPC interpreters in the Chinese context, which leads to the consensus that the in-house interpreters are not working as "neutral conduits" or "language machines" but playing an active mediation role in the reconstruction or reframing of political discourses in the high-profile GPC events. However, the gatekeeping role of these institutional interpreters remains underexplored. In addition, the limited discussions on interpreters' gatekeeping in the context of GPC interpreting in China have led to totally different conclusions. For example, after analysing the interpreting data of six Chinese GPCs held in response to the outbreak of SARS in 2003, Sun (2013) concludes that the interpreters play a role of "institutional aides or insiders" but not "institutional gate-keepers" (ibid: 179). By contrast, Gu's (2019a) critical examination of the rendition of foreign journalists' questions in the Premier-Meets-the-Press conferences lends clear support to the GPC interpreters' role as "institutional gatekeepers who control the flow of information" (ibid: 16).

Interestingly, studies on community interpreting (Wadensjö 1998; Davidson 2000; Pöllabauer 2012) suggest that interpreters working for government institutions inevitably exercise the gatekeeping role in their interpreting to frame their institutional goals by presenting events and negotiating values from different ideological positions. In light of the evidence found in other related studies (Li 2018; Gu 2019a, 2019b) as well as the present one, we argue that the Chinese in-house interpreters do play a gatekeeping role in GPC interpreting, especially when rendering the questions from journalists during the press conferences. With a custom-built parallel corpus, this chapter aims to investigate the degree and linguistic means of GPC interpreters' gatekeeping by conducting a critical discourse analysis (CDA) of the interpreter's filtering choices at the Chinese foreign minister's annual press conferences (2016–2018).

Towards a working definition of gatekeeping

As Pöllabauer (2012) points out, "gatekeeping" has been repeatedly used in translation and interpreting (T&I) studies as a metaphor to describe or discuss the role of translators/interpreters, but the concept itself is seldom tackled in depth, which in effect leads to the divergent conclusions about the gatekeeping role in T&I literature. Therefore, this section will first introduce the origin and the existing definitions of this concept in different fields, then briefly review the discussions on "gatekeeping" in T&I studies, before offering a working definition of "gatekeeping" for the present chapter.

The concept of "gatekeeping" was first created by the social psychologist Kurt Lewin (1947) to refer to the pivotal role of housewives in controlling the food habits and activities of families through creating behavioural barriers and incentives. It was subsequently developed as a popular metaphor or analytical concept in the fields of communication, information science, and political science, etc., where the focus is put on "different components in the conceptualization of gatekeeping" (Barzilai-Nahon 2009: 2). For example, in communication studies, gatekeeping is defined as "the process by which the billions of messages that are available in the world get cut down and transformed into the hundreds of messages that reach a given person on a given day" (Shoemaker 1991: 1). And in the field of political science, gatekeeping refers to the process of decision making in controlling access to certain services or the process of agenda-setting (e.g. Blanton 2000). To a large extent, communication studies and political science share the understanding of gatekeeping as a process of controlling or filtering (information or service), which can be applied to T&I studies.

In T&I studies, gatekeeping has mainly been discussed in the context of news translation and community interpreting. Fujii (1988) analyses gatekeeping practices in news translation in Japan. His observation reveals that the gatekeeping role of news translators in Japan is not limited to controlling the quantity of message but also involves message transforming, message supplementing and message reorganizing, which function together to meet the target text receivers' needs. More concerned with the theoretical modelling of gatekeeping in news translation, Vuorinen (1997: 161) defines gatekeeping as "the process of controlling the flow of information into and through communication channels".

As for community interpreting, Wadensjö's (1998) discussions on gatekeeping are probably the most influential. She describes gatekeepers in the context of encounters between institutions and clients as "intermediaries between lay people and institutions" who "control the flow of information by introducing, reinforcing and excluding topics according to the rationalities of the institution" (ibid: 67). In this light, both representatives of public institutions and interpreters function as gatekeepers. Inspired by Wadensjö (ibid), Davidson (2000) analyses the gatekeeping of hospital-based interpreters in medical interviews involving Spanish-speaking immigrants in the United States. His fieldwork observation and text analysis lead to the conclusion that these institutional interpreters act, "at least in part, as informational gatekeepers who keep the interview 'on track' and the physician on schedule" (ibid: 383). Drawing on Shoemaker and Vos's (2009) theoretical model of gatekeeping, Pöllabauer (2012) analyses the interpreting practice at two Austrian municipal social service and welfare institutions and identifies several "gates" in the encounters, that is, obstacles "which make (or may make) access to services and/or information more difficult for non-mother-tongue clients than probably for German-speaking clients" (ibid: 228).

This overview of literature shows that T&I scholars have found "gatekeeping" a convenient term to describe the active role of translators/interpreters in institutional settings, but the way they use this concept varies from project to project. On two extremes, Davidson (2000) uses "gatekeeping" metaphorically to summarize his empirical findings without giving a definition, whereas Vuorinen (1997) tackles the term in theoretical depth without offering any data analysis. In between is Pöllabauer (2012), who integrates an established theoretical model of gatekeeping into her data analysis, but the multi-layered model focuses too much on the macro-level analysis, which limits her in-depth textual analysis of the interpreting data.

The present study aims to investigate interpreters' gatekeeping through a systematic analysis of the transcribed interpreting data, and we use the term both as a metaphor and an analytical concept which can be investigated linguistically. The linguistic evidence for interpreters' gatekeeping practices has to do with translation shifts in the interpreting process, such as the "transforming" and "supplementing" shifts found by Fujii (1988). For a more systematic identification of shifts and a more in-depth analysis of the interpreting data, the present study draws on systemic functional linguistics (SFL), which views language as organized around three major strands of meaning, that is, three metafunctions: ideational, interpersonal and textual. The ideational metafunction is concerned with construing experience, the interpersonal metafunction with enacting or negotiating social relations, and the textual metafunction with the organization of ideational and interpersonal meanings (Martin and Rose 2007). It is worth noting that translation shifts in the textual metafunction are often motivated by their system differences rather than the translator/interpreter's ideological concerns, resulting from the fact that Chinese is a topic-prominent language while English is a subject-prominent language (Baker 2001: 153). Therefore, a working definition of interpreters' gatekeeping is proposed here as the ideologically motivated filtering of the source speaker's messages in the interpreting process, by withholding, modifying, or supplementing the ideational/interpersonal meanings.

Data, theoretical framework and methodology

GPCs in this chapter refer to the state-level government press conferences in China. The most influential GPCs in China are the press conferences held annually at the closing of the plenary sessions of the National People's Congress (NPC) and the National Committee of the Chinese People's Political Consultative Conference (CPPCC) (Li 2018: 4), when the premier or foreign minister is invited to answer questions raised by journalists from home and abroad, with consecutive interpreting service offered by experienced in-house interpreters from the Ministry of Foreign Affairs. Aiming to publicize China's voices to the international media, these interpreter-mediated GPCs are high-profile political-diplomatic events live broadcast to the whole world.[1]

The data for the present study are collected from Foreign Minister Wang Yi's annual press conferences during the NPC and CPPCC sessions between 2016 and 2018. The footages of the three interpreter-mediated events were downloaded from YouTube and then manually transcribed in a verbatim manner to produce a textual corpus that faithfully represents the original speeches. Bi-directional consecutive interpreting service between Chinese and English for the events was offered by the same interpreter, Sun Ning, who has worked at the Department of Translation and Interpreting (DTI), Ministry of Foreign Affairs (MOFA) since 2003. Since the 1950s, the translators/interpreters from DTI have been responsible for the translation/interpreting of diplomatic events involving the central government leaders and important political documents (Shi 2009), so they "represent the top-level of the translating/interpreting profession in China" (Ren 2004: 61). Although our data only involve one interpreter, his interpreting is considered representative of GPC interpreting in China, because he has received the same intensive training within the institution as his colleagues (ibid). The total size of the corpus (Corpus A) is 62,676 tokens (one English word or one Chinese character is counted as one token).

Previous studies on the GPC interpreting in the Chinese context have mostly focused on the interpreting of Chinese leaders' responses rather than the journalists' questions, but the latter actually is a more "dynamic" and "negotiated" section, featuring "the clash of different ideological beliefs" between the Chinese government and international journalists (Gu 2019a: 3). To fill this gap, the present study focuses on the interpreter's gatekeeping in rendering journalists' questions. Thus a mini-corpus (Corpus B) consisting of only the journalists' questions (61 questions[2] in total) and their renditions is extracted from Corpus A, with a size of 12,529 tokens. The minister's responses (as well as the chairperson's utterances) and their renditions in Corpus A will be used as contextual reference. Different from Gu's (2019a) focus on the premier's press conferences, we choose to look at the foreign minister's press conferences, because the foreign minister's press conferences have a consistent theme of "China's foreign policy and external relations", which attract more sensitive questions from international journalists, making them more ideal sites to examine interpreters' gatekeeping. Also different from Gu's (2019a) exclusive focus on the foreign journalists' questions, we'll look at questions asked by all journalists for comparative purposes.

For the convenience of comparative analysis and discussion, the ST section of data is distinguished into three participation frameworks:[3] Chinese journalists questioning in Chinese (PT1), foreign journalists questioning in Chinese (PT2) and foreign journalists questioning in English (PT3), but the term "Chinese" or "foreign" here refers not to nationality but to whether they represent Chinese or foreign media outlets. In our data, "Chinese journalists" include those who have raised questions on behalf of news outlets sponsored or monitored by the Chinese government, such as *People's Daily*, CCTV, CGTN, *China Daily*, *Global Times*, Beijing TV, *The Paper*, China Radio International, China News Service, Xinhua News Agency, etc., whereas "foreign journalists" include those who have raised questions representing news media outside of China, such as Reuters, Bloomberg, *The Straits Times*, Kyodo News, *Press Trust of India*, Radio France, TASS, NBC news, CNN, *Tanzania Standard Newspaper*, Philippine News Agency, etc. To establish comparative "units of analysis" (Kenny 2011), the STs and TTs are manually aligned at the clause level whenever possible. Table 6.1 illustrates the composition of the mini-corpus.

To investigate the interpreter's gatekeeping in rendering journalists' questions in the political-diplomatic setting of GPCs, this study adopts a corpus-based CDA approach informed by SFL. The corpus-based method has its advantage in producing quantitative results about recurring patterns, while the CDA approach (van Dijk 1995; Fairclough 2003) has its strength in scrutinizing linguistic choices to reveal the ideology and power relations behind the discursive practice. The integrated approach between the two has proved instrumental for T&I projects aiming to look at both the recurrent patterns of translating/interpreting choices and the ideological positioning or stance-taking behind these choices (e.g. Zhan 2013; Pan 2015; Kim 2017; Gu 2018; Wang and Feng 2018). Given the scope and purpose of the present study, we will follow Gu (2018, 2019a, 2019b) in employing CDA mainly for the critical comparisons between STs and TTs rather than confine ourselves to any of the major CDA schools established in the context of monolingual studies.

Within the broad framework of descriptive translation studies (DTS), shifts are considered a "true universal of translation" (Toury 1995: 57) and a useful tool to describe the ST–TT relationship and the translator/interpreter's choices. Defined

Table 6.1 Composition of the mini-corpus (Corpus B)

Participation framework	Number of questions	Length of ST (tokens)	Length of TT (tokens)
Chinese journalists questioning in Chinese (PT1)	31	4,784	1,819
Foreign journalists questioning in Chinese (PT2)	17	2,647	993
Foreign journalists questioning in English (PT3)	13	993	1,293
Subtotal	61	8,424	4,105

as "small linguistic changes occurring in translation of ST to TT" (Munday 2001: 55), translation shifts involve both "obligatory shifts" and "optional shifts", with the former "dictated by differences between linguistic systems" and the latter "opted for by the translator for stylistic, ideological or cultural reasons" (Bakker et al. 2004: 228). In this study, we only look at the optional linguistic shifts chosen by the interpreter despite the availability of close equivalents between Chinese and English, which will serve as potential evidence of the interpreter's gatekeeping motivated by his ideology and institutional alignment with the Chinese government.

For the systematic analysis of shifts in the interpreting data, we will draw on SFL, which has always been "a valuable resource for critical discourse analysis" as it is also "oriented to the social character of texts" (Fairclough 2003: 6). As mentioned earlier, both the ideational and interpersonal metafunctions of language are relevant to interpreters' gatekeeping, but each is realized through a series of complex systems. In addition, ideational and interpersonal shifts often co-occur in the same ST–TT pair of clause, for the clause is by nature "a multifunctional construct" (Halliday and Matthiessen 2004: 168). Thus, to narrow down our analysis to a manageable level, the present study will only look at the interpersonal metafunction, which is typically realized through systems including MOOD (ibid; Halliday and McDonald 2004), SPEECH FUNCTION (ibid; Martin and Rose 2007), and APPRAISAL (Martin and White 2005). In fact, all these interpersonal systems are complex, with APPRAISAL being the most complicated in particular, which can be further categorized into the subsystems of ATTITUDE, ENGAGEMENT and GRADUATION (ibid). As the present study intends to critically examine the interpreter's gatekeeping choices rather than give a comprehensive account of the interpersonal systems, we do not intend to conduct quantitative analysis of interpersonal shifts in each specific system. Instead, we will identify all the interpersonal shifts guided by these interpersonal systems in SFL and classify them broadly into additions, omissions and modifications of interpersonal meanings, and then calculate the frequency of these shifts[4] against the number of ST clauses in each participation framework for quantitative comparison. After that, we will discuss to what extent these interpersonal shifts reveal the interpreter's gatekeeping and probe deeper into the ideologically salient types of interpersonal shifts related to specific systems for qualitative analysis.

Quantitative analysis

Based on the manual coding, we count the frequency of the three types (omission, addition and modification) of interpersonal shifts in the three different participation frameworks and then calculate the degree of interpersonal shifts as the frequency of shifts divided by the number of ST clauses. Quantitative results are summarized in Table 6.2.

Obviously, the general degree of interpersonal shifts in the rendition of journalists' questions at the foreign minister's press conferences is very high (75.8%): a total of 495 interpersonal shifts occur in the rendition of 653 ST clauses. To be

Table 6.2 Occurrence of interpersonal shifts in different participation frameworks

Participation framework	Omission	Addition	Modification	Interpersonal shifts in total	Number of ST-clauses
Chinese journalists questioning in Chinese (PT1)	232 (66.9%)	20 (5.8%)	9 (2.6%)	261 (75.2%)	347
Foreign journalists questioning in Chinese (PT2)	120 (64.2%)	10 (5.3%)	22 (11.8%)	152 (81.3%)	187
Foreign journalists questioning in English (PT3)	55 (46.2%)	9 (7.6%)	18 (15.1%)	82 (68.9%)	119
Total	407 (62.3%)	39 (6.0%)	49 (7.5%)	495 (75.8%)	653

more specific, 407 shifts of omission (62.3%), 49 shifts of modification (7.5%) and 39 shifts of addition (6%) in terms of interpersonal meanings occur in the interpreting. So there is a predominant tendency towards withholding certain interpersonal meanings of the ST. Although some of the omissions may be caused by the interpreter's cognitive constraints, close reading of the concordances suggests that most of these interpersonal shifts can be explained by the interpreter's ideological beliefs and his institutional position, which will be illustrated in the next section.

In terms of the different participation frameworks, it is noticeable that shifts of omission occur more frequently in rendering Chinese questions into English (PT1: 66.9%; PT2: 64.2%) than in rendering English questions into Chinese (PT3: 46.2%). This can be attributable to the difference in their intended target audience. When the interpreter renders a Chinese question into English, the foreign minister has already heard the source Chinese question clearly and will most probably use the time of consecutive interpretation to plan his response rather than listen to how the question is rendered into English. In this case, the target audience of the TT is primarily the English-speaking journalists representing the international media. As journalists, they are more concerned with the content of the questions raised by other journalists and the foreign minister's responses, instead of a word-for-word rendition of the remarks or comments in their questions. That explains why linguistic resources construing interpersonal meanings are frequently omitted in the English renditions of Chinese questions. By contrast, when the interpreter renders journalists' questions from English to Chinese, the target audience of the TT is primarily the foreign minister, along with other Chinese-speaking journalists representing Chinese media. Since the foreign minister is both the addressee and auditor of the Chinese TT, it is important for the interpreter to offer adequate rendition of the English questions so that the minister can have a comprehensive understanding of not only the question but also the journalist's stance. This leads to a much lower degree of omission in terms of interpersonal meaning.

Another noticeable pattern lies in the shifts of modification. It appears that the interpreter more frequently modifies the interpersonal meanings of the ST when rendering questions of foreign journalists (PT3: 15.1%; PT2: 11.8%) than when rendering those of Chinese journalists (PT1: 2.6%). This can be explained by the fact that foreign journalists tend to raise more sensitive and face-threatening questions than Chinese journalists, and the interpreter considers it necessary to modify foreign journalists' questions so that the interpreted questions into Chinese (PT3) sound more polite and acceptable to the foreign minister and the interpreted questions into English (PT2) sound more proper and politically correct as major points of departure (Gu 2019b: 3) in the outward communication of China's voices initiated by the Chinese government.

Qualitative analysis

The foregoing quantitative analysis suggests a high degree of gatekeeping on the part of the interpreter in rendering journalists' questions at the foreign minister's press conferences. This section aims at a qualitative analysis of typical examples to discuss the communicative effect of the interpersonal shifts and the ideological motivations behind these gatekeeping choices. Close critical reading of the aligned data reveals that the interpreter's gatekeeping through interpersonal shifts manifests itself most saliently in the following six categories: (1) omission of complete ST clauses realizing the speech function of thanking, greeting or statement (topical, subjective and attitudinal) in PT1 (Example 1) and PT2 (Example 2); (2) omission of force-raising graduation resources in PT1 (Example 3) and PT2 (Example 2); (3) addition of identity statements (Example 4) or complete questions (Example 5) in PT3; (4) addition of engagement or attitude markers in PT1(Example 6) and PT2 (Example 7); (5) modification of engagement or attitude in PT3(Example 8) and PT2 (Example 9); (6) modification of mood in PT2 (Example 2 and Example 10).

Omission of complete ST clauses of thanking, greeting or statement

The first type of interpersonal shifts concerns the semantic system of SPEECH FUNCTION. Interpersonally viewing clause as "giving" or "demanding" either "goods-&-services" or "information", Halliday and Matthiessen (2004: 108) describe *statement, question, command* and *offer* as the four primary speech functions of the clause. Martin and Rose (2007: 226) extend the system into 13 categories, which include *greeting* and *exclamation*. Based on our observation of the interpreter-mediated dialogues between the foreign minister and the journalists, we propose to add *thanking* to the list. We find that ST clauses realizing the speech function of *thanking, greeting* or *statement* (topical, subjective and attitudinal) are often omitted completely in the English interpreting of journalists' Chinese questions.

Example 1 (2017 *People's Daily*)

ST: 外长您好[A]。我是人民日报的记者。我的问题是关于中国外交的[B]。我们都知道[C]，这几年中国外交越来越有声有色，亮点纷呈。那么，如果请您用一个词或者几个词来总结一下十八大以来中国外交的风格或者特点，您会选择什么样的词汇？您的理由是什么？谢谢[D]。

LT:[5] Good morning, Minister [A]. I'm a journalist from *People's Daily*. My question is about China's diplomacy [B]. We all know that [C] these years China's diplomacy is increasingly active and colourful. So, if I ask you to use one word or a few words to sum up the style or features of China's diplomacy since the 18th CPC Congress, what words would you choose? What are your reasons? Thank you [D].

TT: People's Daily. In the last few years, China's diplomacy has been more active and dynamic. If you are to use a few words to sum up China's diplomacy since the 18th CPC Congress, what would they be? And why do you choose these words?

As illustrated by Example 1, the Chinese-speaking journalists usually begin their turn of talk by giving polite greetings to the foreign minister (Clause A), introduce their question by a topical statement (Clause B), raise their question and then end their utterance politely with "谢谢" [thank you] (Clause D). Before raising the question, they often add a subjective statement such as "我们都知道" [we all know that] (Clause C) or "我们注意到" [we notice that], which fall into the category of *concur* in terms of the ENGAGEMENT system, overtly proclaiming themselves as "agreeing with, or having the same knowledge as" the audience (Martin and White 2005: 122). All these clauses of thanking, greeting, topical and concurring statements are regularly omitted in the English TT. Apparently, the interpreter does not consider it necessary to reproduce the journalists' polite expressions of thanking and greeting in the English TT, because the politeness has already been communicated to the minister in the ST, and the target audience of the English TT would not care so much about the journalists' manners. The topical statements are helpful in the Chinese ST to help the minister prepare for his response, but they are considered redundant in the English TT because they can be easily extracted from the exact questions. The concurring statements reflect the journalists' subjective efforts at such high-profile press conferences to justify their questions by aligning the audience with themselves on their positions, but these efforts are not so important to the TT audience as the questions themselves. Therefore, they are also frequently filtered out in the interpreting. All these omissions make the English TT sound more concise and objective, which suits the English-speaking audience's needs at such long-lasting conferences.

More interestingly, when the Chinese questions are raised by foreign journalists, the interpreter (in addition to the omissions discussed earlier) tends to omit long attitudinal statements marking biased opinions against China's political stance, as illustrated by Example 2.

Example 2 *(2016 CNN)*

ST: 外交部发言人多次表明，中国不接受、不参与的这个立场。<u>但问题就是说，这是一个被国际社会所承认的法院，那他的判决宣布之后，不管中国的立场如何，中国如果不调整或改变政策或行为的话，那就会很明显地违反了一项国际法的判决。</u>美国的白宫的<u>高级</u>官员也明确表示，这个判决宣布之后将会对中菲双方同样具有约束力。所以我的问题就是，呃，有人就表示，这样的如果中国在判决之后还是坚持自己的行为的话，<u>会给美国和他的盟友在南海的行为其实是提供了更多这个基于国际法的法理依据</u>。

LT: The Foreign Ministry spokesperson has repeatedly announced China's position of not accepting and not participating. <u>But the problem is, this is a tribunal acknowledged by the international community. After the announcement of its ruling, if China does not adjust or change its policies or acts, it will apparently violate international law, despite China's stance.</u> <u>Senior</u> White House officials in the US have also <u>clearly</u> said that the ruling is going to be binding on both China and the Philippines after its declaration. So my question is, um, some people point out that if China still persists in its actions after the ruling, <u>it will give the United States and its allies more legal basis in line with the international law for their actions.</u>

TT: China has expressed its position of not accepting and not participating in the arbitration. White House officials have said the ruling is going to be binding on both China and the Philippines. And after the ruling is made public, if China still does not accept the outcome, <u>will it give the United States and its allies more reasons to do what they want?</u>

This is the segment of a long utterance by an American journalist on the South China Sea issue during the 2016 press conference. Focusing on the arbitration case initiated by the Philippines against China, the CNN journalist apparently takes sides with the American government in supporting the arbitration and gives a long statement (a series of clauses) to describe the tribunal established at the unilateral request of the Philippines as "acknowledged by the international society" before asking the minister to respond to the likely ruling. This position is clearly not acceptable to China, as the Chinese government believes in the international practice that arbitration must be based on mutual state consent. While the White House's position in the following utterance is reproduced clearly into English, the interpreter chooses to exclude the statements expressing the journalist's personal stance against China; thus, the foreign journalist's negative attitude towards China is downplayed in the English TT.

In fact, most clauses realizing the speech functions of *thanking* and *greeting* are also omitted in the rendition of journalists' questions from English to Chinese, in order to save time. However, the topical statements and the attitudinal statements are mostly reproduced into the Chinese TT, probably because the foreign minister as the target listener of the TT needs to rely on them to understand the question and get prepared for it.

Omission of force-raising graduation resources

The second category of interpersonal shifts concerns the system of GRADUATION (subsystem of APPRAISAL) (Martin and White 2005), which deals with the upscaling or downscaling of attitude and engagement meanings according to either prototypicality or intensity/amount. The first is referred to as *focus*, which involves *sharpening* or *softening* resources; and the second is referred to as *force*, which involves *raising* or *lowering* resources. In our data, we find that force-raising graduation resources are often omitted in interpreting journalists' questions from Chinese into English.

One case in point is Example 2, where the graduation resources used to raise the force of the voice against China are omitted. After expressing his personal stance against China on the South China Sea issue, the CNN journalist goes on to cite "美国的白宫的高级官员" [senior White House officials in the US] as an authoritative voice who has "明确" [clearly] expressed the same stance as the journalist's: the ruling is going to be binding on both China and the Philippines after its declaration. The force-raising resources "高级" [senior] and "明确" [clearly] are both omitted, to the effect that the cited voice sounds less authoritative and less forceful in the English TT. This filtering choice is most probably motivated by the interpreter's ideological alignment with the Chinese government, who maintains that the arbitration is neither binding nor conducive to the settlement of disputes in the South China Sea.

In cases where China's position towards other countries is concerned, the force-raising graduation resources are omitted, probably not because the interpreter intends to downplay China's attitude but because the interpreter is aware of the different rhetorical conventions between Chinese and English. A typical case is Example 3.

Example 3 (2016 *The Cambodia Daily*)

ST: 中国也<u>始终</u>把东盟作为周边外交的合作方，优先方向，<u>坚定</u>支持东盟在区域合作中的中心地位。

LT: China has also <u>always</u> viewed ASEAN countries as a priority for cooperation in its neighbourhood diplomacy and <u>firmly</u> supports ASEAN's centrality in regional cooperation.

TT: China views ASEAN countries as a priority in its neighbourhood diplomacy and supports ASEAN's centrality in regional cooperation.

Example 3 is a statement from a friendly Cambodian journalist during the 2016 press conference. Here the journalist states China's position towards ASEAN in a tone typical of the Chinese official discourse, so it can be considered as an implicit quote of China's official statement about its position towards ASEAN. The ST segment illustrates the typical Chinese political discourse where the graduation resources such as "始终" [always] and "坚定" [firmly] are often used to raise the force of attitudinal meanings. But according to Pinkham (2000) who used to work as a polisher at Foreign Languages Press and the Central Translation Bureau, these words tend to be overused in Chinese political texts compared with English, and the literal translation will sound like Chinglish with many "redundant intensifiers" (ibid: 36). By omitting the two force-raising graduation resources in the rendition, China's supportive position towards ASEAN is communicated to the international media in a way more acceptable to the English-speaking audience.

Addition of identity statements or complete questions

The third type of interpersonal shifts also concerns the system of SPEECH FUNCTION. Despite the overall tendency towards omission rather than addition in the interpreting, additions of complete clauses realizing the speech function of identity *statement* or *question* are found in the rendition of foreign journalists' utterances from English into Chinese, which clearly point at the interpreter's conscious gatekeeping.

Example 4 (2016 Journalist from Zambia)

ST: Thank you. Good morning, Minister. As China's economy has been slowing down . . .

TT: 我是赞比亚的记者。由于中国的经济增速放缓. . .

BT: <u>I'm a journalist from Zambia.</u> As China's economy has been slowing down . . .

Example 4 is the beginning of the questioning section from a Zambian journalist during the 2016 press conference. Before her utterance, the chairperson has explicitly invited "the journalist from Zambia" to ask the next question. For some reason this journalist forgets to give the expected self-introduction at the beginning of the questioning section. Interestingly, the interpreter dramatically adds the statement of identity in the Chinese TT based on what he has heard from the chairperson, which shows his efforts to maintain the norm of the discourse pattern of the questioning section in the Chinese TT and to facilitate the minister's comprehension of the following questions by providing necessary contextual information.

Example 5 (2017 Tanzania Standard Newspaper)

ST: It's over a year since the Forum of China-Africa Cooperation Summit in Johannesburg. Can you brief us on the implementation of the outcomes for this summit of last year, one year ago? Also, is there any problem of China-Africa cooperation in this year and one year ago?

TT: 中非合作论坛约翰内斯堡峰会已经过去一年多了，请问峰会成果的落实情况怎么样？在这一年，中非合作会面临怎样的问题？<u>会有哪些新的进展？</u>

BT: It's been over a year since the Forum of China-Africa Cooperation Summit in Johannesburg. Please allow me to ask, how is the implementation of the outcomes of this summit? What problems will China-Africa cooperation face this year? <u>What new progress will there be?</u>

Example 5 is a segment of the questioning section from a Tanzanian journalist during the 2017 press conference. After stating the situation that one year has passed since the Forum of China-Africa Cooperation Summit in Johannesburg, she raises two relevant questions: one is on "the implementation of the outcomes for this summit", and the other is about the "problem" in China–Africa cooperation, which sounds rather pessimistic. Fully aware of the Chinese government's positive attitude towards China–Africa cooperation, the interpreter notably adds a third question in the Chinese TT on the "new progress" in China–Africa cooperation, which dramatically reframes the journalist's attitude towards China–Africa cooperation into a more optimistic one. It is important to note that the minister indeed talks about the progress before the problem in his response, which demonstrates the significant effect of the interpreter's gatekeeping in rendering the journalist's questions.

Addition of engagement or attitude markers

The fourth salient type of interpersonal shifts concerns the interpersonal systems of ENGAGEMENT and ATTITUDE, which are two subsystems of APPRAISAL developed by Martin and White (2005). ATTITUDE is concerned with positive or negative feelings, which includes *affect* (emotional feelings), *judgement* (ethical attitudes towards behaviour) and *appreciation* (aesthetic evaluation of things and phenomena).

Interpreting as institutional gatekeeping 119

ENGAGEMENT involves the linguistic resources by which the speaker/writer brings other voices into the text, either to contract (e.g. *counter*, *concur*), or expand (e.g. *acknowledgement*, *distance*) the dialogic space for alternative voices. Although *acknowledgement* (e.g. "he says that") and *distance* ("he claims that") both function as expansive resources, there is a crucial difference between them in that *distance* suggests the speaker's negative attitude towards the presented voice while *acknowledgement* marks the speaker's neutral stance. Based on our interpreting data, additions of engagement or attitude markers primarily occur in the interpreting of journalists' questions from Chinese to English.

Example 6 (2018 *Global Times*)

ST: 在国际上呢也开始了新一轮"中国威胁论"的炒作，比如说，认为中国正在用"锐实力"来影响世界等等。
LT: A new round of hype about "China threat" theory has started in the world. For example, some say that China is using its "sharp power" to influence the world.
TT: . . . those in the world who try to paint China as a threat, who say that China will use its so-called "sharp power" to influence the world.

Example 6 is a segment of the questioning section from a Chinese journalist during the 2018 press conference. Here she reports a new round of "China threat theory" in the Western media in order to ask the minister for his response. It is obvious that the Chinese journalist also does not align with these Western voices, for she uses the engagement resource "炒作" [hype] in the first clause to express her distance. But her second clause adopts a more neutral position, as only the engagement resource of acknowledgement "认为" [think/believe] is used. In the rendition of the second clause, the interpreter adds a distance marker "so-called", which clearly presents this third voice as questionable. This addition reveals the interpreter's ideological position against these Western voices.

Example 7 (2016 *Lianhe Zaobao*)

ST: 中国也带头创建了亚投行，输出了那个大型的那个基础设施。
LT: China has also initiated to build the Asian Infrastructure Investment Bank and has exported large-scale infrastructure.
TT: China has initiated to build the Asian Infrastructure Investment Bank and is helping other countries building large-scale infrastructure.

Example 7 is an utterance from a Singaporean journalist on China's investment in the Middle East, Africa and Latin America during the 2016 conference. Before citing some commentators who "see China's goal as wanting to overhaul the international order", here she states China's actions in these regions with neutral verbs such as "创建" [create/build] and "输出" [export], but the interpreter adds the attitude resource "helping other countries", clearly construing a positive judgement towards China's actions. Through this gatekeeping choice, the English TT is framed to view the Chinese government's investment as friendly and helpful, contrary to the position of "some commentators".

These two examples show that the interpreter's addition of engagement or attitude markers in the rendition of journalists' utterances from Chinese to English either distances the journalists and himself away from biased Western voices against China or foregrounds positive judgemental attitudes towards China in the English TT. These choices are clearly motivated by the interpreter's institutional alignment with the Chinese government.

Modification of engagement or attitude

The fifth type of interpersonal shifts also concerns the system of ENGAGEMENT and ATTITUDE. As illustrated by Table 6.2, the modification shifts in terms of interpersonal meanings mostly occur in the rendition of foreign journalists' questions. The following two examples illustrate how engagement and attitude meanings in foreign journalists' utterances are modified by the interpreter.

Example 8 (2016 Reuters)

ST: This is giving the world the impression that perhaps China is trying to hide something in the South China Sea, or that perhaps its claims, or perhaps the Chinese government is not confident about its claims in the South China Sea.

TT: 这给大家带来的一个印象，好像是中国要隐藏什么，或者是中国对于自己的主张不够自信。

BT: This is giving people the impression that perhaps China is trying to hide something, or perhaps China is not confident about its propositions.

Example 8 is part of the questioning section from a British journalist at the 2016 conference. The journalist starts with stating the background that China does not permit foreigners, including foreign journalists, to visit its islands in the South China Sea, and then gives his comment in the cited segment, followed by a series of challenging questions such as asking when China will permit foreign journalists to visit. By using the distance marker "claim", he expands the dialogical space between China's voices and alternative voices, and at the same time distances himself away from China's voice. The interpreter, however, renders "claims" into "主张" [propositions], which marks acknowledgement, expressing a neutral stance. The engagement shift here in effect downplays the journalist's negative attitude towards China, which is presumably motivated by the interpreter's ideological alignment with the Chinese government.

Example 9 (2017 CNN)

ST: 那么我们也注意到，习近平主席最近提到中国要引导国际社会塑造一个更加公正合理的国际新秩序。这也被很多人解读为是中国要打破美国在二战之后建立的这套国际体系，以自己为主导的新体系取而代之。

LT: We also notice that President Xi recently mentioned China will guide/lead the international community to build a more just and rational new international order. This is understood by many people to mean that China is going to break the international order established by the US after WWII and replace it with the new world order dominated by itself.

TT: And President Xi said, China will work with the international community to build a just and equitable new world order.

Example 9 is a segment of the questioning section from an American journalist during the 2017 press conference. Here the journalist quotes President Xi's remarks at the Feb. 17 national security seminar that "China will guide/lead the international community to build a more just and rational new international order" in order to bring about the question on whether China aims to take up the global leadership role from the United States, as widely discussed by Western media. In fact, the Chinese verb "引导" is a little ambiguous and can be translated either as "lead" or "guide" depending on the context. As Webster (2017) points out, careful reading of President Xi's full speech will lead to the correct understanding that Xi meant to emphasize China's role as a "participant, defender (especially in international security), and proactive reformer in the existing international system" rather than a global leader. However, in the context of the CNN journalist's utterance followed by his statement that President Xi's remarks are viewed by many as the intention to replace the US-dominated old world order with China-dominated new world order (note that the underlined sentence, which is not rendered into TT, also illustrates the interpreter's gatekeeping by omitting long statements expressing negative attitude towards China, as in Example 2), the ST verb "引导" invokes a negative judgement about China and constructs China's image as an aggressive country aiming to seize global leadership. Apparently aware of this controversy and Minister Wang's likely response, the interpreter wittily renders the potentially aggressive "引导" into "working with", which invokes a positive judgement of China as a cooperative and responsible country. The interpreter's gatekeeping choice of attitudinal shift reconstructs China's image as a responsible and friendly country willing to make greater contributions to a more just and rational international order, which well matches the following response by the foreign minister.

Modification of mood

The last type of interpersonal shifts concerns the system of MOOD (Halliday and McDonald 2004), which is the grammatical system to realize the interpersonal semantics of SPEECH FUNCTION. In both English and Chinese, mood is classified into three basic types: *imperative*, *declarative* and *interrogative*, with interrogatives further classified into *polar* (*yes/no*) questions and *elemental* (*wh-*) questions. Different from English in which the ordering of subject and finite (verbal operator) is crucial to the realization of mood, mood types in Chinese are typically realized by the clause particle, the interrogative word and the intonation (ibid: 330–343). Yet it is not hard to find equivalents (and hence identify shifts) in the translation of mood between the two languages. The modification of mood also primarily occurs in the rendition of foreign journalists' utterances, because their questions tend to be more challenging and fact-threatening than those by Chinese journalists. The interpreter's gatekeeping choice of mood shift can be illustrated by Example 2.

While addressing the sensitive South China Sea issue, the CNN journalist raises his concerns about the United States and its allies' response to China's actions in the declarative mood, which could literally be rendered as "if China still persists in its actions after the ruling, it will give the United States and its allies more legal basis in line with the international law for their actions". This declarative statement would give the impression that the United States and its allies are justified to take action against China if China does not accept the ruling, which is apparently against the stance of the Chinese government. The interpreter here gatekeeps the ST message by changing the declarative mood into interrogative (a polar question, to be exact): "if China still does not accept the outcome, will it give the United States and its allies more reasons to do what they want?" In this way, the Minister is empowered to judge whether this assumption is valid or not, rather than passively receive it as an existing assumption. Salient mood shifts also include changes between polar questions and elemental questions, as illustrated by Example 10.

Example 10 (2018 Bloomberg)

ST: 美国总统特朗普说，他愿意采取一切工具来防止中国的国有经济模式破坏国际竞争，那么请问，<u>中国是否也愿意采取一切工具来反击？如果是的话，中国将会采取哪些工具呢？</u>

LT: US President Donald Trump said he will use all tools at his proposal to prevent China's state economic model from undermining international competition. So, I'd like to ask, <u>will China also use all tools at its proposal to strike back? If so, what tools will China use?</u>

TT: U.S. President Donald Trump has said he will use all tools at his proposal, disposal to prevent China's state economic model from undermining international competition. <u>How will China respond to that?</u>

This is part of the questioning section of an American journalist at the 2018 conference. In the context of the frequent trade frictions between China and the United States, the journalist cites US President Trump's aggressive statement and then asks Minister Wang to give his response. The Chinese ST includes two questions, one polar question followed by an elemental question. The polar question demands the minister to tell whether China is willing to use all tools at its proposal to strike back, and the elemental question demands the minister to tell what kinds of tools China will use. This combination of polar and elemental questions is highly face-threatening to the minister because China has consistently proposed "win-win cooperation" between the two countries. By rendering the two questions into a simplified elemental question "How will China respond to that?" the interpreter positions the minister to respond to President Trump's remarks in his own way without having to directly address the journalist's provocative questions. This mood shift from polar to elemental significantly helps downplay the tension between the United States and China in the English TT received by the international media.

Discussion

The SFL-informed critical discourse analysis of interpersonal shifts in the consecutive interpreting of the Chinese foreign minister's press conferences (2016–2018) shows that the interpreter practices a high degree of gatekeeping in rendering the journalists' questions. Instead of being a "conduit" with "extreme personal non-involvement" (Roy 2002: 348), the interpreter significantly controls and filters the original messages in the interpreting process by withholding, modifying and supplementing the interpersonal meanings in the ST.

ST clauses realizing the speech function of thanking, greeting or statement (topical, subjective and attitudinal) are often omitted completely in the English interpreting of journalists' Chinese questions, either because their communicative purposes have been well conveyed to the minister in the Chinese ST and they are not so relevant to the interest of the English TT audience (Example 1), or because the ST clauses contain long attitudinal statements expressing biased opinions against China and the interpreter deems its rendition into English as both unnecessary and misleading (Example 2 and Example 9). Force-raising graduation resources are also frequently omitted in interpreting journalists' questions from Chinese into English, either to downplay the journalist's negative stance against China on sensitive issues (Example 2) in the English TT or simply to render the English TT more compatible with English rhetorical norms of using intensifiers less often (Example 3).

All these omissions make the English TT sound more concise and objective, which saves time for the communication of more important messages. By contrast, when the interpreter renders journalists' questions from English to Chinese, a much lower percentage of omissions occur (see Table 6.2), because the Chinese TT receiver is the foreign minister, who relies on the TT to have a comprehensive understanding of the question and the journalist's stance so as to carefully prepare for his response. This contrast can be attributed to the practice of "audience design" (Bell 1984), which means the interpreter makes his linguistic choices according to the primary audience he has in mind.

Compared with the omissions, additions and modifications occur much less frequently among the interpersonal shifts (see Table 6.2). However, despite the interpreter's overall tendency towards a reduced rendition for the sake of time, the supplementation and modification of interpersonal meanings do point to salient patterns that reflect the interpreter's gatekeeping role. In the interpreting of foreign journalists' utterances from English to Chinese, complete clauses realizing the speech function of statement or question are sometimes added. The supplementation of the journalist's identity statement in Example 4 shows the interpreter's efforts to maintain the norm of the Chinese GPC discourse pattern and to offer necessary contextual information of the question to the minister. The addition of the complete question in Example 5 demonstrates the interpreter's efforts to reframe the journalist's attitude towards China's diplomatic relations into a more optimistic one and thus offer a more positive frame for the minister's response accordingly. In the interpreting of journalists' questions from Chinese to English, however, the interpreter tends to add the interpersonal resources marking engagement or attitude, either to distance the journalist away from the negative voices against China (Example 6) or to foreground a positive attitude towards China (Example 7) in the English TT.

Modifications of interpersonal meanings primarily occur in the rendition of foreign journalists' utterances because they tend to utter more statements expressing negative attitudes towards China and raise more sensitive and face-threatening questions than Chinese journalists. Modifications of engagement and attitude either downplay the foreign journalist's negative attitude towards China (Example 8) or invoke a positive attitude towards China (Example 9) in the TT. Modifications of mood manifest itself either in changing a declarative statement against China's stance into an interrogative polar question, thus empowering the minister to judge the validity of the statement (Example 2), or changing a provocative polar question into an open elemental question so as to give the minister more flexibility in addressing the question (Example 10).

Results of both quantitative and qualitative analysis suggest that the interpreter's gatekeeping practices are motivated by his ideological alignment with the Chinese government. As an employee at the Department of Translation and Interpreting affiliated to the Ministry of Foreign Affairs, the GPC interpreter (Sun Ning, in the present study) is not only a professional interpreter but also a "diplomatic worker" and "government representative" (Guo 2004: 14); therefore, he is equipped with a special "institutional power" (Mason and Ren 2012: 233) to gatekeep journalists' questions at these high-profile GPCs. His more frequent omission of ST clauses and interpersonal resources in Chinese-English interpreting than the other direction shows his alignment with the minister as his "principal of service" (Wang 2012: 207). His choices of omitting, adding and modifying interpersonal meanings in effect facilitate the communication of the journalist's question, empower the minister to address the question with flexibility, enhance the positive image of China or filter out the negative voices towards China in the journalist's utterances, all of which reflect his institutional alignment with the Chinese government. A close reading of the minister's responses in Corpus A reveals the significant effect of the interpreter's gatekeeping choices.

These findings are highly compatible with Gu's (2019a, 2019b) research on the interpreting of the Chinese Premier's press conferences but are contradictory to Sun's (2013) conclusion on the role of interpreters for Chinese government press conferences during the SARS period. In fact, Sun's (ibid) data (e.g. the use of hedging devices to mitigate potential face-threatening acts) also point to the gatekeeping role of GPC interpreters, but the exclusion of interpersonal shifts as evidence for gatekeeping leads her to an opposite conclusion. Different from Gu (2019a, 2019b) who has investigated the interpreters' agency and ideology purely based on qualitative analysis of optional shifts, the present study has integrated quantitative analysis with qualitative analysis, and hence both the degree and means of the interpreter's gatekeeping are revealed.

Conclusion

To conclude, the major contributions of the present chapter include a proposed working definition for interpreters' gatekeeping, an SFL-informed model of CDA analysis for interpersonal shifts in interpreting and systematic discussions on the degree and means of gatekeeping in Chinese GPC interpreting. This study involves more than one single interpersonal system, covering the systems of SPEECH FUNCTION, MOOD and APPRAISAL, in terms of which the manual coding of shifts is highly time-consuming. Therefore, the present analysis involves only one interpreter based on a mini-corpus. It will be desirable to test the patterns of gatekeeping choices found in this study with a larger corpus of GPC interpreting in future research. Apart from interpersonal shifts, future studies could also look at ideational shifts, which we believe will offer alternative evidence for GPC interpreters' gatekeeping.

Acknowledgements

This research is supported by the MOE (Ministry of Education, China) Project of Humanities and Social Sciences (Grant No.: 17YJC740043). Special thanks go to Professor Jeremy Munday, Professor Binhua Wang, Dr Rongbo Fu and the anonymous reviewer for their insightful comments on earlier versions of this chapter.

Notes

1. For example, the press conferences by Chinese Foreign Minister Wang Yi can be watched live via YouTube channels such as "CGTN" and "CCTV Video News Agency".
2. It is not uncommon for a journalist to ask a series of questions rather than one question when given the opportunity, but the series of questions raised by the same journalist are counted as one question here. Originally there are 62 questions altogether, but one rare case of a journalist from a Chinese government-sponsored media outlet questioning in English was discarded in the corpus in order to focus attention on the three major participation frameworks in Table 1.
3. "Participation framework" is a term developed by Goffman (1981) to refer to the complicated participation status of the speaker and hearer in a conversation. Here it is used to mark the different identities of the source speakers and the different languages they use in the GPCs.
4. For the convenience of coding, when the ST clause realizing a specific interpersonal speech function is completely omitted in the rendition, it will be considered as one occurrence of omission.
5. For comparison, a literal translation [LT] of the ST or back translation [BT] of the TT is provided by the author for each example.

References

Baker, M. (2001) *In Other Words: A Coursebook on Translation* (2nd ed.), London and New York: Routledge.

Bakker, M., Koster, C. and van Leuven-zwart, K. (2004) 'Shifts of translation', in *Routledge Encyclopedia of Translation Studies*. M. Baker (ed.), Shanghai: Shanghai Foreign Language Education Press. pp. 226–231.

Barzilai-Nahon, K. (2009) 'Gatekeeping: A critical review', *Annual Review of Information Science and Technology* 43(1): 1–79.

Bell, A. (1984) 'Language style as audience design', *Language Society* 13(2): 145–204.

Blanton, S. L. (2000) 'Promoting human rights and democracy in the developing world: U.S. rhetoric versus U.S. arms', *American Journal of Political Science* 44(1): 123–131.

Davidson, B. (2000) 'The interpreter as institutional gatekeeper: The social-linguistic role of interpreters in Spanish-English medical discourse', *Journal of Sociolinguistics* 4(3): 379–405.

Fairclough, N. (2003) *Analysing Discourse*, London and New York: Routledge.

Fu, R. (2018) 'Translating like a conduit? A sociosemiotic analysis of modality in Chinese government press conference interpreting', *Semiotica* 2018(221): 175–198.

Fujii, A. (1988) 'News translation in Japan', *Meta* 33(1): 32–37.

Goffman, E. (1981) *Forms of Talk*, Oxford: Basil Blackwell.

Gu, C. (2018) 'Forging a glorious past via the "present perfect": A corpus-based CDA analysis of China's past accomplishments discourse mediat(is)ed at China's interpreted political press conferences', *Discourse, Context & Media* 24: 137–149.

Gu, C. (2019a) 'Interpreters caught up in an ideological tug-of-war?', *Translation and Interpreting Studies* 14(1): 1–20.

Gu, C. (2019b) 'Mediating "face" in triadic political communication: A CDA analysis of press conference interpreters' discursive (re) construction of Chinese government's image (1998–2017)', *Critical Discourse Studies* 16(2): 201–221.

Guo, Jiading 过家鼎 (2004) '岁月不曾流逝的记忆 – 外交翻译生涯三十余年点滴谈' (Memories: Over thirty years of diplomatic translation/interpreting), 对外大传播(*International Communications*) (9): 12–14.

Halliday, M. A. K. and Matthiessen, C. (2004) *An Introduction to Functional Grammar* (3rd ed.), London: Edward Arnold.

Halliday, M. A. K. and McDonald, E. (2004) 'Metafunctional profile of the grammar of Chinese', in A. Caffarel, J. R. Martin and C. M. I. M. Matthiessen (eds.), *Language Typology: A Functional Perspective*, Amsterdam: Benjamins. pp. 305–396.

Kenny, D. (2011) 'Translation unit and corpora', in A. Kruger, K. Wallmach and J. Munday (eds.), *Corpus-Based Translation Studies: Research and Applications*, London: Continuum. pp. 76–102.

Kim, K. H. (2017) 'Newsweek discourses on China and their Korean translations: A corpus-based approach', *Discourse, Context & Media* 15: 34–44.

Lewin, K. (1947) 'Frontiers in group dynamics II: Channels of group life; social planning and action research', *Human Relations* 1(2): 143–153.

Li, X. (2018) 'Mediation through modality shifts in Chinese-English government press conference interpreting', *Babel* 64(2): 269–293.

Liao, S. and Pan, L. (2018) 'Interpreter mediation at political press conferences', *Interpreting* 20(2): 188–203.

Martin, J. R. and Rose, D. (2007) *Working with Discourse: Meaning Beyond the Clause*, London and New York: Continuum.

Martin, J. R. and White, P. R. R. (2005) *The Language of Evaluation: Appraisal in English*, London and New York: Palgrave Macmillan.
Mason, I. and Ren, W. (2012) 'Power in face-to-face interpreting events', *Translation and Interpreting Studies* 7(2): 234–253.
Munday, J. (2001) *Introducing Translation Studies*, London: Routledge.
Ouyang, Q. H. (2010) 'Interpersonal mediation of the interpreter in political press conference', in W. H. Zhong (ed.), *Interpreting in China: New Trends and Challenges: Proceedings of the 7th National Conference and International Forum on Interpreting*, Beijing: Foreign Language Teaching and Research Press. pp. 213–225.
Pan, L. (2015) 'Ideological positioning in news translation: A case study of evaluative resources in reports on China', *Target* 27(2): 215–237.
Pinkham, J. (2000) *The Translator's Guide to Chinglish*, Beijing: Foreign Language Teaching and Research Press.
Pöllabauer, S. (2012) 'Gatekeeping practices in interpreted social service encounters', *Meta* 57(1): 213.
Ren, Xiaoping 任小萍 (2004) '外交部高级翻译培训' (Training translators and interpreters for the Ministry of Foreign Affairs), 中国翻译 (*Chinese Translators Journal*) (1): 61–62.
Roy, C. B. (2002) 'The problem with definitions, descriptions and the role metaphors of interpreters', in *The Interpreting Studies Reader*. F. Pöchhacker and M. Shlesinger (eds.), London and New York: Routledge. pp. 345–353.
Shi, Yanhua 施燕华 (2009) '外交翻译60年' (Sixty years of diplomatic interpreting), 中国翻译(*Chinese Translators Journal*) (5): 9–12.
Shoemaker, P. (1991) *Gatekeeping*, Newbury Park, CA: Sage.
Shoemaker, P. and Vos, T. (2009) *Gatekeeping Theory*, New York and London: Routledge.
Sun, T. (2013) *Interpreting China: Interpreters' Mediation of Government Press Conferences in China*, Beijing: Foreign Language Teaching and Research Press.
Toury, G. (1995) *Descriptive Translation Studies and Beyond*, Amsterdam and Philadelphia: John Benjamins.
van Dijk, T. A. (1995) 'Opinions and ideologies in the press', in A. Bell and P. Garrett (eds.), *Approach to Media Discourse*, Oxford: Blackwell. pp. 21–63.
Vuorinen, E. (1997) 'News translation as gatekeeping', in M. Snell-Hornby, Z. Jettmarová and K. Kaindl (eds.), *Translation as Intercultural Communication*, Amsterdam and Philadelphia: John Benjamins. pp. 161–172.
Wadensjö, C. (1998) *Interpreting as Interaction*, Singapore: Addison Wesley Longman.
Wang, B. (2012) 'A descriptive study of norms in interpreting: Based on the Chinese-English consecutive interpreting corpus of Chinese premier press conferences', *Meta* 57(1): 198–212.
Wang, B. and Feng, D. (2018) 'A corpus-based study of stance-taking as seen from critical points in interpreted political discourse', *Perspectives* 26(2): 246–260.
Webster, G. (2017) 'China's "new world order"? What Xi Jinping actually said about guiding international affairs', *Transpacifica*, 23 February. Available at: http://transpacifica.net/2017/02/chinas-new-world-order-what-xi-jinping-actually-said-about-guiding-international-affairs/ (Accessed: 18 November, 2019).
Zhan, C. (2013) *The Interpreter's Role as a Mediator in Political Settings*, Beijing: Foreign Language Teaching and Research Press.

Part III
Discourse analysis of news translation

Part III
Discourse analysis of news translation

7 Stance mediation in media translation of political speeches
An analytical model of appraisal and framing in news discourse

Li Pan and Chuxin Huang

Introduction

Given the close relationship between politics, language and media, it is not surprising to find that political discourse constantly forms a crucial part in media discourse. The intertextual relations between journalistic texts and political texts can further be "across languages and cultures" (Schäffner 2012b: 112). However, while political speech, as a significant political discourse, has long been analysed as a means of "codifying the way public orators used language for persuasive and other purposes" in the Western classical tradition of rhetoric (Chilton 2004: ix), the ways that media accommodate political leaders' speeches of persuasion in their news discourses have been far from sufficiently researched. Political speeches, noted for having "the personal 'stamp'" of the speakers (Newmark 2001: 39), more often than not feature the speakers' personal preference for particular rhetorical devices in expressing attitude and stance.

Concerning the authorship of political speeches, there is no denying that secretaries or speech writers are involved in creating a politician's speech texts (Charteris-Black 2011: 5). But speech writers are required to produce the draft based on agreement with the political speaker and can only use words or rhetorical resources that fit the speaker's image, personal belief and political identity; thus, "speeches can *only* succeed rhetorically when they comply with a distinct political image that is 'owned' by the politician" (Charteris-Black 2011: 6). Since the (Chinese) political leaders have to approve the speech content and choose what to utter before giving an address (Lee 2018: 483) that should ensure the consistency between the speaker's image and rhetorical style, it is fair to say that it is the speaker rather than the speech writers who actually determines the expressions used to address the audience, to build his or her own image and to convey his or her personal beliefs.

Many of the international speeches delivered by the Chinese President Xi Jinping involve frequent use of metaphors to clarify his or the country's standpoint about international as well as national issues. While media at home and abroad tend to quote Xi's metaphors in reporting his speeches, sometimes even using them in their headlines, some news media are inclined to misrepresent Xi's attitude and stance in translating, quoting and contextualising Xi's metaphors (e.g. Dong and Chitty 2012).

Mediation in this study is understood as the authorial intervention into the representation and meaning-making of political metaphors through media translation, quotation and contextualisation. So far, relatively few studies have looked at the media translation, quotation and contextualisation of the metaphors used in political discourse; even fewer studies have probed into the subtle changes of the speaker's original stance towards controversial issues in such quotations in the context of the media discourse.

Since a salient feature of Xi's speeches delivered at international conferences is his skilful use of metaphors in explaining complex Chinese political concepts or clarifying his or the Chinese government's stance on national and international issues, this research compares the translations of Xi's metaphors found in the English reports disseminated by the Chinese, the British and the American news media before examining the ways in which Xi's metaphors are quoted and contextualised in the foreign media discourse. Research questions include: (1) Are there any differences in the English translations of the Chinese president's metaphors in the Chinese, the British and the American media's reports of his speeches? (2) What are the differences in the selected media's framing of Xi's stance in quoting and contextualising his speeches? (3) Why are there differences between the original stance and those accommodated in the English reports towards the issues that Xi uses the metaphors to clarify?

To seek answers for these research questions, this study draws on the appraisal theory developed by Martin and White (2005) as theoretical framework to investigate the English translations and English reports of Xi's two keynote speeches at international conferences. One speech was delivered at the World Economic Forum Annual Meeting in Switzerland on 17 January 2017 (henceforth Davos 2017). The other was at the opening ceremony of the first China International Import Expo in Shanghai (hereafter CIIE 2018) on 15 November 2018. The two speeches were chosen because both of them emphasise the role of global economy and the Chinese government's stance on globalization on international occasions. The English translations have been collected from Xinhua Net, the official site of the Chinese state-run news agency Xinhua News Agency (hereafter Xinhua) and the English news reports on President Xi's speeches from three American and three British news media that are BBC, the *Financial Times* (*FT*), Reuters, the Associated Press (AP), the *Washington Post* (*WP*) and the *Wall Street Journal* (*WSJ*). Since the Chinese metaphors in political speeches feature unique socio-cultural images or connotations and mostly appear once in a speech, they are not covered widely in the media outside China. Thus, this study collects data from these six media outlets because they quoted and rendered the metaphors. Although the literature on media framing indicates that framing is relevant to media agenda, institutional practice or ideological difference, this study does not seek to explore these connections but instead focus solely on the way in which political metaphors sourced from the Chinese president are (mis)represented in media discourse. Based on an analysis of how the news media exploit the metaphorical images and how the translated metaphors are positioned as reported speech in the media discourse, the study aims to compare the stance signalled in Xi's metaphors in his original Chinese speeches and that accommodated in the Anglo-American media's translation and quotation within the context of the English news reports.

Metaphor and metaphor translation

Since Aristotle, metaphor has been considered a powerful linguistic device in persuasion (Charteris-Black 2014). The persuasive power of metaphor lies in the likening of two dissimilar things to make an abstract entity or concept concrete. Viewed from the perspective of cognitive linguistics, metaphors are not just linguistic expressions but also ways of thinking of human mind (Ortony 1993). Such a notion forms the basis of Lakoff and Johnson's conceptual metaphor theory (1980/2003). Stressing the role of metaphor in human's conceptualization and reasoning, conceptual metaphor theory (CMT) holds that "the image-schema structure of the source domain is used in reasoning about the target domain" (Lakoff and Johnson 2003: 254).

Metaphor is one of the most frequently used persuasive devices in political speeches. It changes our understanding and thinking of politics (Charteris-Black 2011: 32). In political discourse, metaphors, apart from signifying the concepts implied in the target domain, embrace "pragmatic 'added value', for example, to express an evaluation of the topic, to make an emotional and persuasive appeal" (Musolff 2016: 4). One salient characteristic of metaphor use in political speech is that "the source concepts can be bent or shaped in any way" and that only limited parts of the source domain are mentioned repeatedly, while the other aspects of the same source domain are never used to explain the target (Musolff 2016: 38). Metaphors in public speeches exploit the unconscious emotional associations of words and values rooted in cultural and historical knowledge; thus, political metaphors are potentially highly persuasive and can trigger unconscious knowledge "to influence our intellectual and emotional responses by evaluating actions, actors and issues" (Charteris-Black 2014: 160). The main purpose of political metaphors in speeches is to frame our view and understanding of political issues by erasing alternative viewpoints (Charteris-Black 2011: 32).

Translation studies started to focus on metaphors in the 1970s and has explored their translatability, translation methods and translation problems or patterns in different linguistic and cultural settings (Dagut 1976; Newmark 1980; Van den Broeck 1981; Mason 1982; Alvarez 1993; Dickins 2005; Schäffner and Shuttleworth 2013). So far, there have been relatively few studies on the translation of political metaphors in media discourse, such as the interpretation of political metaphors in the interview with political figures (Bulut 2012) and media translation of political metaphors (Schäffner 2012a, 2014). Even less explored are the ways in which media frame and mediate political metaphors in news discourse.

Media framing and stance mediation

Media framing is critical to the study of stance mediation in media translation of political metaphors in news discourse. Framing, as the exertion of power, mainly consists of selection and salience:

> to frame is to select some aspects of a perceived reality and make them more salient in a communicating text, in such a way as to promote a particular

> problem definition, causal interpretation, moral evaluation, and/or treatment recommendation for the item described.
>
> (Entman 1993: 52)

The role of framing in news texts is "really the imprint of power – it registers the identity of actors or interests that competed to dominate the text" (ibid., 55).

Framing is also combined with priming and agenda-setting as tools of power to better understand the slant and bias in media discourse and how media influence power distribution (Entman 2007). Baker (2006) defines framing as "an active strategy that implies agency" and involves conscious participation in constructing reality (106), which can be realized in translation as an interpretive frame (107). In our study, media framing is through the selection and foregrounding of certain metaphorical images as reported speech with respect to the stance signalled in media texts and the conditioning of the co-textual elements, which generates particular interpretation and in turn motivates evaluations of the images while obscuring other elements which reflect the original user's value positions.

Previous studies have focused on metaphors as framing devices in media coverage based on content analysis (Baysha and Hallahan 2004; Peeters 2010). Some scholars have also paid attention to certain types of metaphors used in media framing of current events (Wallis and Nerlich 2005; Arrese 2015) or to compare metaphors used in reporting the same events by media of different language (López and Llopis 2010). As for the translation studies on framing, studies have largely centred on media framing in news translation (Baker 2006; Van Doorslaer 2009; Valdeón 2014; Pan 2014, 2015).

Media framing of the translated political metaphors depends on the stance adopted in news discourse. In appraisal theory, stance refers to the "evaluative style", a way of examining "the communicative/ rhetorical effect", and "sub-selections of evaluative options within text" (Martin and White 2005: 163–164). Specifically, stance reflects the patterns in using evaluative resources within a "key" or register that has certain rhetorical or communicative goals and constructs the image of a speaker or writer (164). From the sociolinguistic perspective, Jaffe (2009) explores stance-taking as an essential attribute of communication and suggests that neutrality *per se* takes a stance, because each semantic option is "in contrast to" other linguistic choices (3). Since certain linguistic stances may be linked to one or multiple selves, personal or social identities, "speaker stances" are adopted to "align or disalign themselves with and/or ironize stereotypical associations with particular linguistic forms" (4). Du Bois (2007) defines stance as a public act that includes three aspects – evaluation, positioning and alignment (163). Stance can be taken in language use as speakers or writers evaluate and position what they are to speak or write about and associate or disassociate themselves with the putative audience or the given value positions regarding the salient propositions.

Mediation refers to "movement of resources for meaning-making", and media texts form a text type specialising in "moving resources for meaning-making between texts" (Fairclough 2006: 23). In Jaffe's word, mediation is "afforded by the inherently multivocalic nature of stances that are actualized through other people's voices as they are reported (directly or indirectly), parodied, alluded to, recycled, repeated, ironized, and so forth" (Jaffe 2009: 18). Mediation has been studied under critical discourse analysis (CDA) on news translation, such as the identification of ideological bias in translating political discourse (Aslani and Salmani 2015; Bánhegyi 2017; Daghigh Sanatifar et al. 2018) and the negative mediation in Spanish translated news reports represented by the lexical choices of text producers (Valdeón 2007). Only a few studies have been conducted on stance mediation in news translation within the appraisal framework developed by Martin and White (2005) (Zhang 2013; Pan 2014, 2015). Munday has studied the Spanish interpretations of the inaugural speeches by Obama (Munday 2012) and Trump (Munday 2018) within the analytical model based on appraisal theory so as to investigate "the evaluative input of the translator/interpreter as a third participant in the communication process" (Munday 2018: 181). He analyses the evaluative strength of lexical metaphors as forms of attitudinal invocations in the addresses by the two presidents and how the interpreters and translators have dealt with the evaluative elements in rendering these metaphorical expressions. Up to now, relatively few studies have focused on the stance mediation of the translated metaphors quoted in media discourse.

Theoretical framework

The appraisal theory (Martin and White 2005), developed from the description of interpersonal meaning in systemic functional linguistics (Halliday 1994), has been applied to the studies of the attitude and stance expressed in various genres of discourse. As an analytical model, appraisal theory deals with "the way language construes attitude and enables writers/speakers to position themselves evaluatively with respect to the viewpoints of potential respondents and other speakers/writers" (Thomson et al. 2008).

The appraisal framework comprises three interactive systems – attitude, engagement and graduation (Martin and White 2005). Attitude refers to positive or negative assessment that involves affect (emotional response), judgement (evaluative behaviour) and appreciation (aesthetics of "things"). Engagement deals with the dialogic positioning of the writer/speaker with respect to the putative addressee. Graduation is concerned with the scalability of attitudinal meanings and authorial involvement or intervention in the discourse. Our study will mainly focus on the attitude and engagement resources in the analysis of media discourse with translated political metaphors.

In the attitude system, the attitudinal meanings "tend to spread out and colour a phase of discourse as speakers and writers take up a stance oriented to affect, judgement or appreciation" (Martin and White 2005: 43). Attitudinal invocations are "typically conditioned by the co-text" (Thomson et al. 2008: 221). Metaphors can function as provoked attitude (Martin and White 2005: 65) on the propositions about the topic or the target domain in terms of the source domain with different metaphorical images. Since many lexical items are unstable and co-textually contingent in terms of their intended evaluative meanings, sometimes a lexical item that generates attitudinal meaning in some contexts may convey non-attitudinal meaning elsewhere. This kind of linguistic realization can be also known as the "co-textual conditioning" of "attitudinal instability" (White 2016: 83).

Engagement in the appraisal framework deals with the resources of intersubjective stance with the meanings which construe a heteroglossic backdrop for the text associated with "prior utterances, alternative viewpoints and anticipated responses" (Martin and White 2005: 97). The dialogistic perspective guides us to investigate the linguistic resources the writers/speakers use to advance particular value position or stance reflected in the texts, with the result of alignment or disalignment between the speakers/writers and various positions referenced by the texts as well as the shared beliefs of the construed audience. This taxonomy aims to identify certain dialogic positioning with given meanings and explore what is at stake when one meaning or stance is chosen over another. These resources, classified into entertain and attribute, disclaim and proclaim, may invoke alternative viewpoints (dialogistic expansion) or constrain the scope of dialogistic alternatives (dialogistic contraction). Dialogistic expansion includes the resources of entertain and attribute, also known as the authorial/internal voice and the external voice through attributed material.

The investigation of stance mediation in metaphor translation across various foreign media outlets would be insufficient if we just examined the meanings of evaluative resources in the original or translated metaphorical expressions *per se*, the positioning of which also depends on the evaluative effects coming from elsewhere in the text. "Metaphor interpretation varies with context" (Kövecses 2015: 7). In critical metaphor analysis, persuasion is "a multi-layered discourse function" contingent on the interaction between "intention, linguistic choice and context" (Charteris-Black 2011: 51).

Case analysis

To explore how foreign media mediate the stance and value position in quoting and framing Xi's metaphors extracted from his speeches, the analysis of the metaphor will start with the examination of the preservation and omission of metaphorical images and the differences in lexical choices as evaluative resources. It is followed by the investigation of the possible differences in interpretation and interpersonal meanings of the metaphors due to the co-textual elements surrounding the reported speech or the attitudinal resources from elsewhere in the speech text or media article, or those facts selected and described by the speaker or author in framing the text as a whole.

This study will analyse four metaphorical expressions, two extracted from Xi's keynote speech titled *Jointly Shoulder Responsibility of Our Times, Promote Global Growth* (translation by Xinhua) at Davos 2017 and two from his speech titled *Work Together for an Open Global Economy That is Innovative and Inclusive* (translation by Xinhua) at CIIE 2018. Both the original and translated speech texts were edited and released by Xinhua after Xi addressed the two events. The original and translated speech texts at Davos 2017 total 6,645 Chinese characters and 4,327 English words, while the Chinese and English versions at CIIE 2018 total 4,742 Chinese characters and 3,151 English words. All the selected metaphors are translated and quoted by the Anglo-American media in reporting the events or related topics. The data for analysis consist of (1) the full transcripts of Xi's original speeches in Chinese posted by Xinhua; (2) the full text of the speeches in English translated by Xinhua; (3) 10 news articles disseminated by the American and British media, in which Xi's metaphors are translated and quoted and which have been retrieved from LexisNexis or the media websites.

Evaluative resources used in different media are to be analysed with the toolkit available in the three subsystems in the appraisal framework in order to examine the media framing and mediation of translated metaphors in three dimensions: (1) the selection and combination of metaphorical images, termed in this chapter as 'co-textual metaphors', (2) the co-textual attitudinal elements inserted into the quoted metaphors, referred to as 'co-textual evaluation of metaphors', and (3) the co-textual conditioning of the media article as a whole, namely 'co-textual positioning of metaphors'.

Co-textual metaphors

In metaphor translation, co-textual metaphors refer to the metaphorical images chosen from the metaphors in the source text and translated to form an interaction with the combination of the images in the target text. To examine the possible attitudinal stance different from that of the original metaphors in the source texts, the original metaphorical images enacted in Xi's speeches (ST) and their corresponding expressions translated by Xinhua (TT) as well as the selected metaphors quoted by the American and British media (TT1 to TT5) are compared with regard to their image deviations and lexical resources.

Example 1 (**Davos 2017 17/01/2017**)

ST 经济全球化曾经被人们视为阿里巴巴的山洞，现在又被不少人看作潘多拉的盒子。
(Literal translation: Economic globalization has been regarded as Ali Baba's cave, and now is seen by many as the Pandora's box.)
TT Economic globalization was once viewed as the treasure cave found by Ali Baba **in The Arabian Nights**, but it has now become the Pandora's box in the eyes of many.

The metaphor in the ST indicates the mixed views of economic globalization in terms of two images – *Ali Baba's cave* with treasures and *Pandora's box* with evils. Both images are retained in the TT and the source of *Ali Baba's cave* – a folk tale from "The Arabian Nights" and the modifier *treasure* are added to explain the attitudinal meaning of this image as the bright side of economic globalization, followed by the conjunction *but* to signify the contrast between the two propositions. The attitudinal invocation of the metaphor towards economic globalization is realized through the interaction of the two images implying opposing views, thus allowing either positive or negative evaluations.

TT1 (BBC 17 January 2017) He also said that while some consider globalisation a sort of "Pandora's box" **full of all the world's evils**, it cannot be blamed for the plight of Syrian refugees or the 2008 financial crisis.

TT2 (Reuters 17 January 2017) In his speech, Xi acknowledged that globalization had become a "Pandora's Box", **benefiting certain segments of society while harming others**.

In citing the metaphor, both TT1 and TT2 only preserve and foreground the negative image of *Pandora's box* that conveys the negative views about globalization while omitting the image of *Ali Baba's cave* that provokes the positive attitudinal assessment. They also offer the attitudinal meaning of the image as shown in *full of all the world's evils* in TT1 and *benefiting certain segments of society while harming others* in TT2.

Example 2 **(Davos 2017 17/01/2017)**

ST 不能一遇到风浪就退回到港湾中去，那是永远不能到达彼岸的。

(Literal translation: One cannot return to the harbour when encountering the storm; in this way one will never reach the other shore.)

TT One should not just retreat to the harbor when encountering a storm, for this will never get us to the other shore of **the ocean**.

In Example 2, it is unclear in the ST what the general image of *shore* refers to because the interpretation of its meaning is co-textually contingent on the other metaphorical image elsewhere in the original speech. Therefore, the TT clarifies the image through adding the image of *the ocean*, which can be related to the metaphor of the world economy as an ocean from the preceding part of the speech so as to convey the meaning that countries cannot withdraw from the world economy when they encounter challenges along the way; otherwise, they will never reach the shore of the ocean.

TT1 (*FT* 17 January 2017) "We should not retreat into the harbour whenever we encounter a storm or we will never reach **the opposite shore**."

TT2 (AP 17 January 2017) "We should not **develop a habit of** retreating to the harbor whenever encountering the storm, for this will never get us to the other shore of the **ocean**," he said.

In citing the metaphor, TT1 and TT2 retain all the metaphorical images in the ST, while TT2 adds *ocean* to describe the image of *shore*, as indicated in the TT by

Xinhua. It should be noted that TT2 defines the image of *retreating to the harbor* as *a habit*, which cannot be found in the ST.

Example 3 **(CIIE 2018 05/11/2018)**

ST 中国经济是一片大海，而不是一个小池塘。大海有风平浪静之时，也有风狂雨骤之时。没有风狂雨骤，那就不是大海了。狂风骤雨可以掀翻小池塘，但不能掀翻大海。经历了无数次狂风骤雨，大海依旧在那儿！经历了5000多年的艰难困苦，中国依旧在这儿！面向未来，中国将永远在这儿！

(Literal translation: The Chinese economy is a sea, not a small pond. When the sea is calm, there are also wild winds and sudden downpours. Without them, that will not be the sea. Wild winds and sudden downpours can overturn small ponds, but they cannot overturn the sea. Having experienced countless wild winds and sudden downpours, the sea is still there! Having gone through more than 5,000 years of difficulties and hardships, China is still here! Facing the future, China will forever be here!)

TT To use a metaphor, the Chinese economy is not a pond, but an ocean. The ocean may have its calm days, but big winds and storms are only to be expected. Without them, the ocean wouldn't be what it is. Big winds and storms may upset a pond, but never an ocean. Having experienced numerous winds and storms, the ocean will still be there! **It is the same for China**. After going through 5,000 years of trials and tribulations, China is still here! Looking ahead, China will always be here to stay!

This example contains two pairs of metaphorical images – *ocean* and *pond*, *calm days* and *winds and storms*. The Chinese economy is highlighted as large, stable and open as an *ocean* and the challenges in economic development are *winds and storms*. The contrast between the images of *ocean* and *pond* in the face of *winds and storms* reflects the strength of the Chinese economy as an ocean. This metaphor provokes a positive evaluation of the Chinese economy in the face of difficulties and uncertainties. The stance Xi intends to signal is that the country will not back away and instead will continue to advance its reform to overcome the challenges with determination and confidence as it has been in the twists and turns of the past.

The TT clarifies the expression as a metaphor by adding *to use a metaphor* at the beginning. At the end of the metaphorical expression, it adds *it is the same for China*, which extends the target domain of the Chinese economy to include China as a country and project the image of the ocean onto the extensive target domain China.

TT1 (BBC) Appearing to refer to **the trade war** as a "**battering** storm" he said the Chinese economy "is a sea". Storms can "overturn a pond" he said, but "never" a sea.

TT2 (*BBC*) Mr Xi said the Chinese economy was "**a sea**". Storms can overturn a pond, he said, but never a sea.

TT3 (*AP*) China's $12 trillion-a-year economy is "**a sea**, not a small pond" and can withstand **shocks**, he said. "A storm can overturn a small pond, but not a **sea**," he said. "After more than 5,000 years of hardship, China is still here. Facing the future, China will always be here."

TT4 (*WP*) "**Great** winds and storms may upset a pond but not an **ocean**," Xi said, comparing China to **a vast and immovable sea**. "After 5,000 years of trials and tribulations, China is still here. Looking ahead, China will be here to stay."

TT5 (*WSJ*) "The Chinese economy is not a pond but an ocean," Xi said. "**High** winds and storms may upset a pond but never an **ocean**."

All the TTs were released on the same day when the CIIE was opened. This metaphorical expression is probably the most quoted one of the metaphors in Xi's speech at CIIE 2018 by the Anglo-American media in reporting this event. All the TTs highlight the image of the Chinese economy as a sea in the face of storms. TT1, TT2 and TT3 are basically literal translation while omitting the metaphorical image *winds* and retaining the image of *storms*. The three TTs use the image of *sea* to describe the source domain of the Chinese economy, which is portrayed as an *ocean* in the TT by Xinhua. Moreover, TT1 and TT3 are a little different from other TTs in describing the image of *storm* that in ST refers to the challenges facing the economic development in China. In TT1 *storm* is modified with *battering*, which intensifies the negativity and severity of *storm*, but TT1 also narrows the scope of the target domain by specifying the signified as *the trade war* in the authorial voice, thereby inviting the putative readers to interpret this metaphor in terms of a deviated image. TT3 indicates that the metaphorical image of *storm* signifies *shocks*, a term that indicates insecurity and intensifies the negative evaluation of *storm*. Both TT4 and TT5 quote the words in Xinhua's translation with different modifiers before the images of *winds and storms*. Also, in TT4, the image of source domain *an ocean* quoted as external source is transferred to *a sea* in the authorial voice in contrast to the lexical choice by the Chinese media.

Example 4 (CIIE 2018 05/11/2018)

ST 各国都应该努力改进自己的营商环境，解决自身存在的问题，不能总是粉饰自己、指责他人，不能像手电筒那样只照他人、不照自己。

(Literal translation: All countries should strive to improve their business environment and solve their own problems. They cannot always gloss over themselves and blame others and cannot act as a flashlight that only shines on others without shining on themselves.)

TT Countries need to improve their business environment by addressing their problems. They should not just point fingers at others to gloss over their own problems. They should not hold a "flashlight" in hand doing nothing but to check out on the weakness of others and not on their own.

The metaphor in Example 4 derives from the Chinese two-part allegorical saying 袖口里装手电筒 – 只照别人, 不照自己 (literal translation: holding a flashlight in one's cuff – shining on other people without shining on oneself), which means that people always find out the weaknesses of others while ignoring their own. A Chinese two-part allegorical saying contains two parts – the first part "portraying an image of an object, an event, or a situation" and the second part "indicating the meaning intended to be derived from the first part" (Lai 2008). Hence the image of *flashlight* implies a negative evaluation of the target domain. In the ST the target domain of *flashlight* is the countries that need to improve their business environment while the countries as the original target domain are personified as one *holding a flashlight in hand* in the translation by Xinhua. The negative attitude invoked by the other image of *shining on others without shining on oneself* is omitted in the TT, where the attitudinal meaning of the image *flashlight* is rendered.

TT1 (*FT* 05 November 2018) "Each **country** should work hard to improve its own business environment. One cannot always beautify oneself while criticising others, and one can't shine a flashlight on other people without looking at oneself," Mr Xi added.

TT2 (*WSJ* 05 November 2018) **Those who complain about Chinese commercial practices** "should not just point fingers at others to gloss over their own problems," he said. "They should not hold a flashlight that only exposes others while doing nothing themselves."

Both TTs retain the first image of *flashlight* while translating the second image through free translation to explain the negative attitude towards the target domain. The target domain of *flashlight* that refers to the countries in general is retained in TT1 as *each country*, but it is narrowed down to *those who complain about Chinese commercial practices* in TT2, thereby distorting the proposition advanced by the original speaker.

This analysis shows that in media texts, most of the original metaphorical images are preserved through literal translation. Some news reports directly quote the translated versions of Xi's metaphorical expressions produced by the Chinese media Xinhua. Meanwhile, the selected media tend to make some adjustments in translation and attitudinal invocation. In some cases, certain original images are **omitted** in media discourse, for instance, with one of the two images with similar meanings deleted, as shown in Example 3. However, when two images in the ST are intended to respectively offer positive and negative views about the target domain, the quoted materials may retain only one image that provokes particular attitudinal orientation, as in Example 1. Moreover, the original images may be **modified** with isolated attitudinal terms when quoted in media articles, thereby intensifying the attitude provoked by the original metaphor, as reflected in Example 2 and 3. In addition, the metaphorical image of the target domain in the ST is sometimes **narrowed** down to refer to a particular topic out of the original speech co-text in the quoted resources of the media articles, as presented in Examples 1, 3 and 4.

The discourse effect of political metaphors lies in the juxtaposition and interaction of the images within the source domains, through which the readers can understand and interpret the intended meanings of the target domains. The lexical and grammatical items used to present the images of source domains in media discourse may contain attitudinal meanings based on the co-textual settings. Hence the images employed to form the source domains in order to describe the target domains can represent the value positions advanced in the unfolding news articles and provoke evaluations towards the propositions.

Co-textual evaluation of metaphors

The attitude provoked by Xi's metaphors quoted in media articles is in some cases found deviated from his intended position advanced in the metaphorical expressions in his original speeches due to the co-text embedding the metaphors in media discourse.

Positioning in quoting the metaphors

Reporting verbs frame the reported speech introduced into the text and act to associate or disassociate the authorial voice from the attributed material (Martin and White 2005: 112). White's (2012) study on reporting verbs explores both the primary authorial voice of the reporters and "the 'secondary voice', the voice of the quoted source" in relation to "prior utterances and potential responses" (63). He holds that the reporting verbs can indicate "both the 'stance' of the primary authorial voice vis-à-vis the attributed material and the 'stance' of the secondary, quoted source towards this material" (63).

> Example 1 – TT2: In his speech, Xi **acknowledged** that globalization had become a "Pandora's Box", benefiting certain segments of society while harming others.
>
> (Reuters 17 January 2017)

In Example 1, the reporting verb *acknowledged* presents the secondary voice of Xi as "concurring" (White 2012: 65) the proposition that *globalization had become a "Pandora's Box"*. That is so say, Xi admits that globalization had become evil or harmful as a Pandora's box, which is further explained in the remaining attributed material – *benefiting certain segments of society while harming others* positioned by the news writer as Xi's viewpoint in the quoted speech.

However, in the original speech, Xi recognized both the positive and negative views about globalization in terms of the images of *Ali Baba's cave* and *Pandora's box* before addressing his views on the global economy regarding globalization. The two metaphorical images provoke both expectations of and worries about economic globalization among the international community instead of representing Xi's personal views on globalization as something harmful, as expressed in the news. The interaction of the two images is distorted in the reported speech where the positive image of *Ali Baba's cave* is absent, thereby highlighting the negativity of globalization. Moreover, the interpretation of the metaphorical image *Pandora's Box* in the quoted voice is deviated from the message conveyed in the original speech. Hence, the stance taken on globalization in the original speech is mediated in the reported speech in the news report.

Most reported speeches with Xi's metaphors extracted from the news reports as our research data are framed by such "unmarked or neutral" (White 2012: 63) verbs as *said, told, added* or *declared*, thereby leaving the propositions "open to the co-text to present the authorial text as either aligned/disaligned with respect to the position being advanced, or as neutral or disinterested" (Martin and White 2005: 113), but under the dialogistic positioning in the engagement domain, the author may attitudinally intervene in the quoted proposition via other communicative mechanisms, as explored next.

Evaluation in the authorial voice

The negative evaluation of the use of metaphors may be invoked by the evaluative resources in the authorial voice preceding the metaphors attributed to the external voice.

> Example 4 – TT1: That commitment was also **embellished with** a very familiar metaphor. **Appearing** to refer to **the trade war** as a "battering storm" he said the Chinese economy "is a sea". Storms can "overturn a pond" he said, but "never" a sea.
>
> (BBC 5 November 2017)

> Example 4 – TT5: To underscore its **attractiveness** as a market, the president **highlighted** China's population of 1.3 billion and its size as the world's No. 2 economy. "The Chinese economy is not a pond but an ocean," Xi said. "High winds and storms may upset a pond but never an ocean."
>
> (*WSJ* 5 November 2017)

The evaluative element *embellished with* in the authorial voice shows that the author frames a negative attitudinal assessment of the quoted metaphor and its original meaning in Example 4. Besides, both the two extracts project their respective views of what the metaphorical image refers to or the intentions of the original metaphor use onto Xi's metaphor before introducing it as reported speech. TT1 frames the image of *storm* as *the trade war* while TT5 explains Xi's purpose of using the metaphor to emphasise the *attractiveness* of the Chinese economy. Given the analysis of "co-textual metaphors", both the extracts of media articles position the metaphorical expressions in the authorial voice in a way diverged from the value position advanced in the original speech.

The analysis reveals that the original meaning or intention of Xi's metaphors has been mediated in media discourse in the voices of both the news writers and the quoted sources.

Co-textual positioning of metaphors

Aside from reported speech, it is very likely that "there are indicators elsewhere in the text that the writer/speaker more globally supports or rejects the value position being advanced" (Martin and White 2005: 112). The choice of metaphors is influenced by the linguistic elements in the surrounding discourse that is related to the topic of the ongoing discourse (Kövecses 2015: 181, 186). The interpretation and the value position implied in Xi's metaphors may also be contingent on the evaluative resources from elsewhere in the news articles – the headlines, news topics and other attributed sources. These evaluative indicators are combined to support or suppress the quoted metaphors in order to motivate the framing of the value position implied in the metaphors.

In order to further investigate the positioning and stance in the English reports, two news articles are analysed one by one as samples with respect to their headlines, news topics, external voices and Xi's image, China or China-related issues framed in the media coverage in examining whether the quoted metaphorical expressions are supported or suppressed in the co-textual environment.

Davos 2017

> **Headline 1:** *China's Xi tells World Economic Forum there are no winners in trade wars*
>
> (BBC 17 January 2017)

The metaphor in Example 1 is quoted in this report by BBC. The headline is a reported speech of Xi's address, quoting him as expressing a negative attitude towards trade wars. In the body text, aside from Xi's speech, all the other external voices are from the US side, including the criticism from Trump and the warning from his then advisor Anthony Scaramucci on China's trade deal. The quoted speech of Xi's metaphor (Example 1) is followed by a quoted warning of Anthony Scaramucci, who was opposed to China's trade deal and said that the US would win any trade war with China. This warning, which can be interpreted as a response to Xi's position as quoted in the headline, signals an opposite stance towards trade wars. At the same time, with China's trade practice blamed in external voices of the US such as the criticism from Trump on China's exchange rate policy, Xi's metaphors quoted in the report, interpreted as *a rebuke to* Trump, who is seeking a protectionist approach, is consequently suppressed in the co-text. As a whole the suppression is accelerated by the negative assessment of China and its economy across the text.

CIIE 2018

> **Headline 2: Xi tells the world China will boost imports, while swiping at Trump's 'law of the jungle'**
>
> (*WP* 5 November 2018)

In the *Washington Post*'s headline, Xi's speech in CIIE is highlighted as a criticism towards US President Trump. With *swiping at*, an attitudinal indicator flags a negative positioning, the headline positions the reader to interpret Xi's stance as against Trump. As the text unfolds, the quoted metaphor of Chinese economy as an ocean is framed as directing at Trump, with Xi's *hardened tone*, while the other quoted metaphor of a flashlight is framed as *a stiff rebuke of China's critics* in the preceding discourse. As a result, the stance in both the original metaphors is mediated in news discourse. Moreover, the United States' negative response to CIIE is foregrounded in the article, as reflected in the expressions such as *notably absent* and *had no plans for "high-level participation"*. In this report, Xi is the only external voice from China, while the other quoted sources include both positive and negative viewpoints on the country's image or Xi's speech. However, the main focus is on the negative views on China, as shown in the attributed materials about its unfair trade from the US Department of Justice and the US Embassy in Beijing, and about the lack of concrete actions of China in the voice of Jim McGregor, chairman of the consultancy APCO's Greater China practice. In contrast, the only supportive view on China, coming from the prime minister of Pakistan, appears at the end of the article. The quoted metaphors are therefore suppressed by the salience of the negative image of China and Xi's speech across the text.

To sum up, the same as in the body texts of the two sample news articles, some news reports deploy attitudinal markers, mainly negative ones in their headlines, signalling a high degree of authorial intervention in the proposition and indicating certain stances or value positions towards the news topics such as the event or Xi's speech. In addition, the news articles tend to introduce other external voices as a contrast or correspondence to the quoted voice of Xi. In the reports analysed, more often than not, such external sources serve to suppress rather than support the value positions adopted in the quoted metaphorical expressions.

Discussion

The case analysis shows that stance mediation can be realized in all the three dimensions in the media translation of political metaphors. The metaphorical images and the stance, as interrelated as they are in both the original political speeches and the reports on the speeches, are mediated most noticeably in the dimensions of the co-textual metaphors and the co-textual evaluation of the quoted metaphors in the news reports. On the one hand, in media translation of the Chinese political metaphors, the metaphorical images are found somehow altered or selectively translated in the English reports. In Musolff's words, "the source concepts" have been "bent or shaped" in some way (2016: 38). The mediation has been realized not only through the source image deviations but also the lexical choices in (re)presenting the metaphors and the positioning of Xi's metaphors in varied means of reported speech through evaluative and stance-taking resources in the authorial voice. As for the authorship of the selected speeches, the speech writers are required to comply with the intentions and beliefs of the president, as represented by the lexical choices and use of rhetorical resources based on the agreement between the two sides. It suggests that Xi is ultimately held accountable for his utterances, which are "recorded in official sources" and quoted back to him later for the consistency of his political image and rhetorical style (Charteris-Black 2014: 21).

As found in the analysis of the co-textual settings, the American and British media mostly activate negative evaluation towards Xi's metaphors, which results in their own representation and framing of the political leader as well as the issues concerned. For reporting those metaphors Xi deployed in his international speeches to articulate his positions on the issues of global economy and globalization, both the news media in UK and USA seem to rely on the translated versions posted on the official website of the Chinese state media Xinhua and sometimes with adaptation in news coverage. The translated metaphors in journalistic texts are not identical to those in the English transcripts by Xinhua but show some minor differences, particularly indicated in the combination of direct quotes and reported speeches, which contribute to "the positioning and construction of the political actors" (Schäffner 2012b: 115). Moreover, the attitude expressed through the quoted metaphors in media discourse generally diverges from the attitude in the original speeches. The foreign media tend to exploit these quoted metaphorical expressions to frame their news articles with distinct value positions on the issues in question in the original speeches. In other words, apart from selecting metaphorical images to form co-textual metaphors, stance is mediated on the same issues indicated in Xi's discourse with the use of various evaluative resources in quoting those metaphors in narrating the news related to the speeches.

It is also found that the mediation of Xi's political metaphors through selection and salience serves as a framing device in news discourse. The main realization is through the selection of the original metaphorical images and target lexical items to present the metaphors in the news articles. The significance of such selection lies in the fact that the interaction of certain images of the original metaphors realized in lexical items may trigger or intensify evaluations deviated from their intended meanings in the source texts. A case in point is the salience of the negative image of Pandora's box in TT2 of Example 1 to refer to globalization in media discourse in which Xi's stance is mediated in the surrounding discourse with certain attitudinal meanings.

As a whole, the close relation between media framing of the metaphors and the mediation of stance can be best described in two aspects. On the one hand, media framing of the translated political metaphors is influenced by the stance signalled in the media articles towards the images of the country and the original speaker. On the other hand, the framing elements selected by the news writers in translating and quoting the political metaphors rely on the stance signalled in news discourse, which in turn influences the evaluative orientations built across the whole text.

Conclusion

This chapter draws on the appraisal framework to analyse the stance mediation of Xi's metaphors quoted in the foreign media articles. It is found that the value positions adopted by Xi in employing the metaphors in his speeches in the international occasions are altered when only certain metaphorical images are translated, quoted and contextualised as reported speech in the media texts. The analysis of the three dimensions of co-texts of metaphors in the case study suggests that the framing of the political metaphors is made possible through the selection of metaphorical images, insertion of evaluative resources in quoting the metaphors and positioning of the metaphors with appropriation of internal and external voices that contextualises the metaphors and influences its discourse effect by suppressing or supporting the stance accommodated. The framing thus contributes to the mediation of the evaluation of and stance towards the event or issue in question. Therefore, even when the metaphors are faithfully translated and quoted in news reports, the mediation of stance can be facilitated by contextual evaluation, such as that in the headlines and the surrounding words of the metaphors and other parts of news reports.

The analysis provides an insight into the linguistic realizations and co-textual conditioning through which the value positions are mediated and framing is realized in news texts. While a larger data is needed for a fuller overview of mediation through quantitative analysis, this study is useful as a model of analysing the mediation of political metaphors in foreign media's quoting of political speeches in their news reports. It is hoped that it can set the basis for further examination of the systematic patterns and methods in media translation of political metaphors in further research in this regard.

Acknowledgement

This study has been supported by the Philosophy and Social Science Research Project of Guangdong Province (GD19CYY08), the Guangdong Provincial Innovation Research Team Project (2018WCXTD002), the Philosophy and Social Science Research Project of Guangzhou (2019GZGJ67) and the Centre for Translation Studies of Guangdong University of Foreign Studies.

References

Alvarez, A. (1993) 'On translating metaphor', *Meta* 38(3): 479–490.
Arrese, A. (2015) 'Euro crisis metaphors in the Spanish press', *Communication & Society* 28(2): 19–38.
Aslani, M. and Salmani, B. (2015) 'Ideology and translation: A critical discourse analysis approach towards the representation of political news in translation', *International Journal of Applied Linguistics and English Literature* 4(3): 80–88.
Baker, M. (2006) *Translation and Conflict: A Narrative Account*, Abingdon: Routledge.
Bánhegyi, M. (2017) 'Identifying political and ideological bias in translated newspaper articles', *FORUM. Revue internationale d'interprétation et de traduction/International Journal of Interpretation and Translation* 15(1): 1–26.
Baysha, O. and Hallahan, K. (2004) 'Media framing of the Ukrainian political crisis, 2000–2001', *Journalism Studies* 5(2): 233–246.
Bulut, A. (2012) 'Translating political metaphors: Conflict potential of zenci [negro] in Turkish-English', *Meta* 57(4): 909–923.

Charteris-Black, J. (2011) *Politicians and Rhetoric: The Persuasive Power of Metaphor*, New York: Palgrave Macmillan.
Charteris-Black, J. (2014) *Analyzing Political Speeches: Rhetoric, Discourse and Metaphor*, New York: Palgrave Macmillan.
Chilton, P. (2004) *Analysing Political Discourse: Theory and Practice*, London and New York: Routledge.
Daghigh, A. J., Sanatifar, M. S. and Awang, R. (2018) 'A taxonomy of manipulative operations in political discourse translation', *FORUM. Revue internationale d'interprétation et de traduction/International Journal of Interpretation and Translation* 16(2): 197–220.
Dagut, M. B. (1976) 'Can "metaphor" be translated?', *Babel* 22(1): 21–33.
Dickins, J. (2005) 'Two models for metaphor translation', *Target* 17(2): 227–273.
Dong, L. and Chitty, N. (2012) 'Exploring news frames of diplomatic visits: A comparative study of Chinese and American media treatment of vice president Xi Jinping's official tour of the US', *Communication, Politics & Culture* 45(2): 277–292.
Du Bois, J. W. (2007) 'The stance triangle', *Stancetaking in Discourse: Subjectivity, Evaluation, Interaction* 164(3): 139–182.
Entman, R. M. (1993) 'Framing: Toward clarification of a fractured paradigm', *Journal of Communication* 43(4): 51–58.
Entman, R. M. (2007) 'Framing bias: Media in the distribution of power', *Journal of Communication* 57(1): 163–173.
Fairclough, N. (2006) 'Semiosis, ideology and mediation', in *Mediating Ideology in Text and Image*. I, Lassen, J. Strunk and T. Vestergaard (eds.), Amsterdam and Philadelphia: John Benjamins Publishing Company. pp. 19–36.
Halliday, M. A. K. (1994) *An Introduction to Functional Grammar*, London: Edward Arnold.
Jaffe, A. (ed.) (2009) *Stance: Sociolinguistic Perspectives*, Oxford, USA: Oxford University Press.
Kövecses, Z. (2015) *Where Metaphors Come From: Reconsidering Context in Metaphor*, Oxford: Oxford University Press.
Lai, H. L. (2008) 'Understanding and classifying two-part allegorical sayings: Metonymy, metaphor, and cultural constraints', *Journal of Pragmatics* 40(3): 454–474.
Lakoff, G. and Johnson, M. (2003) *Metaphors We Live By*, Chicago: University of Chicago Press.
Lee, T. C. (2018) 'Can Xi Jinping be the next Mao Zedong? Using the Big Five model to study political leadership', *Journal of Chinese Political Science* 23(4): 473–497.
López, A. M. R. and Llopis, M. Á. O. (2010) 'Metaphorical pattern analysis in financial texts: Framing the crisis in positive or negative metaphorical terms', *Journal of Pragmatics* 42(12): 3300–3313.
Martin, J. R. and White, P. R. R. (2005) *The Language of Evaluation: Appraisal in English*, Houndmills, Basingstoke: Palgrave Macmillan.
Mason, K. (1982) 'Metaphor and translation', *Babel* 28(3): 140–149.
Munday, J. (2012) *Evaluation in Translation: Critical Points of Translator Decision-Making*, London and New York: Routledge.
Munday, J. (2018) 'A model of appraisal: Spanish interpretations of President Trump's inaugural address 2017', *Perspectives* 26(2): 180–195.
Musolff, A. (2016) *Political Metaphor Analysis: Discourse and Scenarios*, London and New York: Bloomsbury Publishing.
Newmark, P. (1980) 'The translation of metaphor', *Babel* 26(2): 93–100.

Newmark, P. (2001) *A Textbook of Translation*, Shanghai: Shanghai Foreign Language Education Press.
Ortony, A. (ed.) (1993) *Metaphor and Thought*, Cambridge: Cambridge University Press.
Pan, L. (2014) 'Mediation in news translation: A critical analytical framework', in *Media and Translation: An Interdisciplinary Approach*. D. Abend-David (ed.), New York and London: Bloomsbury. pp. 246–265.
Pan, L. (2015) 'Ideological positioning in news translation: A case study of evaluative resources in reports on china', *Target* 27(2): 215–237.
Peeters, S. (2010) '"The suburbs are exploding" metaphors as framing devices in the French suburban crisis coverage', *Belgian Journal of Linguistics* 24(1): 103–119.
Schäffner, C. (2012a) 'Finding space under the umbrella: The Euro crisis, metaphors, and translation', *Journal of Specialised Translation* (17b): 250–270.
Schäffner, C. (2012b) 'Unknown agents in translated political discourse', *Target* 24(1): 103–125.
Schäffner, C. (2014) 'Umbrellas and firewalls: Metaphors in debating the financial crisis from the perspective of translation studies', in *Tradurre Figure/Translating Figurative Language*, Bologna: CeSLiC. pp. 69–84.
Schäffner, C. and Shuttleworth, M. (2013) 'Metaphor in translation: Possibilities for process research', *Target* 25(1): 93–106.
Thomson, E. A., White, P. R. and Kitley, P. (2008) '"Objectivity" and "hard news" reporting across cultures: Comparing the news report in English, French, Japanese and Indonesian journalism', *Journalism Studies* 9(2): 212–228.
Valdeón, R. A. (2007) 'Translating news from the inner circle: Imposing regularity across languages', *Quaderns: revista de traducció* (14): 155–167.
Valdeón, R. A. (2014) 'From adaptation to appropriation: Framing the world through news translation', *Linguaculture* (1): 51–62.
Van den Broeck, R. (1981) 'The limits of translatability exemplified by metaphor translation', *Poetics Today* 2(4): 73–87.
Van Doorslaer, L. (2009) 'How language and (non-) translation impact on media newsrooms: The case of newspapers in Belgium', *Perspectives* 17(2): 83–92.
Wallis, P. and Nerlich, B. (2005) 'Disease metaphors in new epidemics: The UK media framing of the 2003 SARS epidemic', *Social Science & Medicine* 60: 2629–2639.
White, P. R. (2012) 'Exploring the axiological workings of "reporter voice" news stories: Attribution and attitudinal positioning', *Discourse, Context & Media* 1(2–3): 57–67.
White, P. R. (2016) 'Evaluative contents in verbal communication', in *Verbal Communication*. A. Rocci and L. de Saussure (eds.), Berlin and Boston: Walter de Gruyter GmbH. pp. 77–96.
Zhang, M. (2013) 'Stance and mediation in transediting news headlines as paratexts', *Perspectives* 21(3): 396–411.

8 Representations of the 2014 Hong Kong protests in news translation

A corpus-based critical discourse analysis

Yuan Ping

Introduction

The 2014 Hong Kong protests are also known as the Occupy Central or Umbrella Movement. These terms refer to a series of demonstrations that occurred in Hong Kong in late 2014. It was one of the "critical moments" (Flowerdew 2016: 529) or "key moments" (Bhatia 2016: 549) and the start of a massive social movement in Hong Kong since the handover of sovereignty in 1997. The protests attracted significant local and global media attention. The direct cause of the action was the decision made by the Chinese National People's Congress Standing Committee on the election frameworks and the nomination methods for the 2016 Hong Kong Legislative Council and the 2017 Hong Kong Chief Executive elections. The regulations stipulated that the candidates for these elections were to be selected from a small number of representative committee members rather than through universal suffrage. As a consequence, more than one million demonstrators occupied some major roadways in the city, including several central areas, for 79 days.

Despite the significant role played by the media during the protests, the research on media representations of the 2014 Hong Kong protests (e.g. Sparks 2015; Bhatia 2016; Chan 2017; Feng 2017; Du et al. 2018) has highlighted several aspects of the protests in the local, national and international media. These studies compare the representations of the 2014 Hong Kong protests in the monolingual press, either in the Chinese-language or the English-language press. However, the representations of the protests in the bilingual, multilingual or translational media were left unnoticed. Thus, the role played by translation in the media coverage of the 2014 Hong Kong protests seemed to be left unnoticed. This study seeks to conduct a corpus-based critical discourse analysis of the 2014 Hong Kong protests in the original news discourses produced by their source media and of how the protests are (re)framed in news translation provided by the selected media outlets from the Chinese mainland, Hong Kong, the United Kingdom and the United States.

Corpus-based critical discourse analysis

Traditional methods to study news discourse mostly involve critical discourse analysis (CDA), and this has been used extensively to examine the relationship between ideology and language in the news. The CDA approach mainly draws on Fairclough's (1992, 1995) three-dimensional framework, which first involves a semantic analysis of linguistic features in the discourse at the lexical, grammatical and pragmatic levels, then incorporates the investigation of the discursive practices that are associated with its language usages and, finally, considers the socio-cultural contexts where the texts are produced.

Like many other critical approaches, the CDA approach has potential drawbacks. CDA has received some constructive criticism (e.g. Stubbs 1994; Widdowson 1995; Orpin 2005; Baker et al. 2008) over the past few decades. One of the limitations of this approach is that it relies on a small sample of data. Indeed, Stubbs (1994: 204) raises the issue of scale when he argues that "significant amounts of text must be stored on computer and searched, and quantitative methods must be used to describe the patterns". Fairclough (2013: 45) also notes that "a single text on its own is quite insignificant: the effects of media power are cumulative, working through the repetition of particular ways of handling causality and agency, particular ways of positioning the reader, and so forth". Another criticism about CDA lies with the representativeness of the sample and the subjectivity of scholars in carrying out the analysis. Selection bias is a potential concern because critical discourse analysts are inclined to select or "cherry-pick" (Baker and Levon 2015: 222) examples that correspond to their point of view.

The problems arising from CDA could be remedied by corpus linguistics because it offers the study of language usage from a large amount of data. The use of corpora can be beneficial for CDA in discovering the relationship between language and ideology because corpora "identify repetitions, and can be used to identify implicit meaning" (Hunston 2002: 123). The quantitative nature of corpus analysis could, therefore, reduce the researcher's bias and enhance the objectivity of the research. Corpus-based approaches also allow for the use of qualitative studies that examine a specific language pattern over a large number of instances, through concordances. Thus, the corpus-based study could avoid the criticism of picking favourable cherries and offers a way of choosing the right cherries for closer analysis. However, one of the weaknesses of corpus approach is that the "data in corpora are de-contextualised" (ibid.); thus, the analyst needs to "spell out the steps that lie between what is observed and the interpretation placed on those observations" (ibid.). This weakness is precisely where the corpus-based CDA comes into play because CDA offers the model of description, interpretation and explanation of the data generated from the initial corpus analysis.

Corpus-based CDA has become a popular research method adopted by corpus linguists and discourse analysts to investigate the representations of a range of social issues or topics in the media (e.g. Baker 2006; Baker et al. 2008; Baker and Levon 2015). These corpus-based discourse analyses, as a triangulation of both quantitative and qualitative methods, have yielded many fruitful discussions and provided keen insights into discursive constructions of various topics that shed light on some substantial issues and relationships in society. Corpus approaches have also been adopted in several studies to examine topoi pertaining to Hong Kong, specifically on the media representation of the 2014 Hong Kong protests (e.g. Chan 2017; Feng 2017; Ho 2018). While these studies have incorporated aspects of corpus methods into CDA to examine corpora of a large number of news texts on the protests, they do not consider any translated discourse. Thus, they have overlooked the differences that may occur between translated and original news discourses, which would reveal the implicit ideology of the news media behind their dominant discursive practices.

Corpus approaches to news translation

Despite an increasing interest in research adopting corpus approaches, there has been a lack of studies done by corpus methods in news translation. Valdeón (2012: 847) attributes this deficiency to the difficulty of gathering news corpora because "very often the researcher is unable to locate the source texts upon which news writers base their material". This ambiguity makes the aligning of source texts with their translations very difficult. As Caimotto and Gaspari (2018: 205) also states, the difficulties of analysing news translation by corpus methods are caused by the nature of news texts as being "heavily mediated and edited", which makes it difficult for the researcher to trace back to their source texts (STs). They argue that Baker's (1995) classification of parallel, multilingual and comparable corpora should be expanded and propose the notion of a "comparallel corpus" (Caimotto and Gaspari 2018: 212) – in which the STs may not easily be identifiable and which may contain target texts (TTs) as a partial translation of STs – for application to the study of the ideology of news texts, by combining corpus-based CDA and translation studies.

Some existing so-called corpus analyses of news translation are not analyses in the classical sense as the researcher employs neither a parallel nor a comparable corpus but rather an electronic pile of documents. Some cross-linguistic corpus-assisted discourse studies claim to adopt a comparable corpus, but the news texts are not translations in the strict sense of the word. Károly (2012) is perhaps the first researcher to carry out a real corpus study involving actual translations of news texts (Valdeón 2012). Similarly, McLaughlin (2015) explores the frequencies of lexical items in two corpora of translated news texts. However, these two corpus studies remain at the textual level, mainly examining the syntactic or lexical aspects of news translation. The most relevant corpus study that goes beyond the textual level and looks into the socio-political aspect is probably Kim's (2017) corpus-based study of news discourses on China in *Newsweek* and their Korean translations between 2005 and 2015. Kim's study examines the discursive construction of Chinese national identity and the linguistic changes in translation through the comparison of collocates of "China" in STs and TTs, followed by a closer analysis of these collocations in their concordance lines.

Few studies adopt corpus methods other than corpus-based critical discourse analyses, for example, exploring the relationship between textual features and social contexts. One researcher who does so is Ji (2017), who examines the translations of environmental news on *BBC Chinese*, through computer-assisted frame analysis by using the UCREL Semantic Analysis System (USAS)[1] and exploratory factor analysis. Her corpus analysis reveals shifts in evaluative language between the original and translated materials, which reflect the distinct reporting strategies that *BBC Chinese* adopts towards various genres of environmental news for the different target readerships.

However, corpus-based news translation research is still scarce compared with other textual approaches. One of the limitations of this approach is the pitfall of decontextualisation, which reminds the researcher not to overlook the contexts in its concordances. Besides, none of the existing research in translation studies thus far has examined news discourses related to Hong Kong by adopting a corpus approach.

Corpus data and methodology

This section gives a detailed explanation of the corpus data and the different analytical procedures involved in the corpus-based CDA for analysing the news corpora.

Corpus data

Since there was no existing corpus of news texts on the 2014 Hong Kong protests in English or Chinese, a corpus needed to be compiled for analysis. The news corpus used in this study is composed of four comparable sub-corpora. For the sake of convenience, this corpus is named as the "English and Chinese News Translation Corpus" (hereinafter referred to as ECNTC). Figure 8.1 is a snapshot of the news corpus taken from the Sketch Engine software.

As for its content, the news corpus is composed of translated English and Chinese news articles on the 2014 Hong Kong protests published in *Reference News* (*RN*) from the Chinese mainland, *EJ Insight* from Hong Kong, *BBC Chinese* from the UK and *NYT Chinese* from the US between 28 September and 15 December 2014, the core period of the protests. These media outlets were chosen for the

Language ↓	Name	Words	
English	The New York Times English	88,896	...
English	Reference News English	57,532	...
English	EJ Insight English	18,356	...
English	BBC English	47,265	...
Chinese Traditional	EJ Insight Chinese	30,483	...
Chinese Simplified	The New York Times Chinese	88,504	...
Chinese Simplified	Reference News Chinese	26,663	...
Chinese Simplified	BBC Chinese	20,882	...

Figure 8.1 A snapshot of the ECNTC in Sketch Engine

Table 8.1 Media outlets selected in this study

Country/region	Source text	Target text	Type	Language direction
Chinese Mainland	Various	RN	Newspaper	English > Chinese
Hong Kong	Hong Kong Economic Journal	EJ Insight	News website	Chinese > English
UK	Various	BBC Chinese	News website	English > Chinese
US	NYT	NYT Chinese	News website	English > Chinese

study because they are regarded as representative media outlets and have a large circulation or readership in their own countries or regions. Information about the selected media outlets is outlined in Table 8.1.

The collection of translated news articles involves automatic searching on the news websites of keywords such as *Hong Kong*, *occupy* and *umbrella* or their Chinese equivalents, followed by a manual screening of search results. Translated articles are identified because the translator is named in the translated articles on the news websites. The original news articles were subsequently collected by searching for news sources according to the dates of publication attributed in the translated articles in the LexisNexis and WiseNews[2] databases. This collection method significantly reduces the time spent on searching for specific news articles and also increases the comprehensiveness of the articles collected.

Once all the news texts had been collected, they were then compressed into an archive file and uploaded to the online corpus software Sketch Engine with reference to each news outlet and each language pair. Table 8.2 displays the details (language, name, articles, words and tokens) of the corpus information by each news outlet. The corpus consists of a total of 1,266 news articles on the 2014 Hong Kong protests with approximately 166,532 Chinese characters (201,509 tokens) and 212,049 English words (244,170 tokens), of which 202 are translated into Chinese and 22 into English. The sizes of sub-corpora range from 18,356 words (*EJ Insight* English Corpus) to 88,896 (*NYT* English Corpus). The sizes of the original corpora of *RN*, *EJ Insight* and BBC are more than twice as large as their translated corpora, while the original corpus of *NYT* is slightly larger than its translated corpus. This size difference between the source and translated corpora indicates that a TT is normally shorter than its ST due to omission, which is considered to be a key strategy in news translation (Bielsa and Bassnett 2009: 8).

The type-token ratio refers to the proportion of tokens (running words) to types (different words) in a corpus. Table 8.2 illustrates that the type-token ratio of all the English corpora is significantly higher than that of their Chinese counterparts despite the language direction. The type-token ratio of the traditional Chinese corpus is lower than other simplified Chinese corpora. When the *RN*, BBC and *NYT* texts are translated from English to Chinese, they use less diverse lexis in their texts. When the *EJ Insight* texts are translated from Chinese to English,

Table 8.2 Corpus information by news outlet

Language	Name	Articles	Types (different words)	Tokens (running words)	Type-token ratio	Average sentence length (words)
Chinese simplified	RN Chinese	71	26,663	32,202	82.80	25.66
	BBC Chinese	40	20,882	25,287	82.58	26.04
	NYT Chinese	91	88,504	105,739	83.70	25.27
Chinese traditional	EJ Insight Chinese	436	30,483	38,281	79.63	37.27
Total	**Chinese Corpus**	**638**	**166,532**	**201,509**	**82.64**	**28.56**
English	RN English	242	57,532	66,888	86.01	27.79
	BBC English	270	47,265	54,601	86.56	26.65
	NYT English	94	88,896	102,079	87.09	27.37
	EJ Insight English	22	18,356	20,602	89.10	25.85
Total	**English Corpus**	**628**	**212,049**	**244,170**	**86.84**	**26.92**

they employ a wider variety of lexis. The average sentence length of translated corpora is shorter than that of untranslated corpora. This finding partially agrees with Laviosa-Braithwaite (1996), who has discerned a lower lexical density in translated texts and a shorter mean sentence length in the news and narrative texts caused by simplification. This result supplements Xiao's (2010) findings, who reports that the translated Chinese has a lower lexical density in relation to native Chinese, but the mean sentence length depends on specific text genres. However, the type-token ratio may be affected by the relatively small sizes of corpora. Having explained the decisions made as to the content and structure of the corpora, the next section introduces some methodological issues concerning the analysis of the news corpora.

Methodology

This chapter adopts a corpus-based CDA (Baker 2006), which has gained increasing popularity in recent years. It combines the "useful methodological synergy" (Baker et al. 2008: 273) of corpus linguistics with CDA. Corpus-based CDA is inspired by the discourse-historical approach (Wodak 2001). It could be carried out in several stages beginning with the investigation of lexical devices such as keywords and frequency by using corpus methods and followed by a close and detailed qualitative examination of collocations surrounding these items in their concordance lines. Corpus linguistics offers a quantitative analysis of language usage from a large amount of data, thus potentially reducing the researcher's bias and enhancing the objectivity of the research. Corpus-based approaches also allow for the use of qualitative studies, which examine a specific language pattern over a large number of instances, through concordances.

Three methodological procedures are employed in the analysis of news translation in terms of high-frequency words, keywords and semantic prosodies. In the first phase, the high-frequency words in the original discourses are compared with those in their translated versions within each news corpus to identify if there are any deviations of thematic issues between the original news discourses and their translated versions and whether some salient lexical items have been accentuated or undermined by the specific news media during the translation process. Secondly, the keywords of translated discourses of different news corpora are compared with each other. The lexical keywords of translated discourses are then divided into various semantic groups for the analysis in the later stage. Using the Word Sketch function of Sketch Engine (Kilgarriff et al. 2004), the third phase examines the verb and adjective forms that collocate with the lemma *movement* and its Chinese equivalent 运动 as both object and subject, and their semantic prosodies, which denote positive or negative associations of the media outlets towards the protests.

Comparison of word frequency

The first strand of corpus analysis involves examining the frequencies of words in the original and translated news corpora. A frequency list is a list of words generated according to their number of occurrences in a corpus (Kenny 2001). This word list can either be ranked alphabetically or by the occurrences of words in a corpus. The most frequently occurring words in a corpus are normally function words that have little lexical meaning, such as prepositions, conjunctions, determiners, pronouns and auxiliary verbs. The remainder of the words is content words that have substantial meaning, such as nouns, adjectives, adverbs and verbs (Stubbs 1996). Table 8.3 shows the top 10 frequently occurring content words in each English and Chinese sub-corpus for all four media outlets. English translations of the Chinese characters are given in brackets. The frequency of the word is listed next to the word.

From the results, we can see that the frequencies of some words are almost the same, both in the original and translated corpora, such as *China, Beijing, Hong Kong, government, movement, police* and *people*. Some words occur noticeably more or less frequently in the translated corpora than they do in the original corpora or vice versa. There may be several reasons for this, such as language conventions, translation norms or different ideological perspectives of the news media. For example, the structure of the reporting verb *said* followed by that-clauses is very common in English news texts. In the *EJ Insight* translated English corpus, 11 out of 37 (29.73%) occurrences of the lemma *say* are followed by that-clauses, compared with 27 out of 632 (4.27%) in the *RN*, 23 out of 332 (6.93%) in the BBC and 106 out of 1,000 (10.6%) in the *NYT* English corpora. This result is consistent with Olohan and Baker's (2000) findings that reporting verbs and that-clauses are more explicit in translated English than in original English. The reporting verb 说 (*say*) is still frequent in Chinese news reports; however, the conjunction *that* is

Table 8.3 Top 10 content words in the STs and the TTs of each media outlet

No.	RN				EJ Insight				BBC				NYT			
	ST		TT		ST		TT		ST		TT		ST		TT	
	Word	Freq	Word	Freq	Word	Freq	Word	Freq	Word	Freq	Word	Freq	Word	Freq	Word	Freq
1	Hong	877	香港 (Hong Kong)	1,254	香港 (Hong Kong)	773	Hong	233	Hong	223	香港 (Hong Kong)	688	Hong	537	香港 (Hong Kong)	1,478
2	Kong	718	中国 (China)	992	人 (people)	301	Kong	158	Kong	181	中国 (China)	541	Kong	290	抗议 (protest)	721
3	said	514	政府 (government)	875	政府 (government)	215	government	101	said	79	抗议 (protest)	265	said	156	说 (said)	691
4	police	334	说 (said)	637	港人 (Hongkonger)	193	movement	98	police	75	北京 (Beijing)	254	police	148	政府 (government)	607
5	protesters	332	英国 (UK)	626	占领 (occupy)	185	students	78	China	67	人 (people)	221	protesters	104	人 (people)	523
6	government	277	抗议 (protest)	484	笔者 (author)	170	occupy	69	protesters	61	政府 (government)	209	government	96	抗议者 (protester)	520
7	China	229	美国 (US)	402	民主 (democracy)	154	people	63	protests	60	报道 (report)	195	Mr	82	中国 (China)	485
8	protests	210	活动 (activity)	347	北京 (Beijing)	141	Beijing	59	people	50	占 (occupy)	195	people	82	警方 (police)	463
9	people	205	表示 (express)	341	代表 (representative)	115	political	55	Beijing	47	学生 (student)	184	protests	71	活动 (activity)	450
10	Beijing	175	民主 (democracy)	307	政治 (politics)	114	economic	53	Chinese	45	行动 (action)	173	protest	70	北京 (Beijing)	368

often omitted due to language differences. This study considers the variables of language conventions and translation norms that might be at play and pays particular attention to the shifts related to ideological factors.

Considering that the original corpora of *RN*, *EJ Insight* and *BBC Chinese* are twice as large as their translated corpora, the analysis is based on the presumption that word frequencies in these translated corpora are about half of those in their untranslated ones. The original and translated *NYT* corpora are of a similar size. As a result, the word frequency of its ST should be about the same as it is in its TT. Ideally, the translated word frequencies would not exceed the threshold of their original ones, at least. Otherwise, a word is considered to be strengthened in the translation. If the frequency of a word in its translated corpus is significantly lower than half of that in its original corpus, the word is regarded as being weakened in its translation. After a comparative analysis of frequencies to find what words have been strengthened or weakened in translation, the next step is to take a closer look at their concordances to arrive at some explanation of this effect. The following sections compare the keywords between their STs and TTs. These words are selected because they occur considerably more in their TTs than in their STs or other TTs.

Comparison of keywords

The second strand of corpus analysis compares the keywords of the translated news corpora to find out the similarities and differences between the discourses produced by each media outlet. The keywords function of Sketch Engine compares the frequency lists of two corpora. Words that are unusually frequent in a corpus are identified as keywords and are ranked by their "keyness" score, which is calculated according to the statistical analysis of "log-likelihood ratio" (Dunning 1993: 68). Keyness analysis could be employed to discover both differences as well as similarities between two corpora (Gabrielatos 2018). The frequency list of a small specialised corpus is usually compared with that of a large general corpus known as a reference corpus. This analysis selects English Web 2013 (enTenTen13) as the reference corpus for its English corpus, Chinese Web 2011 (zheTenTen11) for its simplified Chinese corpus and Chinese Traditional Web (TaiwanWaC) for its traditional Chinese corpus. The English Web corpus[3] and the Chinese Web corpus[4] are part of the TenTen corpus family and are made up of texts collected from the Internet in 2013 and 2011 with sizes of 19 billion English words and 1.7 billion simplified Chinese characters respectively. The Chinese traditional web corpus[5] is a similar corpus with a considerably smaller size of 260 million traditional Chinese characters. The reasons for choosing these reference corpora are firstly, they are made up of texts collected from the Internet in recent years, secondly, the sizes of these corpora are reasonably large and thirdly, they all contain a selection of news texts.

This section aims to investigate the same and different discourses that the translated news corpora intend to reinforce. In this analysis, keywords of translated corpora are compared with those of another media outlet to find out their similarities and differences. The keywords of translated news corpora are first tagged according to the UCREL Semantic Analysis System (USAS)[6] by using its automatic English and Chinese taggers respectively. They are then scrutinised, since many words remain unmatched, especially some pronouns and abbreviations. These unmatched words are then tagged manually according to the tag sets. The lexical keywords are categorised into different semantic groups in relation to their topics or themes. The grouping of these "semantically related words" (Baker 2006: 86) provides an overview as to how the event is represented in the translated discourses produced by the news media. Table 8.4 shows the comparison of the top 25 keywords grouped by their semantic meanings.

Table 8.4 Comparison of top 25 keywords in the translated news corpora by different semantic groups

	RN Chinese	EJ Insight English	BBC Chinese	NYT Chinese
Personal names	林郑月娥 (Carrie Lam), 卡梅伦 (David Cameron), 彭定康 (Chris Patten), 梁振英 (Leung Chun-ying)	Tung, Lam, Lian, Yizheng, Leung	习近平 (Xi Jinping), 梁振英 (Leung Chun-ying), 彭定康 (Chris Patten), 刘慧卿 (Emily Lau)	梁振英 (Leung Chun-ying), 黄之锋 (Joshua Wong), 储百亮 (Chris Buckley), 傅才德 (Mike Forsythe), Chris, Buckley, ALAN, WONG, Wong
Geographical names	中环 (Central), 金钟 (Admiralty), 旺角 (Mong Kok)	Hong, Kong, SAR, mainland, Admiralty, Mong, Kok	旺角 (Mong Kok)	金钟 (Admiralty), 中环 (Central), 旺角 (Mong Kok)
Government and public domain	立法会 (LegCo), 港府 (HK government), 特首 (Chief Executive), 长官 (chief), 香港人 (Hongkonger)	Scholarism, KMT, LegCo, Hongkonger, Hongkongers	特首 (Chief Executive), 香港人 (Hongkonger)	立法会 (LegCo), 香港人 (Hongkonger)
Social actions	占中 (Occupy Central), 示威 (demonstration), 抗议 (protest), 示威者 (demonstrator), 抗议者 (protester)	Occupy, protester, handover	占中 (Occupy Central), 示威 (demonstration), 抗议 (protest), 抗议者 (protester), 示威者 (demonstrator)	占中 (Occupy Central), 示威 (demonstration), 抗议 (protest), 抗议者 (protester), 示威者 (demonstrator)
Causes	政改 (political reform), 普选 (universal suffrage)	suffrage	政改 (political reform), 普选 (universal suffrage)	

(*Continued*)

Table 8.4 (Continued)

	RN Chinese	EJ Insight English	BBC Chinese	NYT Chinese
Processes	拘捕 (arrest), 禁制令 (injunction), 清场 (clearance)	bailiff	催泪弹 (tear gas), 雨伞 (umbrella), 清场 (clearance), 占领区 (occupation)	催泪 (tear), 胡椒 (pepper), 雨伞 (umbrella), 路障 (barricade), 营地 (campsite), 清场 (clearance)
Other	法新社 (AFP), 南华 (SCMP), 路透社 (Reuters)	Bourse, CSSTA, GaveKal	责编 (editor), 英媒 (British media), 卫报 (The Guardian), 金丝雀 (canary), 每日 (Daily), 电讯报 (Telegraph), 推特 (Twitter)	

From the table, we can see that the media outlets focus on various aspects, such as pronouns, government, social actions, causes and processes. They employ different personal and geographical names in their news stories and share some common keywords such as *Leung Chun-ying, Occupy Central, Mong Kok, Hongkonger, protester, protest, demonstrator* and *demonstration*, which remain prominent in all translated news corpora. Despite their similarities, each media outlet emphasises more keywords from different semantic groups to frame its news discourses. For instance, *RN* selects plenty of sources from the other media like Reuters, Agence France-Press (*AFP*) and the *South China Morning Post* (*SCMP*). *BBC Chinese* highlights much information from the British press such as the *Guardian* and the *Daily Telegraph* as the website summarises information from several British media and incorporates "英媒 (British media)" into its headlines. Even within the same semantic group, each media outlet tends to emphasise different aspects of keywords. As Gabrielatos (2018: 228) puts it, "the identification of key items is only the first stage, as a manual analysis is required to establish the use of the items in context". The following steps would be to contextualise the representations of several keywords with reference to individual and geographical names, government, social actions, causes and processes.

Semantic prosodies of keywords

Semantic prosodies of keywords is perhaps one of the most frequently used textual devices in news translation because the language of evaluation can reveal the stance or values of news outlets towards an issue, and thus they are most likely to be altered to reflect the variation of attitudes shown by different news outlets.

Semantic prosody can be defined as "a subtle element of attitudinal, often pragmatic meaning" (Sinclair 1998: 20). It reveals "positive or negative associations that become attached to words based on their usage" (Olohan 2004: 82). However, it is difficult through manual scrutiny to retrieve such linguistic patterns because they are invariably embedded in an unwieldy quantity of texts that, as Louw (1993: 159) argues, "can only be properly traced by computational methods". There are some corpus-based studies that suggest the usefulness of semantic prosody in qualitative evaluation of news discourse (e.g. Bednarek 2006). The following section uses the function of Word Sketch, one of the features of the Sketch Engine. It retrieves information regarding the collocational behaviour of words according to their grammatical relations. This feature saves time and constitutes a more systematic and productive approach than manual inspection and intuitive speculation.

This section undertakes a contrastive analysis of semantic prosodies and collocations in the English and Chinese corpora. When it comes to the 2014 Hong Kong protests, the news media tend to focus on various aspects of the protests, evident in the keywords analysis. With the development of the demonstrations, people hold divergent attitudes regarding the event, particularly among student protesters and ordinary citizens. When reporting the news, media outlets also bring their own opinions into news reports. This strand of analysis aims to investigate the attitudes of the media or translators towards the movement and if there are any subtle shifts in their attitudes between original and translated discourses. The selected media outlets adopt different prosodies and epithets in association with the event. One focus in this study is the semantic prosodies of the keyword *movement* in the English corpora and its Chinese equivalent 运动 in the Chinese corpora. This keyword is selected because it is a relatively common keyword in both the English and Chinese news corpora, which provide comparatively adequate data for contrastive analysis. This keyword could be used as an object following an adjective or a verb. It could also be used as a subject modified by an adjective or followed by a verb. The analysis only considers the threshold of words that occur more than once in its respective corpus. Otherwise, they are considered statistically invalid "as the low frequency may result in unreliable quantification" (Xiao and McEnery 2006: 110).

The selected media outlets adopt various semantic prosodies for the movement and its Chinese equivalent 运动, as shown in Table 8.5. Frequent collocates of *movement* and its Chinese equivalent 运动 include *occupy, central, umbrella* and *protest* in English and 占中 (*Occupy Central*), 抗议 (*protest*) and 民主 (*democracy*) in Chinese. The movement is more likely to be associated with positive connotations and named as 雨伞运动 (*Umbrella Movement*) in the *EJ Insight*, BBC and *NYT* corpora than it would be in the *RN* corpora. The former three media outlets relate the Occupy Central Movement to the Sunflower Movement in Taiwan several times, which never occurs in the *RN* corpora. The *EJ Insight*, BBC and *NYT* corpora tend to employ a large number of modifiers relating to democracy or civil rights, including nouns such as *pro-democracy, democracy, civil rights* and adjectives like *democratic*. These words are translated into 亲民主 (*pro-democracy*), 民主 (*democracy*) and 民权 (*civil rights*), with positive connotations in Chinese.

Table 8.5 Word sketches of *movement* and its Chinese equivalent 运动 in the news corpora

		RN		EJ Insight		BBC		NYT	
		English	Chinese	Chinese	English	English	Chinese	English	Chinese
Modifiers	Noun	occupy central pro-democracy umbrella democracy protest	民主 (democracy) 抗议 (protest)	佔中 (Occupy Central) 民主 (democracy) 雨傘 (umbrella)	umbrella occupy sunflower civil central	occupy umbrella central protest civil democracy sunflower pro-democracy	雨傘 (umbrella) 太阳花 (sunflower) 抗议 (protest) 民主 (democracy)	protest pro-democracy umbrella occupy democracy central sunflower civil rights	雨伞 (umbrella) 民主 (democracy) 占中 (Occupy Central) 抗议 (protest) 亲民主 (pro-democracy) 民权 (civil rights) 太阳花 (sunflower)
	Adjective	illegal	大规模 (mass) 失控 (out-of-control)						
Verbs	*movement*/运动 as an object	hijack crush		消耗 (diminish) 利於 (conducive)	condemn denounce oppose		声援 (support)	criticize support	支持 (support) 批评 (criticise)
	movement or 运动 as a subject	wane		釋出 (generate)	undermine transform demonstrate				持续 (endure) 唤醒 (rouse) 赢得 (win)

By contrast, the *RN* English corpus comprises a mixture of modifiers with positive and negative connotations. Apart from positive nouns such as *pro-democracy* and *democracy*, which are significantly underused in its translated corpus, it employs negative adjectives such as *illegal, out-of-control* and *mass* to modify the movement. Example 1 displays how the negative attribute *illegal* is used to modify *movement* in the original *RN* corpus. As the example shows, this negative word is used in a news article by AFP to denote, verbatim, words used by the spokesperson from the Chinese foreign ministry to criticise the last governor of Hong Kong Chris Patten for instigating the movement and is well maintained in its *RN* Chinese translation.

Example 1

ST: China reacted angrily to Patten's comments on Wednesday, accusing him of "inciting the **illegal** Occupy Central Movement in Hong Kong."   *RN* English 2014.11.06.en

TT: 在香港末代总督彭定康呼吁伦敦采取更多举措，支持前殖民地香港的民主活动后，中国周三对他提出警告，"有关人员应立即停止怂恿'占中'**违法**活动的言行。"   *RN* Chinese 2014.11.06.zh

GLOSS: *After the last governor of Hong Kong Chris Patten called on London to take more measures to support the democratic activities in its former colony, China warned him on Wednesday that "the relevant personnel should immediately stop the words and deeds for inciting the 'Occupy Central' **illegal** activities."*

In addition to modifiers, each media outlet utilises a large number of verbs with *movement* both as a subject and an object. The *RN* English corpus contains most of the verbs with negative connotations such as *wane* (3), *hijack* (2) and *crush* (2). Example 2 from the *SCMP* shows that when *movement* is used as a subject, the public support for it was waning. When *movement* is used as an object, it was hijacked or crushed. Example 3 from the *Washington Times* depicts a vulnerable image of the movement that was taken control of by force. The sentence relates to the discourse from the US government in blaming the Chinese government for the intention to crack down on the student protests. However, these negative verbs, associated with the word *movement*, were both reserved in the translated *RN* corpus.

Example 2

ST: As grievances mount, support for the civil disobedience movement is **waning**.   *RN* English 2014.10.17.en

TT: 随着不满情绪日益增加，人们对这一项运动的支持在**减弱**。   *RN* Chinese 2014.10.17.zh

GLOSS: *As dissatisfaction increases, people's support for this movement is **weakening**.*

Example 3

ST: Massive pro-democracy demonstrations in Hong Kong teetered on the brink of violence Friday, putting the Obama administration in an increasingly precarious position over whether or not to take an aggressive public stand behind the protesters by warning Chinese authorities against violently **crushing** the movement.

RN English 2014.10.06.en

TT: 香港支持民主的大规模示威周五处于暴力边缘，令奥巴马政府在是否需要通过警告中国当局不要暴力**镇压**这场运动，从而公开、坚决地表明支持抗议者的立场方面陷入越来越危险的境地。

RN Chinese 2014.10.06.zh

GLOSS: *The massive demonstration in support of democracy in Hong Kong was on the verge of violence on Friday, when the Obama administration was in an increasingly dangerous situation in terms of whether it should warn the Chinese authorities against violently* **suppressing** *the movement and thus openly and resolutely demonstrate support for the protesters.*

The translator of *EJ Insight* retains both positive and negative feelings and keeps most of these verbs in its translated corpus. The *EJ Insight* corpus places the movement in a quandary: on the one hand, as shown in Example 4, it is condemned by local residents who stand in line with the authorities; on the other hand, the movement has generated tremendous enthusiasm, which is conducive to a sustainable movement.

Example 4

ST: 這些不願為「真普選」付出代價的人，遂與政府同調，**譴責**「雨傘運動」！

EJ Insight Chinese 2014.12.01.zh

GLOSS: *Those who are unwilling to sacrifice for "genuine universal suffrage" are coordinated with the government in* **condemning** *the "Umbrella Movement"!*

TT: These are people who do not share with other Hongkongers the common aspiration to a free vote – let alone are prepared to make any sacrifices for it – so they speak with the same voice as the authorities in **condemning** the movement.

EJ Insight English 2014.12.01.en

The BBC and *NYT* corpora mainly adopt verbs that are in favour of the movement, as can be seen from Example 5, 6 and 7. As Example 5 shows, the BBC Chinese corpus foregrounds the movement in a positive light by using *movement* as an object that collocates with the verb of being supported by expatriates living in Hong Kong through a form of running a marathon.

Example 5

ST: Two of Hong Kong's top ultra-runners completed a 102km "Umbrella ultra-marathon" on Wednesday to show their **support** for the Occupy Central movement. — BBC English 2014.10.29.en

TT: 两名澳大利亚侨民以102公里"超级马拉松"长跑来**声援**雨伞运动。 — BBC Chinese 2014.10.29.zh

GLOSS: *Two Australian expatriates **support** the Umbrella Movement with a 102-kilometre "super marathon" run.*

Similarly, the *NYT Chinese* corpus maintains an overwhelming majority of positive verbs. Example 6 depicts Occupy Central as a fragile movement that had already sustained itself for over a month but is in jeopardy due to tensions and confusion. The Chinese website represents the view that the movement has roused the democratic consciousness of a whole generation of Hong Kong people and people who did not care about politics and that it won extensive sympathy and global attention. As an object, the movement collocates with being supported by the US politicians who were lobbied by the democracy advocates, as shown in Example 7. Many of these words with positive connotations were reserved in the BBC and *NYT* Chinese corpora, which are already salient in their original corpora.

Example 6

ST: Organizers of a planned vote among Hong Kong's pro-democracy demonstrators abruptly canceled it on Sunday, exposing tensions and confusion over how to **sustain** the movement after protesters occupied major streets to demand free elections. — *NYT* English 2014.10.27.en

TT: 原打算在香港的亲民主示威者中进行一次投票活动的组织者周日突然宣布取消投票，暴露出要求自由选举的示威者占领了香港一些街道一个月后，在如何将运动**维持**下去上的紧张气氛和意见混乱。 — *NYT* Chinese 2014.10.27.zh

GLOSS: *The organisers who originally planned to conduct a poll in pro-democracy demonstrations in Hong Kong suddenly announced the cancellation of the vote on Sunday, exposing the tensions and confusions in how to **maintain** the movement after the demonstrators who demanded free elections occupied some streets in Hong Kong for a month.*

Example 7

ST: The N.E.D. also hosted a briefing in Washington last April featuring two of Hong Kong's most influential advocates of democracy in recent decades, Martin Lee and Anson Chan, who angered Chinese leadership by lobbying American politicians to **support** the democracy movement. *NYT* English 2014.10.11.en

TT: NED 今年4月还在华盛顿举办了一场新闻发布会，会上的主角是近几十年来，香港最有影响力的两位民主倡导者 – 李柱铭和陈方安生。他们曾游说美国政治人物**支持**民主运动，并因此激怒了中国政府。 *NYT* Chinese 2014.10.11.zh

GLOSS: *The NED held a press conference in Washington in April this year. The protagonists of the conference were the two most influential democratic advocates in Hong Kong, Martin Lee and Anson Chan. They have lobbied American politicians to* **support** *the democratic movement and have thus angered the Chinese government.*

Overall, the *RN* discourses tend to be linked with words that have unfavourable connotations and possess a generally negative attitude towards the movement through the perpetuation of negative adjectives and verbs from the source media. *EJ Insight* takes a neutral position by preserving an equal number of both positive and negative commentaries on the movement. In contrast, *BBC Chinese* and *NYT Chinese* demonstrate an initially implicit positive attitude towards the movement by maintaining the original positive connotations of the movement in their Chinese translations.

Concluding remarks

This study starts off with the objective of evaluating the discrepancies in news translations by employing a corpus-based CDA approach. The study considers the contrastive differences that exist between the English and Chinese language conventions and pays particular attention to the shifts caused due to ideological factors and hidden stances of the media outlets. Some discourses have become stronger or weaker in their translated corpora compared with the original corpora. These discourses from different semantic groups constitute a metadiscourse that the media outlets undertake to convey. Situated in diverse socio-political contexts, each media outlet possesses its distinct editorial stance on the 2014 Hong Kong protests in its news coverage. For instance, *RN* highlights the consequences of breaking the law and crime and the impact the protesters have on the local economy and the life of local people. The BBC and *NYT Chinese* websites endorse the protests by depicting violent confrontations between the brutal police and peaceful protesters, while *EJ Insight* stands typically between the two factions, providing rational criticism of both sides.

The analyses of semantic prosodies indicate that there are few significant evaluative shifts between the translated and untranslated news discourses within the same media outlet. A possible explanation is that media outlets are likely to select original discourses that are in line with their editorial stances. However, there may be significant differences between the translated discourses produced by different media outlets. For example, the BBC and *NYT* Chinese websites often relate the Occupy Movement with democracy, and this is given prominence and imbued with positive connotations. The democratic associations are significantly less prominent in *RN* discourses and are mixed with less favourable connotations.

This study proposes a methodological framework that could be used in the analysis of news translation and suggests that corpora techniques may inform and be integrated into the analytical framework of CDA at the textual level, as this significantly promotes the objectivity of the study. The thematic analysis by incorporating corpus tools such as the comparison of keywords sheds lights on the determination of the critical elements of original discourses that are strengthened or weakened during the translation process. The comparison of frequency lists also offers an efficient method to identify the discourses, particularly in circumstances where original and translated discourses are not in parallel, a relatively common feature of news translation. The analyses of semantic prosodies assist in distinguishing the repositioning of participants within the text through epithets. On the other hand, corpus analysis could be used as a means to validate the findings generated from CDA. Nevertheless, corpus methods have little capacity to inform CDA beyond the textual level via para-textual elements such as layout and images. In general, the corpus-based CDA can only describe what and how discourses change from original to translated texts, but it does not explain why such shifts may occur. Thus, additional contextual analysis is required in order to disclose such changes in details.

The main weakness of this study is the paucity of the news corpora, which resulted in insufficient data for the analysis of semantic prosodies in particular. Further studies could increase the size of the news corpus by incorporating more media outlets in the coverage of the event or a series of events by the same media outlets. Another limitation of this study is that a large number of Chinese characters remain untagged in the UCREL Chinese tagging system, as Ji (2017: 153–154) also points out at the end of her study. This limitation would undoubtedly affect the reliability of this research.

Acknowledgement

This work was supported by the China Scholarship Council – University of Leeds Scholarship and the Faculty of Arts, Humanities and Cultures Research Dissemination Award. An earlier version of this chapter was presented at the 6th International Association for Translation and Intercultural Studies Conference in Hong Kong. The author would like to express his deep gratitude to Professor Jeremy Munday, Professor Binhua Wang and Professor Meifang Zhang for their valuable comments and helpful suggestions.

Notes

1 The UCREL Semantic Analysis System (USAS) is an automatic semantic tagging system developed by the Centre for Computer Corpus Research on Language at Lancaster University. It is currently available in 14 languages. http://ucrel.lancs.ac.uk/usas/ (Accessed: 20 March 2019).

2 LexisNexis is a large database of news information, including international newspapers and legal documents. WiseNews is a large news database that provides access to a wide range of Chinese-language newspapers and magazines.
3 Sketch Engine. (2013) 'enTenTen – English corpus from the web'. Available at: https://www.sketchengine.eu/ententen-english-corpus/ (Accessed: 6 July, 2020).
4 Sketch Engine. (2011) 'zhTenTen – Chinese corpus from the web'. Available at: https://www.sketchengine.eu/zhtenten-chinese-corpus/ (Accessed: 6 July, 2020).
5 Sketch Engine. (2011) 'TaiwanWac – Chinese corpus from the web'. Available at: https://www.sketchengine.eu/taiwanwac-chinese-corpus/ (Accessed: 6 July, 2020).
6 University Centre for Computer Corpus Research on Language. 'UCREL Semantic Analysis System (USAS)'. Available at: http://ucrel.lancs.ac.uk/usas/ (Accessed: 6 July, 2020).

References

Baker, M. (1995) 'Corpora in translation studies: An overview and some suggestions for future research', *Target* 7(2): 223–243.
Baker, P. (2006) *Using Corpora in Discourse Analysis*, London: Continuum.
Baker, P., Gabrielatos, C., Khosravinik, M., Krzyżanowski, M., McEnery, T. and Wodak, R. (2008) 'A useful methodological synergy? Combining critical discourse analysis and corpus linguistics to examine discourses of refugees and asylum seekers in the UK press', *Discourse & Society* 19(3): 273–306.
Baker, P. and Levon, E. (2015) 'Picking the right cherries? A comparison of corpus-based and qualitative analyses of news articles about masculinity', *Discourse & Communication* 9(2): 221–236.
Bednarek, M. (2006) *Evaluation in Media Discourse: Analysis of a Newspaper Corpus*, London: Continuum.
Bhatia, A. (2016) 'Discursive construction of the "key" moment in the Umbrella Movement', *Journal of Language and Politics* 15(5): 549–566.
Bielsa, E. and Bassnett, S. (2009) *Translation in Global News*, London: Routledge.
Caimotto, M. C. and Gaspari, F. (2018) 'Corpus-based study of news translation: Challenges and possibilities', *Across Languages and Cultures* 19(2): 205–220.
Chan, T. (2017) 'The Umbrella Movement in the media: A corpus-driven analysis of newspapers in Hong Kong and China', *Journalism and Discourse Studies*. Available at: www.jdsjournal.net/uploads/2/3/6/4/23642404/chan-jdsjournal-may2017.pdf (Accessed: 3 June, 2019).
Du, Y. R., Zhu, L. and Yang, F. (2018) 'A movement of varying faces: How "Occupy Central" was framed in the news in Hong Kong, Taiwan, Mainland China, the UK, and the U.S.', *International Journal of Communication* 12: 2556–2577.
Dunning, T. (1993) 'Accurate methods for the statistics of surprise and coincidence', *Computational Linguistics* 19(1): 61–74.
Fairclough, N. (1992) *Discourse and Social Change*, Cambridge: Polity Press.
Fairclough, N. (1995) *Critical Discourse Analysis: The Critical Study of Language*, London: Longman.
Fairclough, N. (2013) *Language and Power* (2nd ed.), London: Routledge.
Feng, D. (2017) 'Ideological dissonances among Chinese-language newspapers in Hong Kong: A corpus-based analysis of reports on the Occupy Central Movement', *Discourse & Communication* 11(6): 549–566.
Flowerdew, J. (2016) 'A historiographical approach to Hong Kong Occupy: Focus on a critical moment', *Journal of Language and Politics* 15(5): 527–548.

Gabrielatos, C. (2018) 'Keyness analysis: Nature, metrics and techniques', in *Corpus Approaches to Discourse: A Critical Review*. C. Taylor and A. Marchi (eds.), London: Routledge. pp. 225–258.

Ho, J. (2018) '"Sensible protesters began leaving the protests": A comparative study of opposing voices in the Hong Kong political movement', *Language & Communication* 64: 12–24.

Hunston, S. (2002) *Corpora in Applied Linguistics*, Cambridge: Cambridge University Press.

Ji, M. (2017) 'A corpus analysis of translation of environmental news on BBC China', in *Textual and Contextual Analysis in Empirical Translation Studies*. S. Laviosa, A. Pagano, H. Kemppanen and M. Ji (eds.), Singapore: Springer. pp. 129–157.

Károly, K. (2012) 'News discourse in translation: Topical structure and news content in the analytical news article', *Meta* 57(4): 884–908.

Kenny, D. (2001) *Lexis and Creativity in Translation: A Corpus-Based Study*, London: Routledge.

Kilgarriff, A., Rychly, P., Smrz, P. and Tugwell, D. (2004) *The Sketch Engine*, 11th EURA-LEX International Congress, Lorient, 6–10 July. Lorient: Université de Bretagne Sud. pp. 105–115. Available at: http://euralex.org/category/publications/euralex-2004/ (Accessed: 20 March, 2019).

Kim, K. H. (2017) 'Newsweek discourses on China and their Korean translations: A corpus-based approach', *Discourse, Context and Media* 15: 34–44.

Laviosa-Braithwaite, S. (1996) *The English Comparable Corpus (ECC): A Resource and a Methodology for the Empirical Study of Translation*. PhD thesis, University of Manchester Institute of Science and Technology, Manchester.

Louw, B. (1993) 'Irony in the text or insincerity in the writer? The diagnostic potential of semantic prosodies', in *Text and Technology: In Honour of John Sinclair*. M. Baker, G. Francis and E. Tognini-Bonelli (eds.), Amsterdam: John Benjamins. pp. 157–176.

McLaughlin, M. L. (2015) 'News translation past and present: Silent witness and invisible intruder', *Perspectives* 23(4): 552–569.

Olohan, M. (2004) *Introducing Corpora in Translation Studies*, London: Routledge.

Olohan, M. and Baker, M. (2000) 'Reporting *that* in translated English: Evidence for subconscious processes of explicitation?', *Across Languages and Cultures* 1(2): 141–158.

Orpin, D. (2005) 'Corpus linguistics and critical discourse analysis: Examining the ideology of sleaze', *International Journal of Corpus Linguistics* 10(1): 37–61.

Sinclair, J. (1998) 'The lexical item', in *Contrastive Lexical Semantics*. E. Weigand (ed.), Amsterdam: John Benjamins. pp. 1–24.

Sparks, C. (2015) 'Business as usual: The UK national daily press and the Occupy Central movement', *Chinese Journal of Communication* 8(4): 429–446.

Stubbs, M. (1994) 'Grammar, text, and ideology: Computer-assisted methods in the linguistics of representation', *Applied Linguistics* 15(2): 201–223.

Stubbs, M. (1996) *Text and Corpus Analysis: Computer-Assisted Studies of Language and Culture*, Oxford: Blackwell.

Valdeón, R. A. (2012) 'Presentation', *Meta* 57(4): 847–849.

Widdowson, H. G. (1995) 'Discourse analysis: A critical view', *Language and Literature* 4(3): 157–172.

Wodak, R. (2001) 'The discourse-historical approach', in *Methods of Critical Discourse Analysis*. R. Wodak and M. Meyer (eds.), London: Sage. pp. 63–94.

Xiao, R. (2010) 'How different is translated Chinese from native Chinese? A corpus-based study of translation universals', *International Journal of Corpus Linguistics* 15(1): 5–35.

Xiao, R. and McEnery, T. (2006) 'Collocation, semantics prosody, and near synonymy: A cross-linguistic perspective', *Applied Linguistics* 27(1): 103–129.

9 Reframing China in conflicts
A case study of English translation of the South China Sea dispute

Binjian Qin

Introduction

The furthered application of the discourse analytical approach into news shows that news does not objectively mirror realities but reconstructs the reality through many people's eyes (Caldas-Coulthard 2003) with "value laden, ideologically determined discourse" (White 2006: 37). Such reconstruction of realities also occurs in news translation, in which the same event may be reframed into different narratives. It is especially true in the news related to international conflicts, because the parties involved may "seek to undermine each other because they have incompatible goals, competing interests, or fundamentally different values" (Baker 2006: 1), and these kinds of competing narratives are prominent in news translation by media with contrasting ideological tendencies (see Pan 2012). However, it should be noted that even in the same news medium, news stories may be varied after they are translated into another language. Some researchers (such as Kang 2007) have realised and probed into such issues, focusing on the mediated stance within the same news agency towards the same event, but such investigation is still rare in news translation between Chinese and English provided by China's state-run media.

In order to fill this research gap, drawing on appraisal theory proposed by Martin and White (2005) and the reframing strategies introduced by Baker (2006), this chapter scrutinises the English translation of news on the South China Sea dispute by Xinhuanet, a Chinese state-run news media organisation. It aims to examine the stance re-instantiation in the English version and scrutinise how China is reframed in the translated news reports. Moreover, this chapter also explores the possible causes of such deviation.

Related theoretical concepts

Appraisal, stance and attitude

Linguistic mechanisms of writers' expression of opinions has been a heated topic among linguists. Different approaches have been adopted in the investigation of this field, with major concepts such as evidentiality (e.g. Chafe 1986), affect (e.g. Ochs and Schieffelin 1989), hedging (e.g. Hyland 1998), evaluation (e.g. Hunston and Thompson 2000), appraisal (e.g. Martin 2000) and stance (e.g. Biber and Finegan 1988). These research paradigms as a whole shed light on "our understanding of the ways in which speakers and writers encode opinions and assessments in the language they produce" (Grey and Biber 2012: 15). Appraisal theory is the most representative theoretical approach investigating subjectivity of discourse in recent years, and it mainly focuses on the concepts of appraisal, evaluation and stance; therefore, the notions of these terms, which usually overlap with each other, will be clarified in this section.

Appraisal is referred to as the "semantic resources used to negotiate emotions, judgements and valuations, alongside with resources amplifying and engaging with these evaluations" (Martin 2000: 145). Appraisal shares close relations with the term 'evaluation' (Martin and White 2005; Zhang 2013) and can be seen as "a set of systems within systemic functional linguistics that has been developed to map evaluation in texts" (Macken-Horarik and Isaac 2014: 67). It is an ambiguous concept defined as "the broad cover term for the expression of the speaker or writer's attitude or stance towards, viewpoints on or feelings about the entities or propositions that he or she is talking about" (Hunston and Thompson 2000: 5). Stance is also an ambiguous concept with various definitions. It has been defined as the explicit expression of feelings, judgements and attitudes (Biber and Finegan 1988). Even though stance shares some common grounds with evaluation, they can be distinguished from the perspective of instantiation developed by Biber and Finegan (1988). In the cline of evaluative instantiation, appraisal is viewed as generalised systemic potential, and stance is the instantiation of evaluative options in a text (Martin and White 2005). In other words, stance can be seen as "the constraints of the configurations of appraisal that characterise such type of texts" (Hood 2012: 55) and the specific choices of appraisal resources are referred to as evaluation. That is, appraisal is a system of evaluative meaning, and stance is actualised by different configurations of evaluative resources.

In order to investigate stance instantiation, this chapter applies the attitudinal resources in the appraisal system. The appraisal system is composed of three categories: attitude, engagement and graduation. In this chapter, the attitude category is found to be more relevant to the investigation in question. According to Martin and White (2005), attitude is concerned with "our feelings, including emotional reactions, judgments of behaviour and evaluation of things" (p. 35). It consists of three sub-categories: affect, judgement and appreciation. Affect deals with "registering positive and negative feelings: do we feel happy or sad, confident or anxious, interested or bored?" which includes "un/happiness, in/security and dis/satisfaction" (Martin and White 2005: 42, 49); judgement "deals with attitudes towards behaviour, which we admire or criticise, praise of condemn", which can be divided into "social esteem" and "social sanction" (Martin and White 2005: 42, 52); and appreciation "involves evaluations of semiotic and natural phenomena, according to the way in which they are valued or not in a given field", which contains "reaction, composition and valuation" (Martin and White 2005: 42–43, 56).

Stance is most obviously expressed by "meanings which have a largely stable attitudinal meaning across of wide range of contexts" (White 2006: 42). That is, the stance in a text is most explicitly instantiated by overt attitudinal resources such as *good* or *bad*. Nevertheless, previous works (see Martin and White 2005; White 2006, 2009) demonstrate that, in journalistic discourse, particularly in the 'broadsheet news reports', stance tends to be hidden in more implicit attitudinal meanings and "indirectly position[s] the reader to adopt a particular attitudinal orientation" (White 2009: 32). Therefore, this chapter adopts the classification of realising attitudinal resources in accordance with the explicitness of the attitudinal locutions proposed by White (2006). In Figure 9.1, attitudinal inscription is "the use of locutions which carry an attitudinal value (positive or negative assessment) which is largely fixed and stable across a wide range of contexts" (White 2006: 39) such as *brave, weak* and so forth; attitudinal token "is applied to formulations where there is no single item which, of itself and independently of its current co-text, carries a specific positive or negative value" (White 2006: 39). Moreover, attitudinal tokens are further classified into evocation and provocation. In the category of evocation, the positive or negative attitudes are triggered by means of a focus on purely informational content, such as "George W. Bush delivered his inaugural speech as the United States President who collected 537,000 fewer votes than his opponent" (Martin and White 2005: 40); while in the category of provocation, the positive or negative evaluations are activated by means of formulations in other evaluative ways such as intensification, comparison, metaphor or counter-expectation (White 2006). For example, when talking about the South China Sea arbitration, Chinese media denounced legality of the tribunal when reporting this incident by employing the headline: "Puppet tribunal in South China Sea case does not represent international law" (Xinhuanet 2016).

Frame, framing and reframing

This chapter adopts the reframing strategies concluded by Baker (2006) in narrative theory. Baker (2006: 19) regards narratives as "public and personal 'stories' that we subscribe to and that guide our behaviour". When describing the features of narrativity and how narratives work, Baker (2006) draws on opinions from scholars, such as Somers (1992, 1994, 1997) and Somers and Gibson (1994), who

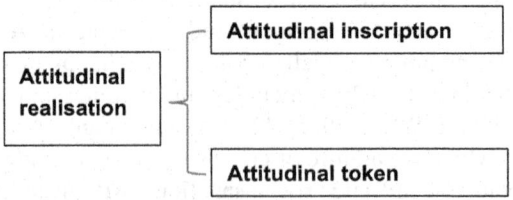

Figure 9.1 Attitudinal realisation strategies
Source: (based on White 2006)

suggest that narratives are constituted through four interdependent features: temporality, relationality, selective appropriation and causal emplotment. Temporality means that narratives are embedded in certain temporal and spatial contexts and their meaning can be derived from these contexts; relationality means that every element in a narrative depends for its interpretation on its place within the network of elements that make up the narrative; it cannot be interpreted in isolation; selective appropriation is the selection of a set of events or elements from open-ended and overlapping events that constitute the experience so as to form a coherent story; causal emplotment turns a series of propositions into an intelligible sequence about which we can make opinions (Baker 2007). Before moving on to the concept of reframing, it is appropriate to clarify the correlations among the notions of frame, framing and reframing.

Frame is defined as, in terms of news discourse, "persistent patterns of cognition, interpretation, and presentation, of selection, emphasis and exclusion by which symbol handlers routinely organize discourse" (Gitlin 2003: 7). Framing, by contrast, is the active sense of frame "as deliberate, discursive moves designed to anticipate and guide others' interpretation of and attitudes towards a set of events" (Baker 2007: 156). Framing is considered to be a strategy to realise different narrative configurations. It can construct different frames via which people "present a movement or a particular position within a certain perspective" (Baker 2006: 106). In terms of news discourse in this study, framing can be seen as representing the realities in news stories by adopting different linguistic mechanisms, particularly evaluative resources, to manifest certain stance in news reports. Bell (1991) and Boyd-Barrett (2007) find that news stories have undergone a further framing process before being disseminated to different target readers. In this additional process, specific methods involve cutting, adding, rearranging and so on (Bell 1991). This resembles the process of news translation in which the news narratives are selected, edited or rewritten. Therefore, news translation is regarded as a kind of reframing in which translators and interpreters resort to various strategies to renegotiate the narrative features in order to "strengthen or undermine particular aspects of the narratives they mediate, explicitly or implicitly" to "produce a politically charged narrative in the target context" (Baker 2006: 105).

Baker (2006) summarises five types of (re)framing strategies: ambiguity, the selective appropriation of textual material, and the labelling, temporal and spatial framing and repositioning of participants. It has been found that the first three strategies, namely ambiguity, selective appropriation and labelling, are more relevant to the present study. Ambiguity is a strategy to frame a set of events and actions in different ways to promote the competing narratives. Selective appropriation of textual material refers to the omission and addition of textual material to "suppress, accentuate or elaborate particular aspects of a narrative encoded in the source text or utterance, or aspects of the larger narrative(s) in which it is embedded" (Baker 2006: 114). Framing by labelling is a discursive process involving the use of "a lexical item, term or phrase to identify a person, place, group, event or other key element in a narrative" (Baker 2006: 122).

The (re)framing strategies of narrative theory have been applied by various scholars in the research on news translation. Valdeón (2008) studies the selective appropriation of themes and texts by BBC's online service for its Spanish readers and reveals the accentuated Anglophone-centred worldview of BBC by ignoring the events happened in Spanish-speaking world. Harding (2011, 2012) utilises these to carry out research on the translation and the circulation of competing narratives from the wars in Chechnya and finds that the Russian narratives in the terrorist attack are narrowed down in the English translation of news. Pan (2012) deals with the stance and mediation in translating sensitive news discourse on events that happened in China in 2008 by integrating narrative theory and appraisal theory. Cheng (2013) discusses how translators deconstruct the ironic narratives in news translation from English to Chinese and suggests the news translator should "rationally" deconstruct the Western-centred narratives and inform the target readers about Self and Other as well as avoid the use of narratives of extreme nationalism.

In summary, appraisal theory enables detailed analysis of the evaluative resources used to realise stances and attitudes in news reports and helps to find out what kinds of evaluative resources are changed in the translated versions; narrative theory provides a useful tool to describe the strategies used in news translation and to explore how the value-laden news discourses are reframed. Although many scholars have investigated news discourse and translation either from the appraisal perspective (such as Zhang 2013; Munday 2015) or by following the narrative theory (such as Valdeón 2014; Wu 2018), few of them combine these two analytical approaches (Pan 2012), let alone the domain of Chinese-English news translation. Therefore, this chapter attempts to fill this research gap by combining these two theoretical approaches and investigating the stance re-instantiation in Chinese-English news translation.

Data and methodology

The data collected for this study are news reports and their translations on the two most representative incidents in the South China Sea dispute, namely the Huangyan Island standoff between China and the Philippines and the South China Sea arbitration unilaterally initiated by the Philippine government. This chapter opts for the conflicts between China and the Philippines in the overall South China Sea dispute because the contentions between these two parties on the sovereignty of islands and waters have been the core events in this geopolitical dispute in recent years.

Both Chinese and English versions of news are collected from Xinhuanet, a website run by Xinhua News Agency, China's national news outlet. Apart from the Chinese-language version, Xinhuanet also provides news in English and other languages for different target readerships. Both Chinese and English editions provide search engines, which facilitates data collection. As the Huangyan Island standoff broke out on 10 April 2012 and triggered Philippines' unilateral initiation of the South China Sea arbitration, the periods of the news data range from 10 April 2012, the day the standoff broke out, to 31 December 2016. The dataset consists of the news reports and their English translation by Xinhuanet. In this dataset, there are 91 pairs of news narratives, accounting for 82,432 Chinese characters and 39,356 English words.

In terms of the analytical method, there are three major procedures, which are listed here:

Step 1: The evaluative resources in the Chinese and English versions of news reports are identified and quantified. To be more specific, the evaluation resources of attitudinal realisations (attitudinal inscription/token), value positions (positive/negative) and appraised target (China) will be identified and calculated with the research tool of *NVivo 11*;

Step 2: Based on the evaluative resources identified in the previous step, this stage focuses on investigating how the translated version is produced via different framing strategies and how the deviations operate in instantiating news stance via translation. There are three sub-steps:

a Identify the reframing strategies, namely labelling, ambiguity and selective appropriation, used in the deviation of attitudinal resources.
b In each reframing strategy, the deviations will be further classified according to the deviation patterns (inscription to token/token to inscription), their respective value positions and appraised targets.
c Based on the previous sub-steps, detailed analysis will be carried out to demonstrate how the attitudinal resources with different value positions, appraised targets and deviation patterns are reframed with different strategies.

Step 3: The relations between the discourse and socio-cultural practice will be explored. The discussion at this stage aims to explain the possible reasons behind the deviation of attitudes in news translation.

In this study, *NVivo11* is utilised to facilitate the analysis of the data in accordance with the deviation parameters. Following are major steps of using *NVivo11* to conduct the analysis: First, an e-project is established to store the news reports collected for the current study in the container. Second, tree nodes are created by referring to the attitudinal types, attitudinal realisation and value positions in Chinese and English versions, as well as deviation parameters before coding any linguistic resource. For instance, with regard to attitudinal resources, nodes named affect, judgement and appreciation in both Chinese and English are created. The same step goes with the deviation parameters by creating tree nodes that are named as reframing strategies such as labelling, ambiguity and selective appropriation and the evaluative deviations in each strategy. Third, the attitudinal resources are coded into correspondent nodes and then further coded into the nodes created in terms of the deviation parameters. Forth, the function of matrix query can be adopted to discover the correlations between different nodes. For example, with this function, the cases of the linguistic resources with co-existing codes can be displayed. Last, the results of the query can be output into software like Microsoft Excel to generate visual figures and tables.

Results and case analysis

The general quantitative result is shown in Figure 9.2. In positive resources, the selective appropriation is the most frequently used strategy, with 57 cases; ambiguity framing (26 cases) is the second most frequently used strategy, followed by labelling framing with 16 instances. Following the similar trend in positive narrative elements, most of the negative ones are translated by using selective appropriation strategy (18 cases); ambiguity strategy is often used, which has six instances; no instance of labelling deviation is found in the dataset. The following subsections will demonstrate the attitudinal deviation patterns in different reframing strategies: first selective appropriation, then ambiguity framing and finally framing by labelling.

Selective appropriation

Figure 9.3 shows that omitting positive inscription is the most frequently found (25 instances), followed by the pattern of omitting positive token (15 cases). The addition of positive inscription is also a significant part in the deviation patterns, with 10 instances, and adding positive token is less found less often in the data, appearing seven times. Compared to the calculation results of the positive attitude, those in negative evaluation are considerably fewer, with only 15 cases in total. Therefore, we will mainly focus on the positive attitudinal deviation patterns.

The deviation pattern of omitting attitudinal inscription is most frequently found in the selective appropriation of negative attitudinal resources, and the anti-China parties are the major appraised targets in this deviation pattern, for instance:

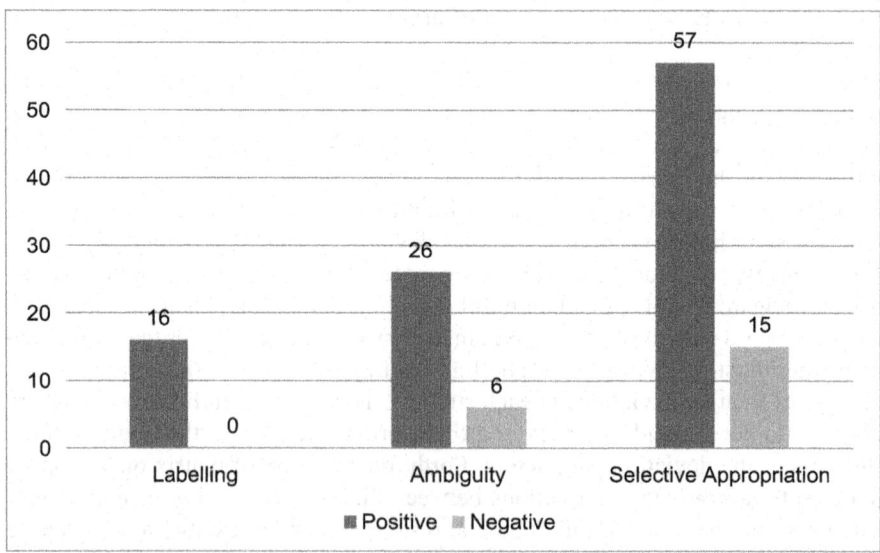

Figure 9.2 Reframing strategies in different value positions

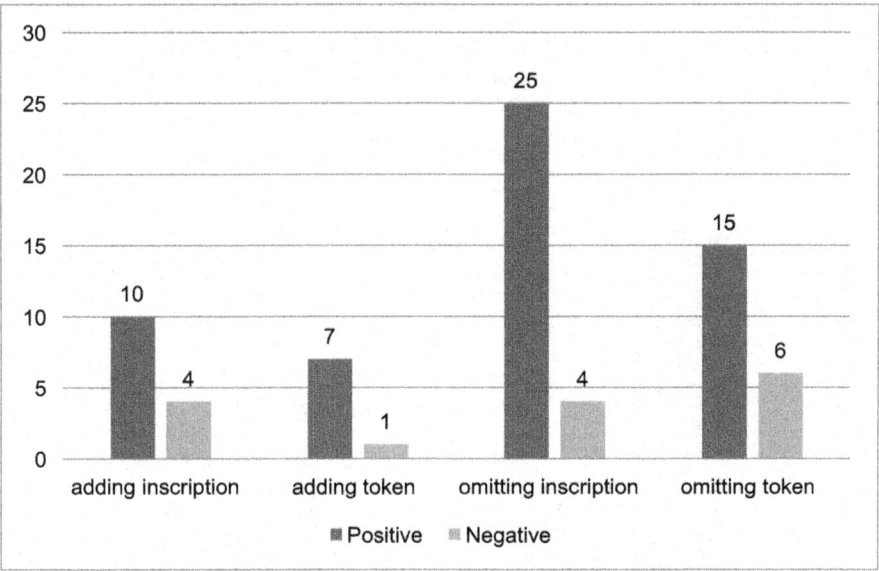

Figure 9.3 Deviation patterns of attitude towards China

Example 1 (Table 9.1)

> Chinese version: 我国***最先进*** 渔政船抵达黄岩岛海域巡航执法
> (新华网, 2012–04–20)

> Literal translation: Our country's ***most advanced*** fishery administration ship reaches Huangyan Island to patrol and enforce laws
> (Xinhuanet, 2012–04–20)

> English version: Chinese patrol ship reaches Huangyan Island after dispute
> (Xinhuanet, 2012–04–20)

Example 1 is chosen from the headline of a news report on a Chinese fishery administration ship's confrontation with the Philippine naval vessels which were besieging Chinese fishermen. The evaluative item listed in the table is the positive attitudinal inscription towards the Chinese fishery administration ship. The positive evaluative item describing the Chinese fishery administration ship as "最先进 (most advanced)" frames the perspective that Chinese government paid special attention to the safety of Chinese citizens besieged by the Philippine naval vessels and sent the best ship to rescue them, which therefore extends an appreciative stance to the Chinese government.

In the English version, however, the positive attitudinal inscription "最先进 (most advanced)" is omitted. The obliteration of the positive attitudinal inscription may filter the misleading impression that China, as one of the world's great

178 *Binjian Qin*

Table 9.1 Omission of positive attitudinal inscriptions

Chinese version	Literal translation	English version
最先进	most advanced	omitted

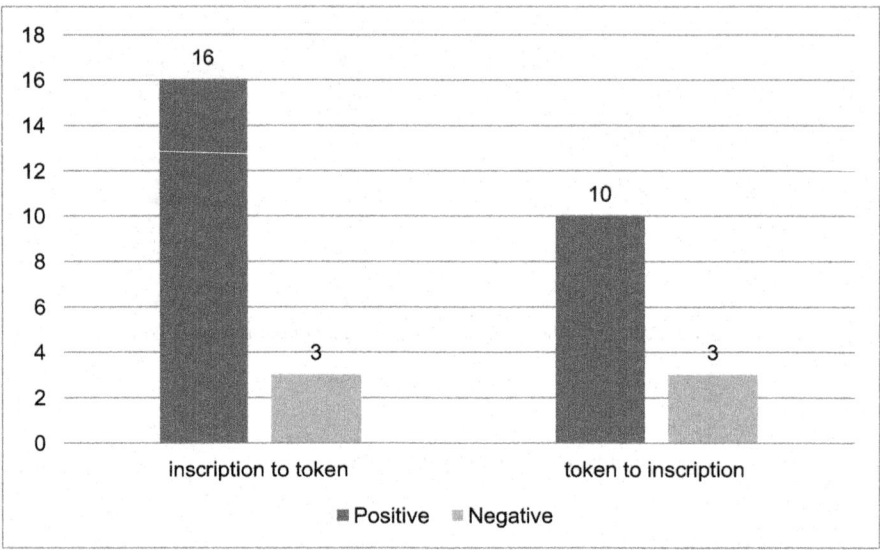

Figure 9.4 Attitudinal deviation patterns in ambiguity

powers, is bullying small neighbouring countries such as the Philippines. In this way, the supportive stance to Chinese government remains, and on the other hand, the Chinese government is depicted in a less aggressive colour.

Ambiguity deviation in reframing news

This subsection will explore the attitudinal deviation patterns in an ambiguous reframing strategy which, as mentioned earlier, represents a set of events or actions by different means. Figure 9.4 shows changing positive inscription into a token is the major pattern, with 16 instances. Turning positive tokens into an inscription also takes a significant part, with 10 instances. Compared to the positive attitude, the negative one plays a much less significant role in the statistics, with only 6 cases in total. In the following, further steps will be taken in the quantification results by analysing the example of the most statistically prominent data.

Example 2 (Table 9.2)

> Chinese version: 中国外交部发言人１１日**明确指出**，菲律宾试图在黄岩岛海域进行所谓"执法"的行为是对中国主权的侵犯，敦促菲方不要再制造事端。

(新华网, 2012–04–12)

Table 9.2 Ambiguity deviation of changing positive attitudinal inscription to token

Chinese version	Literal translation	English version
明确指出	clearly pointed out	said

> Literal translation: Chinese Foreign Ministry spokesman **clearly pointed out** that the so-called law-enforcement actions attempted by the Philippines in the waters off Huangyan Island were an infringement of China's sovereignty, and the spokesman also urged the Philippine side to stop making new incidents.
> (Xinhuanet, 2012–4–12)

> English version: Chinese Foreign Ministry spokesman Liu Weimin **said** at a regular press briefing on Wednesday that the so-called law-enforcement actions by the Philippines in the waters off Huangyan Island was an infringement of China's sovereignty. Liu also urged the Philippines to stop making new trouble and avoid actions that could complicate and aggravate the situation.
> (Xinhuanet, 2012–04–12)

Example 2 is retrieved from a news report on China's reaction on the Philippine navy's besiegement of Chinese fishermen off the waters near Huangyan Island. In the Chinese version, the term "明确指出 (clearly pointed out)" is a positive attitudinal inscription extending the Chinese government's firm and explicit position to safeguard the safety of Chinese citizens and territorial integrity, implying that China would not stand by if the Philippines attempted to do any harm to Chinese people or Chinese territory. In the English version, the term "明确指出 (clearly pointed out)" is rendered as the more neutral word "said". Compared to the Chinese version, the English one is more factual, while it still conveys positive assessment because it can be seen as reporting that China was extending its opposing voice against the Philippine's action in order to protect its national interests.

Labelling deviation in reframing news

This subsection will investigate the attitudinal deviation pattern in the labelling strategy. As presented in Figure 9.5, compared to the negative attitudinal resources, the positive ones are more frequently rendered. There are 12 instances of turning attitudinal inscription into attitudinal tokens and four cases of changing tokens to inscriptions. The calculation also shows that there is no instance of deviating negative attitudinal resources. In the following, we will advance the analysis by illustrating a detailed case investigation.

Example 3 (Table 9.3)

> Chinese version: 中国捍卫国家领土主权和海洋权益的决心**坚定不移**。中国维护国际法治及《联合国海洋法公约》完整性、权威性的态度**坚定不移**。
> （新华网，2016–05–06）

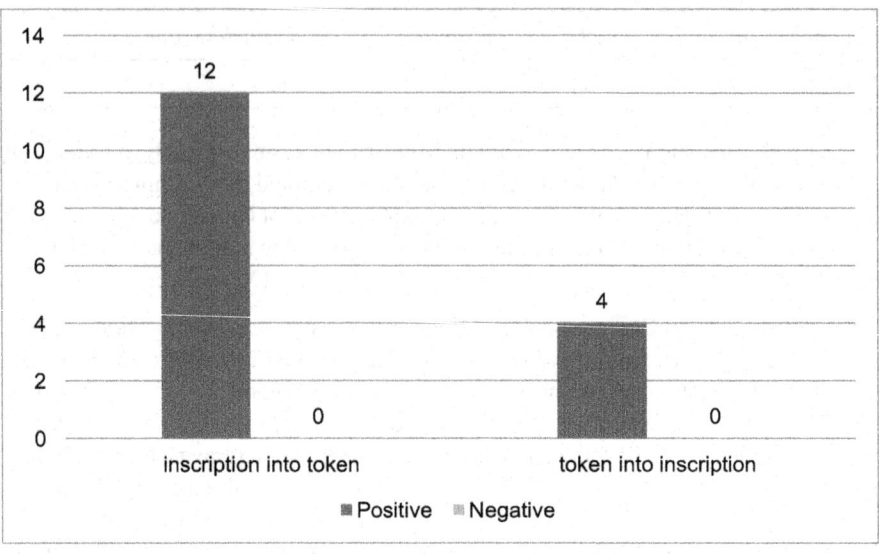

Figure 9.5 Attitudinal deviation patterns in labelling

> Literal translation: News background: China's determination to safeguard territorial sovereignty and maritime rights is *firm and unshakable*. China's attitude to safeguard international rule of law and maintain the integrity and authority of the UN Convention of the Law of the Sea (UNCLOS) is *firm and unshakable*.
> (Xinhuanet, 2016–05–06)

> English version: Backgrounder: China *is determined* to safeguard territorial sovereignty and maritime rights, said the spokesperson. China *will also uphold* the international rule of law and maintain the integrity and authority of the UN Convention of the Law of the Sea (UNCLOS), he said.
> (Xinhuanet, 2016–05–06)

Example 3 is excerpted from a news report on the Chinese government's reaction on the International Tribunal's attempt to force China to accept the verdict of South China Sea arbitration. In the news, the spokesman of Chinese government has indicated that China will not accept the unfavourable verdict. In the Chinese version, China's determination to resist the verdict is labelled as "坚定不移 (firm and unshakable)", a positive attitudinal inscription that explicitly extends China's unswerving position to safeguard its national interests and instantiates a positive stance towards the Chinese government. In addition, the spokesman also uses the term, "坚定不移 (firm and unshakable)" to describe China's attitude to safeguard the international order and the UNCLOS, a significant consensus agreed by the global

Table 9.3 Labelling deviation of changing positive attitudinal inscriptions to tokens

Chinese version	Literal translation	English version
坚定不移	firm and unshakable	is determined
坚定不移	firm and unshakable	will also uphold

community. The two instances of "坚定不移 (firm and unshakable)" construct a parallel and repetition structure that strengthens China's attitude and stance.

In the English version, however, "坚定不移 (firm and unshakable)" is relabelled as "is determined", a positive attitudinal token whose supporting evaluative meaning can be triggered from readers, and the positive attitude can be enhanced by the content of the whole piece of news. The second "坚定不移 (firm and unshakable)" is relabelled into "will also uphold", a positive attitudinal token whose evaluative meaning is implied through the co-text in the news report. In general, the English version is a more informative one whose positive evaluative effect can be triggered via the co-text which illustrates Chinese government's determination. Compared to the Chinese version, the English version instantiates supporting stance in a more blurred way.

Discussion: possible causes for stance re-instantiation

This section will discuss the possible factors that may cause the stance mediation in translating Chinese news into English. In this stage, we have summarised three categories of possible causes: different target readerships, Xinhuanet's institutional protocol and the wider socio-cultural beliefs of China's peaceful rise.

Different target readerships

For Chinese media, one of the major principles of reporting China-related news to the global audience is "broadening the exchange and promoting understanding" (He 2009: 136), and this principle cannot be followed without taking the target readership into consideration. By doing so, news media have to be aware of that there are differences between reporting to the domestic and international audience. In Xinhuanet, the Chinese version of news tends to use politically emotional expressions such as the repeated "坚定不移 (firm and unshakable)" in Example 3 to extend the positive stance towards the Chinese government in the South China Sea dispute.

However, such politically emotional expressions may be seen as a sign of China's international propaganda. The Western readers, especially those in the Anglophone world, obtain their knowledge about China in the narratives produced by America's major media, which tend to demonise China as a threat to the world (He 2009). The frequent use of such phrases may intensify this bias and impede the reception of international target readers to the news because such subjective and emotional expressions may override the objectivity of the news report, which is valued by them (He 2009: 147). Therefore, the translator in Xinhuanet tends to omit such expressions in the English version to, on the one hand, filter the negative evaluation of the anti-China side and, on the other hand, accommodate the reading preference of the international target readers and dissolve their negative stereotype towards China.

Institutional protocols: Xinhuanet as mouthpiece

It has been shown in the previous sections that in Xinhuanet, China is dominantly described in a positive light in both Chinese and English versions. This may be accounted for by the orientation of Chinese media. It has been acknowledged that the major news agencies in China, such as Xinhua News Agency, are mouthpieces of the Chinese Communist Party (CCP) and the Chinese central government (Li 2003). The main function of Xinhua News Agency is to accurately and timely publish the important policies of the CCP and the Chinese central government. Xinhua News Agency sets the standard tone in releasing the major news in China so as to prevent unnecessary speculation and rumours (Xinhua News Research Institute 1990). That is, Xinhuanet, which is affiliated with the Xinhua News Agency, has to stay in line with the CCP and Chinese central government and "establish China's positive national image in the international community" (He 2009: 276). The mouthpiece orientation of Xinhuanet can possibly explain the tendency in which the China-related narrative elements, including other countries and organisations that take a position of approval towards China, are mostly framed and reframed in a positive tone. Example 2 is a case in point. Although China's tough position is scaled down by changing "明确指出(clearly pointed out)" into "said", a factual description verb, China is still depicted in a positive tone because China's attitude to the Huangyan Island standoff is unequivocal: the Philippines should stop their action in South China Sea. That is, despite the Chinese government's stated willingness to solve the dispute via negotiation, it will not concede the sovereignty.

Socio-cultural beliefs: the peaceful rise of China

In recent years, the Chinese government has gradually adopted the strategy of "striving for achievements" to replace the strategy of "keeping low profile" in the foreign policy domain (Yan 2014: 153; Qin 2014: 286). This is identified in the Chinese government's policy on the South China Sea dispute. From 2009, the Chinese government started to prioritise maritime security, and the strategy taken by the Chinese government has been a shift from "passive defence (setting aside disputes, concession and initiation of joint development) to a more active one of safeguarding and consolidating maritime rights and interests (Yin 2017: 59). While this kind of change is not absolute and the strategic continuity still exists, the Chinese government still attaches great importance to bilateral cooperation and the overall situation in the South China Sea region (ibid). Chinese President Xi Jinping also emphasised the relationship between "greater good and self-benefits" in international relations (Xinhuanet 2013). Therefore, China is on the one hand firmly safeguarding the maritime rights and interests and on the other hand seeking the cooperation and harmony in the South China Sea region. This social ideological factor may play a role in the stance re-instantiation of the news reframed by Xinhuanet. Take Example 1 as a case. The Chinese version shows Chinese government's determination to safeguard the maritime sovereignty by sending the "最先进 (most advanced)" patrol ships to Huangyan Island area, where the Philippine navy captured Chinese fishermen. While in the English text such description of the patrol ship is omitted, this also represents the stance that the Chinese government still pursues harmony and cooperation in the region.

Conclusion

This chapter has investigated the issue of how China is framed and reframed in the in the news reports and their English translations in South China Sea dispute by Xinhuanet. Both quantitative and qualitative analysis demonstrates that the Chinese versions of news reports generally hold a positive stance towards China. With such a stance, China is framed as the more powerful side in the dispute which holds a tough position and makes no promise. However, although the English versions reframe China as the positive side in the dispute, the positivity is usually blurred or toned down by filtering China's overwhelming strength and implying China's willingness to solve the dispute thorough negotiation. Such deviations can be explained from three possible aspects: different target readerships, the institutional protocol of Xinhuanet as a mouthpiece of Chinese Communist Party and the Chinese central government, and the socio-cultural belief that China is seen as a peacefully rising country which pursues regional harmony and stability.

References

Baker, M. (2006) *Translation and Conflict: A Narrative Account*, London and New York: Routledge.
Baker, M. (2007) 'Reframing conflict in translation', *Social Semiotics* 17(2): 151–169.
Bell, A. (1991) *The Language of News Media*, Oxford: Blackwell.
Biber, D. and Finegan, E. (1988) 'Adverbial stance types in English', *Discourse Processes* 11(1): 1–34.
Boyd-Barrett, O. (2007) 'Alternative reframing of mainstream media frames', in *Media on the Move: Global Flow and Contra-Flow*. D. K. Thussu (ed.), London: Routledge. pp. 201–220.
Caldas-Coulthard, C. R. (2003) 'Cross-cultural representation of "otherness" in media discourse', in *Critical Discourse Analysis*. G. Wilss and R. Wodak (eds.), London, UK: Palgrave Macmillan. pp. 272–296.
Chafe, W. (1986) 'Evidentiality in English conversation and academic writing', in *Evidentiality: The Linguistic Coding of Epistemology*. W. Chafe and J. Nichols (eds.), Norwood, NJ: Ablex Publishing Corporation. pp. 261–272.
Cheng, Wei 程维 (2013). '"再叙事"视阈下的英汉新闻编译' (On the English-Chinese News Translation from a "re-narration" perspective), 中国翻译 (*Chinese Translators Journal*) (5): 100–104.

Gitlin, T. (2003) *The Whole World Is Watching: Mass Media in the Making & Unmaking of the New Left*, Berkeley: University of California Press.

Grey, B. and Biber, D. (2012) 'Current concepts of stance', in *Stance and Voice in Written Academic Genres*. K. Hyland and C. S. Guinda (eds.), Houndmills, UK: Palgrave Macmillan. pp. 15–33.

Harding, S. A. (2011) 'Translation and the circulation of competing narratives from the wars in chechnya: a case study from the 2004 Beslan hostage disaster', *Meta: Journal des traducteurs* 56(1): 42–62.

Harding, S. A. (2012) 'Making a difference? Independent online media translations of the 2004 beslan hostage disaster', *Translator Studies in Intercultural Communication* 18(2): 339–361.

He, Guoping 何国平 (2009) 中国对外报道思想研究 (*Policy Study on Reporting China for Global Audience*), Beijing: Communication University of China Press.

Hood, S. (2012) 'Voice and stance as APPRAISAL: Persuading and positioning in research writing across intellectual fields', in *Stance and Voice in Written Academic Genres*. K. Hyland and C. S. Guinda (eds.), Houndmills: Palgrave Macmillan. pp. 51–68.

Hunston, S. and Thompson, G. (2000) 'Evaluation: An introduction', in *Evaluation in Text: Authorial Stance and the Construction of Discourse*. S. Hunston and G. Thompson (eds.), London: Oxford University Press. pp. 1–28.

Hyland, K. (1998) *Hedging in Scientific Research Articles*, Amsterdam: John Benjamins.

Kang, J. H. (2007) 'Recontextualization of news discourse', *The Translator* 13(2): 219–242.

Li, Liangrong 李良荣 (2003) '论中国新闻媒体的双轨制 – 再论中国新闻媒体的双重性' (On the dual-track system of Chinese News Media: A revisit on the duality of Chinese News Media), 现代传播 (*Modern Communication Journal of Beijing Broadcasting Institute*) (4): 1–4.

Macken-Horarik, M. and Isaac, A. (2014) 'Appraising appraisal', in *Evaluation in Context*. G. Thompson and L. Alba-Juez (eds.), Amsterdam and Philadelphia: John Benjamins. pp. 67–92.

Martin, J. R. (2000) 'Beyond exchange: Appraisal systems in English', in *Evaluation in Text: Authorial Stance and the Construction of Discourse*. S. Hunston and G. Thompson (eds.), London: Oxford University Press. pp. 142–175.

Martin, J. R. and White, P. R. R. (2005) *The Language of Evaluation: Appraisal in English*. Hampshire: Palgrave Macmillan.

Munday, J. (2015) 'Engagement and graduation resources as markers of translator/interpreter positioning', *Target* 27(3): 406–421.

Ochs, E. and Schieffelin, B. (1989) 'Language has a heart', *Text* (9): 7–25.

Pan, L. (2012) *Stance Mediation in News Translation: A Case Study of Sensitive Discourse on China 2008*. Unpublished Doctoral Thesis, University of Macau, Macao.

Qin, Y. (2014) 'Continuity through change: Background knowledge and China's international strategy', *The Chinese Journal of International Politics* 7(3): 285–314.

Somers, M. (1992) 'Narrativity, narrative identity, and social action: Rethinking English working-class formation', *Social Science History* 16(4): 591–630.

Somers, M. (1994) 'The narrative construction of identity: A relational and network approach', *Theory and Society* 23(5): 605–649.

Somers, M. (1997) 'Deconstructing and reconstructing class formation theory: Narrativity, relational analysis, and social theory', in *Reworking Class*. J. R. Hall (ed.), Ithaca, NY: Cornell University Press. pp. 73–105.

Somers, M. and Gibson, G. (1994) 'Reclaiming the epistemological "other": Narrative and the social constitution of identity', in *Social Theory and the Politics of Identity*. C. Calhoun (ed.), Oxford and Cambridge: Blackwell. pp. 37–99.

Valdeón, R. A. (2008) 'Anomalous news translation: Selective appropriation of themes and texts in the internet', *Babel* 54(4): 299–326.

Valdeón, R. A. (2014) 'From adaptation to appropriation: Framing the world through news translation', *Linguaculture* (1): 51–62.

White, P. R. R. (2006) 'Evaluative semantics and ideological positioning in journalistic discourse', in *Mediating Ideology in Text and Image: Ten Critical Studies*. I. Lassen, J. Strunck and T. Vestergaard (eds.), Amsterdam: John Benjamins. pp. 37–67.

White, P. R. R. (2009) 'Media power and the rhetorical potential of the "hard news" report: Attitudinal mechanisms in journalistic discourse', *Käännösteoria, ammattikielet ja monikielisyys. VAKKI: n julkaisut* (36): 30–49.

Wu, X. (2018) 'Framing, reframing and the transformation of stance in news translation: A case study of the translation of news on the China-Japan dispute', *Language and Intercultural Communication* 18(2): 257–274.

Xinhuanet 新华网 (2013) '习近平：让命运共同体意识在周边国家落地生根' (Xi Jinping: Let the concept of community of shared future accepted by neighbouring countries). Available at: www.xinhuanet.com/2013-10/25/c_117878944.htm (Accessed: 16 May, 2018).

Xinhuanet 新华网 (2016) Commentary: Puppet tribunal in S. China Sea case does not represent int'l law. Available at: http://news.xinhuanet.com/english/2016-07/14/c_135513603.htm (Accessed: 16 May, 2018)

Xinhua News Research Institute 新华社新闻研究所 (1990) '中共中央宣传部、中央对外宣传小组、新华通讯社关于改进新闻报导若干问题的意见' (Opinions on improving news reporting by Publicity Department of the CPC Central Committee, External publicity group of the CPC central committee and Xinhua News Agency), in 新闻工作文献选编 (*Selected Documents on News*), Beijing: Xinhua Publishing House.

Yan, X. (2014) 'From keeping a low profile to striving for achievement', *The Chinese Journal of International Politics* 7(2): 153–184.

Yin Jiwu 尹继武 (2017) '中国南海安全战略思维:内涵、演变与建构' (China's strategic thinking toward South China sea: Concept, evolution and construction), 国际安全研究 (*Journal of International Security Studies*) 35(4): 33–61.

Zhang, M. (2013) 'Stance and mediation in transediting news headlines as paratexts', *Perspectives* 21(3): 396–411.

Part IV
Analysis of multimodal and intersemiotic discourse in translation

10 Translations of public notices in Macao

A multimodal perspective

Xi Chen

Introduction

A public notice is a notice shown publicly, offering "directing, prompting, restricting or compelling" (Lü 2004: 38) information. It may be released by governments or other institutions to give information about what they are planning to do and what they have done, to call for the public's attention to things and surroundings, or to call for people's cooperation. Due to the limited physical space, the language in public notices is generally terse and succinct, conveying essential information in concise phrases, expressions or sentences (Leong 2010: 111).

Public notices can be divided into single-modal and multimodal ones. The former only contains the language, while the latter usually includes language and image. Nowadays, the emergence of more and more image information in different media has marked the coming of the image era. Multimodal public notices have been widely used in our daily life, and the types and varieties of multimodal public notices have increased a lot. In multimodal public notices, language and image are no longer independent semiotic systems but cooperate to achieve meaning potentials.

The studies on public notices have emerged in China in the 21st century, and there has been a research upsurge since 2007 (Liu 2016: 53). At present, plenty of studies have been conducted on public notices used in various situations, such as tourist attractions, transportation vehicles, business places, medical institutions, judicial organisations, etc. Meanwhile, a large number of studies have been conducted on public notice translation from different perspectives (Dai and Lü 2005; Leong 2010; Li 2016; Liu 2016; Lü 2017; Wang and Yang 2018), such as functionalist theories, pragmatics, semiotics, cognitive theories, intercultural communication, communication studies, etc. However, most of the studies on public notice translation only focus at the linguistic level, and few pieces of research consider the multimodal resources and their functions in public notices.

Bilingual public notices are extensively used in many Chinese-speaking regions, such as the Chinese Mainland, Hong Kong and Macao. Macao was a colony of Portugal for more than 300 years. With its unique historical background, the Macao Special Administrative Region (SAR) is now an international tourist city where Eastern and Western cultures blend and develop with each other. Moreover, the historical factors have influenced language usage in Macao. At present, the official languages of Macao SAR are Chinese and Portuguese, and English is also widely used on many occasions, especially in business and tourism activities. Most of the public notices in Macao are bilingual (Chinese and English/Portuguese) or trilingual (Chinese, English, Portuguese). However, this does not mean that most Macao people are bilingual or trilingual. The choice of language in public notices actually reflects different target audiences of different public notices, which may include Macao residents, Hong Kong residents, residents from the Chinese mainland, foreign immigrants and overseas visitors. Therefore, in this study, the different texts in public notices are regarded as translated versions rather than bilingual or trilingual productions. In Macao, the communications between different lingual and cultural backgrounds lead to the frequent use of bilingual or trilingual public notices, which provides resourceful research data for the study of public notice translation. Nevertheless, few studies have been conducted specifically on the translation of public notices in Macao (Zhang 2006; Chen 2014). Up till now, there are only a few studies on the translation of public notices in Macao from a multimodal perspective.

This chapter aims to investigate the translated public notices in Macao from a multimodal perspective. With a self-built database of multimodal public notices in Macao, based on the visual social semiotics (Kress and van Leeuwen 1996, 2001, 2006), it first analyzes the verbal realization of appellative function in the translation of public notices and then examines the visual realization of interpersonal function in the images of public notices. Finally, it discusses the multimodal cooperation between language and image in public notices.

Related literature

As the investigation of translated public notices in Macao includes both the textual analysis of words and the visual analysis of images in multimodal public notices, the related theories and concepts of text typology and visual social semiotics are briefly reviewed in this section to lay the theoretical foundation for further analysis. The text typology assists in the employing of suitable translation methods to translate different kinds of public notices, while visual social semiotics can be used as a helpful tool to interpret images in multimodal public notices.

Text typology and public notice translation

Katharina Reiss (1971/2000) introduces a new model of translation criticism based on the functional relationship between source text (ST) and target text (TT) and points out that judgment should be based on the function of the text in the process of translation evaluation. Based on Karl Bühler's (1934/1965) categorization of three functions of language, Reiss puts forward a text typology for translators, dividing the texts into three types – informative, expressive and operative – and states that specific translation methods should be chosen according to different text types and the function of the texts determine the translation methods. The links between the three text functions and their translation methods are shown in Table 10.1:

Table 10.1 Reiss's Text Topology and Links to Translation Methods (Munday 2016: 115)

Text type	Informative	Expressive	Operative
Language function	Informative (representing objects and facts)	Expressive (expressive sender's attitude)	Appellative (making an appeal to text receiver)
Language dimension	Logical	Aesthetic	Dialogic
Text focus	Content-focused	Form-focused	Appellative-focused
TT should	Transmit referential content	Transmit aesthetic form	Elicit desired response
Translation method	'Plain prose', explicitation as required	'Identifying' method, adopt perspective of ST author	'Adaptive', equivalent effect

Reiss (1977/1989: 109) states that "the transmission of the predominant function of the ST is the determining factor by which the TT is judged" and suggests that specific translation methods should be used according to text type (Reiss 1977: 20). Public notice, whose major function is to call for the desired response in the TT receiver, belongs to the operative text, and such appellative-focused text should be translated with "adaptive" method so as to achieve equivalent effects among target readers.

In addition, in the Chinese-speaking regions, it is found that a certain number of Chinese public notices contain some poetic forms, such as parallelism and rhyme, which makes them readable and easy to remember. The poetic public notices, which are operative texts with poetic forms, are also widely used in Macao (Chen 2014). How to translate these poetic public notices then becomes a problem for consideration.

Christiane Nord's (1997/2005) further classification of the text functions might help to solve this problem. In her translation-oriented model of text functions, there are four main functions in translation: referential function, expressive function, appellative function and phatic function. "Directed at the receivers' sensitivity or disposition to act, the appellative function ('conative' in Jakobson's terminology) is designed to induce them to respond in a particular way" (Nord [1997/2005] 2001: 42). The appellative function is further divided into three types: direct appellative function, indirect appellative function and poetic appellative function. Poetic appellative function "operates in poetic language appealing to the readers' aesthetic sensitivity" (Nord [1997/2005] 2001: 43). With aesthetic poetic form and appellative function, poetic public notice fits the category of poetic appellative function, and its translation should follow the principles of appellative function. The appellative function is receiver-oriented. "While the source text normally appeals to a source-culture reader's susceptibility and experience, the appellative function of a translation is bound to have a different target." (ibid) It means that the appellative function will not work without the receiver's cooperation. In this study, many multimodal public notices also contain poetic texts, so the realization of their appellative function in translation will be a crucial point.

Visual social semiotics

Multimodality can be applied to the investigation of semiotic resources and intersemiotic relations. In the research on multimodality, three main approaches are adopted: social semiotic multimodal analysis (Kress and van Leeuwen 2001; van Leeuwen 2005), systemic functional grammar (SFG) multimodal discourse analysis (O'Toole 1994; O'Halloran 2004, 2005) and multimodal interactional analysis (Scollon and Scollon 2003; Norris 2004).

The foundations of social semiotic multimodal analysis are Halliday's theories of social semiotics and SFG (Halliday 1978, 1994). According to SFG, the language can express three types of meanings: to represent our experiences of the world (ideational metafunction), to establish social relationships (interpersonal metafunction) and to form coherent communication of the whole (textual metafunction).

Based on Halliday's social semiotics and SFG, Kress and van Leeuwen (1996, 2006) propose a "grammar of visual design" and offer a descriptive framework to describe the visual realization of semiotic meanings in the image. Kress and van Leeuwen's visual social semiotics provides a powerful tool for the research of visual images, and different studies have been conducted on different types of visual images (Chen 2018; Jewitt and Oyama 2001; Harrison 2003; Lirola 2006; Moya Guijarro and Pinar Sanz 2008; Moya Guijarro 2011, 2014; Painter et al. 2013). In fact, visual social semiotics is also applicable for the multimodal analysis of public notices, but few studies have been conducted in this field.

There are four major elements in Kress and van Leeuwen's model: representational resources that visually represent the material world, interactive resources that visually interpret the interaction between the viewer and what is represented in a visual design, modality judgements that concern the reliability or credibility of visual messages and compositional arrangements that relate to the information value and visual emphasis of visual resources. Through this descriptive framework, Kress and van Leeuwen manage to analyze how these semiotic resources in the image are used to represent the world in a specific method, to express interpersonal meaning and to achieve coherence.

According to visual social semiotics, ideational metafunction is "the ability of semiotic systems to represent objects and their relations in a world outside the representational system or in the semiotic system of a culture" (Kress and van Leeuwen 1996: 47). The semiotic resources to realize the ideational function include represented participants, processes and circumstances. In visual images, the interpersonal metafunction is to establish relations between (1) the represented participants (in the visual image); (2) the viewer and the represented participant; (3) the producers (artists/designers) of the image and viewer (Kress and van Leeuwen 1996: 114). Kress and van Leeuwen (2006) further distinguish four types of systems associated with the interpersonal function: image act and gaze, social distance and intimacy and horizontal angle and involvement, as well as vertical angle and power. The four systems work interpersonally, as they demonstrate how what is represented in a visual composition interacts with the viewer (Matthiessen 2007: 20). The textual metafunction in visual images integrates the representational and interactive meaning of the image to each other. The semiotic resources to realize the textual metafunction include information value, salience and framing. In this study, the multimodal analysis will focus on the interpersonal metafunction of the visual images.

Data and methodology

Data

The data of this chapter are from a self-built database of multimodal public notices in Macao. In Macao, the electronic copies of most public notices released by the government can be found on the website of the government. The author collected the electronic copies of the published multimodal public notices from the Macao SAR website and built up a small database. The content of multimodal public notices in this study can be divided into verbal and visual materials. Verbal materials refer to the texts in public notices. Owing to the author's language competence, only the English and Chinese texts will be examined in this study, and the Portuguese texts are not included in the textual analysis. For the convenience of the study, the Chinese texts in these public notices are regarded as the STs and English texts as the TTs. Based on the examination of different public notices in Macao, it is found that the multimodal public notices can be mainly divided into two kinds in terms of the representation contents: multimodal public notices with photograph images and multimodal public notices with cartoon images.

Analytical framework

This study first conducts a text analysis of the verbal materials to examine the verbal realization of appellative function in the translation of public notices. Second, it makes a multimodal analysis of the visual materials to investigate the visual realization of interpersonal function in the images of public notices. Finally, it discusses the interaction between the verbal and the visual in public notices.

Moreover, an analytical framework of interpersonal function and its realization in the image is proposed based on the visual social semiotics (Kress and van Leeuwen 1996, 2001, 2006). The interpersonal function in the image of multimodal public notice is examined through the following features: (1) image act and gaze, (2) social distance and intimacy, (3) horizontal angle and involvement, (4) vertical angle and power and (5) modality.

In the system of image act and gaze, Kress and van Leeuwen (2006: 117–119) differentiate between (i) images from which something is required of the viewer or particular actions/behaviours (demands) are carried out through visual contact (gaze, gesture, etc.) and (ii) images that only present information (offers) that

Table 10.2 Interpersonal function and its realization in the image

Features	Meaning system	Realization
Image act and gaze	Demand	Gaze at the viewer
	Offer	Absence of gaze
Social distance and intimacy	Intimate/personal	Close-up shots
	Social	Medium shots
	Public	Long shots
Horizontal angle and involvement	Involvement	Frontal angle
	Detachment	Oblique angle
Vertical angle and power	Viewer power	High angle
	Equality	Eye-level angle
	Representation power	Low angle
Modality	High modality	High degrees of accuracy or abstraction
	Low modality	Low degrees of accuracy or abstraction

can be either acknowledged or contradicted but lack human or quasi-human eye-contact between the represented participants (RPs) and the viewer. "The choice between 'demand' and 'offer' is not only used to suggest different relations with different 'others', to make viewers engage with some and remain detached from others; it can also characterize pictorial genres. (Kress and van Leeuwen 2006: 120). For instance, the "demand" picture is preferred in television news reading and the posed magazine photograph because these contexts require a sense of connection between the viewers and the authority figures, celebrities and role models they depict. The "offer" picture is preferred in the feature film, television drama and scientific illustration.

Within the system of social distance and intimacy, the degree of intimacy is established between the depicted RPs and the viewer and is determined by how close the RPs appear to the viewer in an image (Kress and van Leeuwen 2006: 124–129). The different scales are related to the choice between the close-up, medium shot and long shot, which result in different feelings of intimacy. For example, close-ups only show the head and shoulders of the subject; "the object is shown as if the viewer is engaged with it" (Kress and van Leeuwen 2006: 127–128). Thus, close-ups create intimacy between the RP and the viewer, as the image is in close proximity to the viewer. In long shots, the object is portrayed full length and "there is an invisible barrier between the viewer and the object" (ibid), while in medium shots, "the object is shown in full but without much space around it" (ibid), which produces an intermediate level of intimacy or distance.

In terms of the visual mode attitude, it is established by the way in which the RPs and the viewer are located from the horizontal and vertical perspectives (Kress and van Leeuwen 2006: 129–143). On the one hand, the horizontal angle encodes whether the viewer is involved with the RPs or not. It includes two types of angles: the frontal angle that creates emotional involvement with the RPs, and the oblique angle that produces detachment from the RPs. On the other hand, the vertical angle relates to different power relationships, depending on the upward or downward point of view along a vertical axis when the RPs are viewed. Two types of power relationships are created by the vertical angle: the relationship between the RPs and the viewer and the relationship between the RPs within an image (Kress and van Leeuwen 2006: 140–143). For instance, if an RP is seen from a high angle, the viewer has power over the RP; if an RP is seen from a low angle, the RP has power over the viewer; if the image is at eye level, then the RP and the viewer have equal power status and there is no power difference involved. (Kress and van Leeuwen 2006: 140) For the relationship between the RPs within an image, similar power relationships are also produced. Two RPs in a visual composition may be depicted face to face, indicating an equal power relationship between them; however, if one RP is looking up or down at the other, different power relationships are presented between them. (Painter et al. 2013: 17)

In addition, images also possess different degrees of modality relating to different levels of credibility. In the system of modality, with no specific choices with clear boundaries, there are only different degrees of credibility ranging from minimalist to naturalist representations. Besides, "modality judgements are social, dependent on what is considered real in the social group for which the representation is primarily intended" (Kress and van Leeuwen 2006: 156). Kress and van Leeuwen (2006: 165–166) also differentiate between four coding orientations of visual modality: scientific modality, sensory modality, abstract modality and naturalistic modality. At present, naturalistic modality remains the dominant one in our society. To achieve naturalistic modality, the more an image resembles what it is in the real world, the higher the degree of modality it has (ibid). One example of images with high naturalistic modality is the photograph. Compared with other modes of representations, such as drawings, illustrations and paintings, the photograph "is the one most easily assimilated into the discourses of knowledge and truth for it is thought to be an unmediated simulacrum, a copy of what we considered the 'real'" (Shapiro 1988: 124). Therefore, if a photograph is used in the image, its high modality will help the viewer regard the depicted RPs as "what is" rather than "what might be". Furthermore, the resemblance of an image to RPs in the real world is determined by eight modality markers in the image: colour saturation, colour differentiation, colour modulation, contextualization, representation, depth, illumination and brightness (Kress and van Leeuwen 2006: 160–162).

Case analysis

In this section, three cases are selected to analyze different kinds of multimodal public notices in Macao. The first case deals with public notices with different multimodal representations. On some occasions, a series of public notices are released by the same institution in different years. These public notices include the same information or have the same function, but they are shown through different multimodal representations, which is an interesting phenomenon and worth investigating. The second case relates to multimodal public notices with photograph images, while the third case analyzes multimodal public notices with cartoon images.

Public notices with different multimodal representations

Figures 10.1–10.3 are a series of public notices with the same content but different multimodal representations. They were all released by the Macao Public Security Police from 2011 to 2014 with the same function of reminding people to beware of pickpockets. In these three public notices, the key information in the verbal material includes two parts: remind people to beware of pickpockets and provide the aid information (emergency hotline: 999 and call for help: 28573333). The key information in the ST is "提防小手". In Chinese, "小手" is another name of "扒手", which refers to the thieves or pickpockets in crowded places, such as buses, railway stations, shopping malls, downtown markets, etc. In the TTs of these three public notices, the ST is translated into a direct appellative sentence, "Beware of pickpockets", which successfully transmits the information with the appellative function of public notices.

Figure 10.1 is a public notice released by the Macao Public Security Police in 2011. In the most prominent position of the image, there is a cartoon figure of a young girl. The girl is shown through the middle shot and frontal angle, producing close social distance and a sense of involvement with the viewer. In the upper side of Figure 10.1, the appellative text "提防小手" is printed in red, with the Chinese character "小" highlighted in white and green, which just accords with the pictorial detail of a close-up of a thief's hand highlighted with the orange frames. In addition, a part of the Chinese character "手" is cartoonized into a thief's hand, in accordance with "小手" in the text. The background of public notices and the apparel of the cartoon image consist of colours with high colour saturation, such as light orange, blue and green. Also, the emergency hotline and call for help information are both highlighted with conspicuous colour contrast, which attracts viewers' attention to such significant information. With the high degree of colour saturation and colour differentiation, the visual material in the public notice is eye-catching. However, compared to the photograph with naturalistic modality, a cartoon produces a lower degree of modality. Thus the visual material is not closely related to real life, with the low degree of conceptualization and representation in the image. To sum up, the appellative function of the verbal materials matches with the interpersonal function of the visual materials in this multimodal public notice.

Figure 10.2 is a public notice released by the Macao Public Security Police in 2012. The background of Figure 10.2 is in blue and grey with a low degree of colour saturation, so a sense of solemn visual perception is produced. The appellative text "提防小手" is printed in a prominent red colour on the left vertical side of the image, and there is a framed close-up photograph of a thief stealing from other's pocket in the upper right corner of the image, in accordance with the verbal text "小手" highlighted in white. The information about the emergency

Figure 10.1 PN released in 2011

Figure 10.2 PN released in 2012

Figure 10.3 PN released in 2014

Table 10.3 Interpersonal function and its realization in Figures 10.2–10.4

Features	Figure 1		Figure 2		Figure 3	
	Meaning system	Realization	Meaning system	Realization	Meaning system	Realization
Image act and gaze	Offer	Absence of gaze	Offer	Absence of gaze	Offer	Absence of gaze
Social distance and intimacy	Close social distance	Middle shot (almost the whole figure)	Public distance, Close personal distance	Long shot (torsos of several people), Close-up shot	Far personal distance	Middle shot (from waist up)
Horizontal angle and involvement	Involvement	Frontal angle	Detachment	Oblique angle	Detachment	Oblique angle
Vertical angle and power	Equality	Eye-level angle	Equality	Eye-level angle	Equality	Eye-level angle
Modality	Medium	Cartoon, colour saturation, colour differentiation, conceptualization, representation	High	Photograph, colour saturation, colour differentiation, conceptualization, representation	High	Photograph+Cartoon, colour saturation, colour differentiation, conceptualization, representation

hotline and call for help is also highlighted with conspicuous colour contrast, which accords with the appellative function in the verbal texts. In addition, it is noteworthy that, compared with Figure 10.1 with cartoon images, there are several photograph images of thieves and pickpockets in the middle of Figure 10.2, but the colour saturation of these photograph images is reduced, which represents a sense of black-and-white photograph to the viewer. These photograph images of thieves and pickpockets are shown in a long shot, creating the public distance with the viewer. Moreover, on the right side of this public notice, seven small close-up photographs are added, providing information on different strategies to beware of pickpockets, such as cover your bag with hands when you are sitting, put your backpack in front when you are taking a bus, etc. A photograph, by the nature of its technology, can produce a much stronger sense of reality than illustrations and paintings. The producer of the image usually uses the photograph's high naturalistic modality to represent the truth or reality for the viewer. Therefore, the use of photographs in this public notice effectively increases the higher modality in the image and contributes to the realization of high interpersonal function in the visual materials.

Figure 10.3 is a public notice released by the Macao Public Security Police in 2014. Different from the previous two ones, this public notice consists of both photograph and cartoon images. This public notice is divided into two parts by frames: the upper side of cartoon images and the lower side of photographs. In the upper side, the verbal text "提防小手" is highlighted in yellow, and above the verbal text, there is a cartoon image of a policeman arresting a pickpocket. The background of the upper side is full of cartoon buildings, but their architectural style and the flag of Macao SAR reveal that it is set in Macao. According to the modality marker "contextualization", the fully articulated and detailed background can increase the high naturalistic modality in the image. (Kress and van Leeuwen 2006: 161) So although these are only cartoon images, the detailed Macanese background helps to increase the naturalistic modality and produces a sense of involvement with the viewer. In the lower side, four photographs of pickpocketing scenes are arranged within frames. The colour saturation in the backgrounds of these photos is reduced, which decreases the degree of conceptualization and representation in the photos, and meanwhile highlights the image of the main RP in these photos: a pickpocket. Moreover, more verbal information is added in these four photograph scenes, which reminds people to beware of pickpockets in catering venues, shops, buses and busy districts, especially when it is crowded. In addition, the bilingual texts "提防小手" are added in each photo, repeatedly strengthen the appellative function of verbal materials. However, in this public notice, the emergency hotline and call for help information are not highlighted with eye-catching colour nor enlarged font, but are placed in the bottom right corner. Therefore, we can find the different emphasis of the interpersonal function in this public notice. In this public notice, more emphasis is paid on transmitting information on being wary of pickpockets in different places.

Multimodal public notices with photograph images

In Macao, quite a large proportion of multimodal public notices include photograph images. Figure 10.4 was released by the Macao Judiciary Police to publicize the basic information about the Police-Community Relations Research Group as well as Reception and Complaints Centre and also call for suggestions, complaints, crime reports and enquiries from the public. In the verbal materials, the ST includes four poetic expressions "警民互动，始于你我；高效执法，基于合作". With Chinese four-character structure and rhyme, the ST is readable and memorable. In the TT, the poetic form is totally abandoned with the key information transmitted. It is translated into simple sentences "Community-police partnership. The key to effective and efficient law enforcement", which realizes the appellative function of public notices to some extent.

As to the visual materials, two photographs are arranged in the middle of Figure 10.4, showing the working status of the Police-Community Relations Research Group and Reception and Complaints Centre. The RPs in the two photos do not have eye contact with the viewer and are presented in a long shot, which forms a greater personal distance between the RPs and the viewer. As the RPs are shown through an oblique angle, a sense of detachment is produced, and the interpersonal function is weakened as well. Also, around the two photographs, there are four highlighted keywords: suggestion, complaint, crime report and enquiry. These four words are in line with the RPs' action in the image and meanwhile emphasize the four main functions of these two organizations. In addition, in the lower half part of Figure 10.4, detailed information about these two organizations are listed, such as the phone number, fax and e-mail of these two organizations, etc. To sum up, in contrast with the public notices that focus on the warnings, the interpersonal function in the image of this public notice focuses on the transmission of information, which meanwhile accords with the appellative function in the verbal text.

Figure 10.5 was released by the Macao Public Security Police to call on the public to report crimes. The key information in the verbal materials is highlighted in green and yellow in the upper part of Figure 10.5. The ST is two poetic expressions "举报不法，全民有责" with Chinese four-character structure and rhyme. In the TT, without the poetic form, it is translated into a simple sentence "Every citizen is responsible for reporting crimes", but it realizes the appellative function of public notices to a great extent. In the visual materials, three photographs constitute a circle in the middle of Figure 10.5, showing different situations of citizens reporting crimes to the police. With the RPs' gaze at the viewer and the gesture of pointing to the viewer, as well as the use of frontal angle, the "demand" and "involvement" meanings are produced, which also strengthens the interpersonal function in the image. Moreover, the RPs' actions in the image are in accordance with the information of "举报" (report) in the verbal text. Meanwhile, the emergency hotline number 999 appears to be especially salient in the red and larger font, attracting viewers' attention to take action and report crimes through phones. In short, in these two multimodal public notices with photograph images, the interpersonal function is well realized in the image and conforms to the appellative function in the verbal text.

Translations of public notices in Macao 203

Figure 10.4 PN on information publicity

Figure 10.5 PN on reporting crimes

Multimodal public notices with cartoon images

Apart from multimodal public notices with photographs, there are also a large number of public notices use cartoon images to transmit information. Figure 10.6 is a public notice released by the Macao Public Security Police to remind people not to drive while under the influence of alcohol or drugs. The verbal text "毒驾醉驾，代价庞大" is highlighted by the colour contrast of white font and the blue-green background. With the Chinese four-character structure, rhyme and alliteration, the ST "毒驾醉驾，代价庞大" is poetic and easy to remember. In the TT, it is translated into "Drug Driving. Drunk Driving. Can Ruin your life." The parallel structure, alliteration and rhyme in the TT tactfully preserve the poetic form and readability in the ST, and in the meantime it also achieves the appellative function of public notices.

In the visual materials, the low degree of colour saturation and colour differentiation of cold colours convey a sense of gloom. Two large cartoon figures almost take up the whole image. One cartoon figure holds a little car in one hand, and throws pills into his mouth with the other hand, which accords with the information "drug driving"; while the other cartoon figure holds a little car in one hand, and pours liquor into his mouth with the other hand, which is in line with the information "drunk driving". These two cartoon RPs are illustrated in black with exaggerated facial expressions and gestures, providing an eye-catching visual effect to viewers. Moreover, below the two RPs, there are some scenes of car accidents and casualties, which echo the serious consequences of driving while under the influence of alcohol or drugs in the verbal text. Meanwhile, the use of cartoon images to represent these accidents and casualties may reduce the real bloodiness produced by photographs. In brief, the visual expression of exaggerated cartoon images helps to realize the interpersonal function and attract the viewer's attention to this public notice. The verbal and the visual interact with and supplement each other, aiming to achieve both the appellative and interpersonal functions in the public notice.

In China, during the Chinese Lunar New Year and Spring Festival, the elders usually give the youths some red pockets with money inside as a symbol of blessing and luckiness. This is an old Chinese tradition, and each person will thus receive plenty of red pockets during the Spring Festival. In recent years, more and more people have begun to recycle the used red pockets to contribute to environmental protection. Figure 10.7 is released by Macao Environmental Protection Bureau to call on people to recycle red pockets, which is a public notice with typical Chinese cultural background. In the verbal materials, the ST "回收利是封好 Easy" is printed in the middle of the image, with "利是封" highlighted in the yellow and larger font. "利是封" (Li Shi Feng) is another name of "红包" (red pocket) in Cantonese-speaking regions. In the TT, the ST is directly translated into a simple sentence "Recycling the red pockets is very easy". In addition, along the upper right side of this public notice, there are three supplemented texts "少用新，多重用，唔好嘥", showing the detailed tips on red pocket recycling. "唔好嘥" (Wu Hao Sai) is a Cantonese expression with the meaning of "do not waste". As

Figure 10.6 PN on driving while under the influence of alcohol or drugs

Figure 10.7 PN on red pocket recycle

the majority of citizens in Macao speak Cantonese, such expression in the public notice adds a strong sense of Cantonese culture and makes the public notice easier to be accepted by the people of Macao. In the TT, the three tips "少用新，多重用，唔好嘥" are translated into concise phrases "Use less new. More reusing. No waste.", which is appellative and memorable.

In the visual materials, the red background accords with the colour of red pockets. Its high degree of colour saturation helps to the realization of the interpersonal function of public notice and may make the viewer easily think of the red pockets and Chinese Lunar New Year at first sight. In addition, in the salient position of the image, several cartoon RPs are illustrated, such as plum blossoms, a cartoon God of Wealth, a cartoon fortune tree and a cartoon dancing lion. These RPs are all closely related to the Cantonese cultural traditions during the Chinese Lunar New Year. Such use of cartoon images in this public notice may attract the attention not only of adults but also of children to take action in red pocket recycle.

Discussion

Through the analyses of these multimodal public notices, it is found that different multimodal representations have different impacts on the realization of interpersonal functions in public notices.

In terms of the first case, three public notices are released by the same institution in different years, with the same appellative information but different multimodal representations. These different multimodal representations may reveal the change of emphasis in the public notices in different years. Figure 10.1 directly calls on viewers to beware of pickpockets and call the emergency hotline or help number when necessary. With the use of supplemental photograph images providing information on different strategies to beware of pickpockets, Figure 10.2 warns viewers to take action against pickpockets by themselves, such as covering bags with hands when sitting, putting the backpack in front when taking a bus or subway, etc. With four photograph scenes of pickpockets on different occasions, Figure 10.3 especially reminds people to beware of pickpockets in crowded catering venues, shops, buses and busy districts. The different multimodal representations in Figure 10.1–10.3 demonstrate the different emphases in these public notices in different years and, meanwhile, reflect some diachronic changes in the design and reception of multimodal public notices in Macao. The public notices in Macao used to be relatively simple and direct, but in recent years, they tend to make progress in designing and structuring as well as the realization of appellative and interpersonal functions. Especially currently, more complicated multimodal representations, such as comics, are adopted in the multimodal public notices in Macao, which has great potential of transmitting information through story narratives and might be more attractive for viewers.

As to the second case, owing to the high naturalistic modality of photographs, the use of photographs effectively increases the higher modality in the image and contributes to the realization of high interpersonal function in the multimodal public notices. The public notices seem to be more persuasive and convincing in this way. Especially when the RPs in the photographs have eye-contact or indicative action with the viewer, it will further increase the demand and involvement meanings of the public notice, which makes the viewer easier to take action according to the public notices.

In addition, the analysis of the third case provides some reflections on the use of cartoon images in multimodal public notices. On the one hand, when the information in public notices involves some sensitive topics or contents, such as the one about driving while intoxicated in Figure 10.6, the use of cartoon images, whose naturalistic modality is lower than photographs, might reduce the discomfort of viewers towards such inappropriate behaviours in reality. On the other hand, when the target viewers of some public notices include not only adults but also children (e.g. Figure 10.7), the use of cartoon images in such multimodal public notices may increase the interpersonal function and make children easier to take action and cooperate.

Conclusion

This study investigates the translated public notices in Macao from a multimodal perspective. The case studies mainly examine three kinds of multimodal public notices in Macao: multimodal public notices with photograph images, with cartoon images and with a mixture of photograph and cartoon images. The research results show that text and image cooperate with and complement each other to achieve the appellative function in the translation of public notices, as well as the interpersonal function in the images of public notices. Meanwhile, the research results also provide implications for the study and practice of multimodal public notices. In the Chinese mainland, multimodal public notices present many deficiencies, such as non-standard language, translation problems, inappropriate multimodal representations, etc. (Liu 2016) In contrast, in general, multimodal public notices in Macao have done better jobs in translation and multimodal representation, which might offer some references for the design and translation of public notices in the Chinese mainland. Moreover, visual social semiotics may be a useful tool to help public notice illustrators and designers achieve better multimodal representations in public notices. Considering the use of different shots, angles and modality markers to represent the RPs in the image, it will assist them in the realization of interpersonal function in public notices and thus in achieving better reception among viewers. Public notices in Macao are resourceful and worth investigating. It is hoped that future research can explore the public notices in Macao from more inspirational perspectives.

References

Bühler, K. (1934/1965) *Sprachtheorie: Die Darstellungsfunktion der Sprache*, Stuttgart: Custav Fischer.

Chen, Xi 陈曦 (2014) '功能决定形式－探讨港澳地区诗型公示语英译' (English translation of Chinese poetic-style public notices in Hong Kong and Macau from the functionalist perspective), 上海翻译 (*Shanghai Journal of Translators*) (2): 18–23.

Chen, Xi (2018) 'Representing culture through languages and images: A multimodal approach to translations of the Chinese classic Mulan', *Perspectives: Studies in Translatology* (2): 214–231.

Dai, Zongxian and Lü, Hefa 戴宗显、吕和发 (2005) 'On C-E translation of public signs' (公示语汉英翻译研究 – 以2012年奥运会主办城市伦敦为例), 中国翻译 (*Chinese Translators Journal*) 26(6): 38–42.

Halliday, M. A. K. (1978) *Language as Social Semiotic: The Social Interpretation of Language and Meaning*, London: Arnold.

Halliday, M. A. K. (1994). *An Introduction to Functional Grammar* (2nd ed.), London: Edward Arnold.

Harrison, C. (2003) 'Visual social semiotics: Understanding how still images make meaning', *Technical Communication* 50(1): 46–60.

Jewitt, C. and Oyama, R. (2001) 'Visual meaning: A social semiotic approach', in *Handbook of Visual Analysis*. T. van Leeuwen and C. Jewitt (eds.), London: Sage. pp. 134–156.

Kress, G. and van Leeuwen, T. (1996) *Reading Images: The Grammar of Visual Design*, London: Routledge.

Kress, G. and van Leeuwen, T. (2001) *Multimodal Discourse: The Modes and Media of Contemporary Communication*, London: Arnold.

Kress, G. and van Leeuwen, T. (2006) *Reading Images: The Grammar of Visual Design* (2nd ed.), London: Routledge.

Leong, K. (2010) 'Chinese-English translation of public signs for tourism', *Journal of Specialized Translation* (13): 111–122.

Li, Zhengya 李正亚 (2016) 'A study on English intertextual translation of public signs' (公示语互文性英译研究), 中国科技翻译 (*Chinese Science & Technology Translators Journal*) 29(1): 32–35.

Lirola, M. M. (2006) 'A systemic functional analysis of two multimodal covers', *Revista Alicantina de Estudios Ingleses* 19: 249–260.

Liu, Lifen 刘丽芬 (2016) 'Development and prospect of public sign study in China' (中国公示语研究进展与前瞻), 中国外语 (*Foreign Languages in China*) 13(6): 53–58.

Lü, Hefa 吕和发 (2004) 'Translating expressions on public signs from Chinese into English' (公示语的汉英翻译), 中国科技翻译 (*Chinese Science & Technology Translators Journal*) 17(1): 38–40.

Lü, Hefa 吕和发 (2017) 'Remarks on C-E sign translation in the "new normal" context' (Chinglish 之火可以燎原? – 谈"新常态"语境下的公示语翻译研究), 上海翻译 (*Shanghai Journal of Translators*) (4): 80–87.

Matthiessen, C. (2007) 'The multimodal page: A systemic functional exploration', in *New Directions in the Analysis of Multimodal Discourse*. T. Royce and W. Bowcher (eds.), London: Lawrence Erlbaum. pp. 1–62.

Moya Guijarro, A. Jesús (2011) 'Engaging readers through language and pictures: A case study', *Journal of Pragmatics* 43(12): 2982–2991.

Moya Guijarro, A. Jesús (2014) *A Multimodal Analysis of Picture Books for Children: A Systemic Functional Approach*, Sheffield: Equinox.

Moya Guijarro, A. Jesús and Pinar Sanz, M. Jesús (2008) 'Compositional, interpersonal and representational meanings in a children's narrrative: A multimodal discourse analysis', *Journal of Pragmatics* 40(9): 1601–1619.

Munday, J. (2016) *Introducing Translation Studies: Theories and Applications* (4th ed.), London: Routledge.

Nord, C. (1988/1991) *Text Analysis in Translation: Theory, Methodology, and Didactic Application of a Model for Translation-Oriented Text Analysis*, Amsterdam: Rodopi. (Beijing: Foreign Language Teaching and Research Press, 2006).

Nord, C. (1997/2005) *Translating as a Purposeful Activity: Functionalist Approaches Explained*, Manchester: St Jerome. (Shanghai: Shanghai Foreign Language Education Press, 2001).

Norris, S. (2004) *Analyzing Multimodal Interaction: A Methodological Framework*, London: Routledge.

O'Halloran, K. L. (2004) *Multimodal Discourse Analysis: Systemic Functional Perspective*, London: Continuum.

O'Halloran, K. L. (2005) *Mathematical Discourse: Language, Symbolism and Visual Images*, London: Continuum.

O'Toole, M. (1994) *The Language of Displayed Art*, London: Leicester University Press.

Painter, C., Martin, J. R. and Unsworth, L. (2013) *Reading Visual Narratives: Image Analysis of Children's Picture Books*, London: Equinox.

Reiss, K. (1971/2000) *Translation Criticism: The Potentials and Limitations: Categories and Criteria for Translation Quality Assessment*, Manchester: St Jerome Publishing.

Reiss, K. (1977/1989) 'Text types, translation types and translation assessment' (Translated by A. Chesterman), in *Readings in Translation Theory*. A. Chesterman (ed.), Helsinki: Oy Finn Lectura Ab. pp. 105–115.

Scollon, R. and Scollon, S. W. (2003) *Discourse in Place: Language in the Material World*, London: Routledge.

Shapiro, M. J. (1988) *The Politics of Representation: Practices in Biography, Photography, and Policy Analysis*, Madison, WI: University of Wisconsin Press.

Van Leeuwen, T. (2005) *Introducing Social Semiotics*, London: Routledge.

Wang, Chang and Yang, Yuchen 王畅、杨玉晨 (2018) 'Translation of public signs in TCM hospitals from the perspective of eco-translatology' (生态翻译学视角下TCM医院公示语英译研究), 上海翻译 (*Shanghai Journal of Translators*) (4): 39–43.

Zhang, Meifang 张美芳 (2006) 'Investigating the languages and translations of public notices in Macao' (澳门公共牌示语言及其翻译研究), 上海翻译 (*Shanghai Journal of Translators*) (1): 29–34.

11 Representation of identity in dubbed Italian versions of multicultural sitcoms
An SFL perspective

Marina Manfredi

Introduction

In contemporary multiethnic and multicultural societies, the media play a key role in constructing cultural diversity; audiovisual (AV) products seem to be one of the most powerful means of representing characters' identity, through different codes, including the verbal one. To this purpose, both films and television series are increasingly 'multilingual' in the broadest sense: different standard languages and dialectal varieties are embedded in their dialogues. When it comes to cross-borders and re-contextualising language variation for viewers from different cultural contexts through a translation process, the issue becomes particularly challenging, since, as it is universally acknowledged, audiovisual translation (AVT) imposes textual restrictions.

After the mainstream Hollywood production traditionally based on monolingualism (Bleichenbacher 2008: 21), cinema has not been restricted to a single language, giving rise to contemporary trends of mixed-race representation (Beltrán and Fojas 2008).

In the United States, the first decade of the 21st century saw films such as *Spanglish* (Brooks 2004), about the culture clash between Mexican immigrants and Americans, and *Gran Torino* (Eastwood 2008), where characters spoke French, German, Italian and the Hmong language. Similarly, in the same decade, a comedy such as *Bend it Like Beckham* (Chadha 2002) and a cross-cultural romance set in Glasgow such as *Ae Fond Kiss* (Loach 2004) portrayed the lives of Pakistani immigrants in the United Kingdom who often employed code-switching from English to Punjabi. Apart from the world of cinema, television has shown increasing interest in offering a 'multilingual' vision of society. At the end of the 1980s, the animated television series *The Simpsons* featured an Indian character, Apu Nahasapeemapetilon, the owner of Kwik-E-Mart's store in Springfield, who spoke with a marked Indian accent. Likewise, a South Asian accent is also displayed by Rajesh Koothrappali (Raj), the nerd from the series *The Big Bang Theory* (2007–2019). In more recent times, the on-demand streaming site Netflix frequently aired multilingual series where characters switch between English and Spanish, including the crime drama *Narcos* (2015–2017), about the Colombian cocaine trade, and *One Day at a Time* (2017–), a humorous sitcom whose protagonists are the Alvarezes, a Cuban-American family living in Los Angeles. In the comedy-drama *Orange is the New Black* (2013–2019), characters use both Hispanic English and African American vernacular English. Another success, first broadcast by the CW Channel, then by Netflix, is the US sitcom *Jane the Virgin* (2014–2019), an anglicised telenovela that tells the story of the Villanueva family, who were of Venezuelan origin and migrated to Florida: three generations of women switch between two languages, while the protagonist's grandmother, her *abuela*, only speaks Spanish. Very recently, Netflix aired the immigrant family comedy *Kim's Convenience* (2016–), premiered on the CBC network, which follows the lives of a Korean-Canadian family who owns a convenience store in multicultural Toronto.

In the last two decades, multiethnic sitcoms addressed to a younger audience have come to the fore, such as Disney Channel's *Lizzie McGuire* (2001–2004), a teen-sitcom whose characters are of mixed race, and ABC's *Ugly Betty* (2006–2010), whose heroine, Betty Suárez, has a Latin American background. The language(s) that characters speak reflect(s) their multicultural identity.

More recently, a relatively new subgenre has appeared, that is, multiethnic/multicultural sitcoms addressed to a 'tween-age' audience (see Manfredi 2018), given that the target market audience is represented by kids who are nearly, or have just become, teenagers. Illustrative examples are YTV's *How to Be Indie* (2009–2011) and Disney's *Jessie* (2011–2015), along with its spin-off *Bunk'D* (2015–).

The majority of television series[1] mentioned so far have been dubbed for an Italian audience. This chapter aims to explore what happens when televisual products which reflect a multicultural vision of society travel cross-culturally and are addressed to a new target audience. More specifically, the aim is to investigate whether multicultural sitcoms for tweens show a special concern for representing identity or, conversely, geographical language varieties are not invariably reproduced in the target version, as is typical of AVT and dubbing in particular (Chiaro 2009: 158).

Translating language varieties has long been recognised as one of the greatest challenges translators and adapters have to deal with. Within translation studies (TS), the issue of so-called multilingualism has been largely explored with respect to films (e.g., Heiss 2004; Dwyer 2005; Federici 2009; Zabalbeascoa and Voellmer 2014; Beseghi 2017, to name just a few). However, less attention has been paid to multilingual series and sitcoms (Ranzato 2006; Manfredi 2018; Beseghi 2019). The focus of this chapter will be on televisual products addressed to tweens, such as *How to Be Indie* (Canada, YTV, 2009–2011), *Jessie* (USA, Disney Channel, 2011–2015) and its spin-off *Bunk'D* (USA, Disney Channel 2015–), through the analysis of selected examples.

How to Be Indie, a Canadian sitcom created by V. Santamaria together with executive producers J. May and S. Bolch and produced by Heroic Film Company, premiered on the network YTV and ran for two seasons. The series was also broadcast in the UK on Disney Channel and in Australia on ABC, with dubbed versions released around the world, from Latin America to Africa and also Europe. In Italy, it was broadcast in its dubbed version, *Essere Indie* (2010–2012) and aired on DeAKids, a satellite channel for young people. The sitcom deals with the adventures of the main character, Indira Mehta, nicknamed Indie by her friends, and her family, migrants from India to Canada. The sitcom centres around the issue of cultural diversity for Indie, her family and friends.

Jessie, a United States' sitcom created by P. Eells O'Connell, was an original Disney Channel production that aired for four seasons. It was dubbed in Portuguese, for Brazil and Portugal, and Italy with the same English title. *Jessie* focuses on the adventures of the title character, an 18-year-old woman who moves from a small town in Texas to New York City with her dream of becoming an actress and finds a job as a nanny for the wealthy Ross family. She takes care of their four children, named Emma, Luke, Ravi and Zuri, the latter three adopted from the United States (Detroit, MI), India and Africa (Uganda) respectively. It was followed by its spin-off, *Bunk'D* (2015–) where three of the kids – Emma, Ravi and Zuri – go to Maine for a summer camp, which is the title of the Italian dubbed version, *Summer Camp* (2016–). The theme underlying the story is the promotion and acceptance of cultural diversity.

This chapter deals with dubbing, not only because Italy is historically a dubbing country in the world AVT's map[2] but also because audiovisual products addressed to a younger audience tend to be dubbed all over the world, even in Scandinavian countries, which are used to subtitling. In addition, while in Anglophone contexts dubbing has traditionally been linked to the idea of a non-authentic experience, this specific translation mode has been recently reassessed (Ranzato and Zanotti 2019: 2–3).

The investigation will be limited to examples concerning the verbal code, without touching upon multimodal discourse analysis. Nevertheless, given the multi-semiotic nature of AV products, aspects related to other codes will sometimes be considered.

The chapter aims to suggest that a linguistic framework for the analysis of multilingualism in AVT is needed in TS to account for the wide spectrum of language variation in a systematic way. I argue that a discourse analysis approach such as that offered by systemic functional linguistics (SFL) (Halliday 1994[3]) may best serve this purpose, as the following section seeks to show.

Theoretical framework

The concepts of 'language' and 'language variety' have long been characterised by ambiguity, both for lay people and linguists. Most of the times, a variety has been seen in relation or opposition to 'standard', thus implying a hierarchical relationship. In TS, the notion of 'multilingualism' has been applied to both interlingual and intralingual varieties. The wide range of language variation featured in AV products has been interestingly faced by Corrius Gimbert and Zabalbeascoa (2011: 117) with the concept of 'third language (L3)' (Corrius Gimbert 2005), which includes standard languages, dialects or other forms of language variation such as 'antilanguages' (Halliday 1978). I argue that even such a useful framework may be supplemented with an SFL (Halliday 1994) approach, which may help overcome some problematic issues raised when analysing the language of multiethnic/multicultural sitcoms.

As Munday and Zhang (2015: 329) point out, there has been a growing interest in the analysis of AVT from an SFL perspective (e.g., Bednarek 2010; Piazza et al. 2011; Taylor 2017), although most contributions concern subtitling (e.g., Taylor 2000; Mubenga 2010; Espindola 2012). At least to my knowledge, it has not yet been applied to dubbing and in particular to the translation of language varieties.

A first framework for the analysis of language variation was proposed by Halliday et al. (1964), who put forth a distinction between varieties according to the 'user' and the 'use' of language. Such a framework was further developed, on the linguistics side by Gregory (1967), Gregory and Carroll (1978) and Halliday and Hasan (1985) and, from a translation point of view, by Catford (1965), Gregory (1980) and Hatim and Mason (1990).

In his article about 'varieties differentiation', Gregory (1967), a major developer of SFL theory, suggested the labels 'dialectal' and 'dyatipic' varieties to categorise the "reasonably permanent" features of a language user (Gregory 1967: 184). Within the former, the scholar illustrated the sub-categories of 'idiolect, temporal, geographical, social, standard and non-standard dialect'. The situational category of a user's 'individuality' corresponds to the contextual feature of 'idiolect'. The situational categories of 'temporal, geographical and social provenances' correlate with the contextual categories of 'temporal, geographical and social dialects'. The difference between 'standard' and 'non-standard' dialect is subtler. In Gregory's view, 'standard' is not associated with any regional or social origin but simply refers to the user's "range of intelligibility" within a community, along a cline or continuum (Gregory 1967: 183).

A decade later, Gregory and Carroll (1978: 12) observed that the general public tend to consider 'dialects' as 'poor country cousins' and that the non-specialists also tend to confuse 'accent' and 'dialect'. The scholars explained that 'accent' refers to the "articulatory and acoustic features" of language, while 'dialect' is a superordinate term which comprises lexical, grammatical and phonological characteristics, including 'accent' (Gregory and Carroll 1978: 12). Therefore, a 'geographical' dialect has its recognisable 'regional accent'. Gregory and Carroll (1978: 17) remarked that, although sometimes 'social' and 'geographical' dialects intermingle, the latter usually reflects the physical space.

Describing how language varies 'according to the user' and 'according to the use', Halliday (1978: 35) put forward the distinction between 'dialect' and 'register', which was developed by Halliday and Hasan (1985: 41). User-related varieties, that is 'dialects', are linked to 'who the speaker or writer is', whereas use-related varieties, that is 'registers', are linked to 'what the speaker or writer is doing'. As Halliday and Hasan (1985: 43) pointed out, although 'dialect' and 'registers' are two different categories, there is a close relationship between them.

Catford (1965), applying such notions to translation, subdivided the dimension of 'dialect' into 'proper or geographical', temporal and social. He argued that in dialect translation the criterion to be fulfilled is "'human' or 'social' geographical", rather than "purely locational" (Catford 1965: 86–87).

Gregory (1980: 463) stated that dialects can pose translation problems. Focusing on literary texts, the scholar argued that a writer may choose to use a geographical dialect along with the 'unmarked' literary language of a given context of culture. The translator may decide to look for equivalence through a TL literary dialect, and not necessarily at the same linguistic level: in other words, a marked phonological feature may be rendered through a marked lexico-grammatical choice.

Hatim and Mason (1990) also explored the issue of language variation in relation to translation and focused on the aspect of ideological choices and implications inherent in translating geographical dialects. They argued that the most common strategies to deal with geographical varieties might cause problems (Hatim and Mason 1990: 40–41). On the one hand, normalising a geographical dialect might result in a loss in the TT; on the other hand, replacing that variety with a TL one might produce unintended effects.

In the present chapter, I use the term 'dialectal variety' and 'geographical dialect' in the Hallidayan sense, and I will consider 'a standard dialect' any variety that is understood by its speech community. Furthermore, I will take into account both 'real' and 'pseudo' geographical dialects, given that I will be dealing with fictional television products such as sitcoms, or 'kid-coms' (Manfredi 2018). In order to avoid ambiguity between the notions of 'standard' and 'non-standard' outside SFL, I will use the labels 'unmarked' and 'marked'. Finally, I will discuss examples according to three main translation strategies, that is localisation, foreignisation and neutralisation (see Taylor 2006: 39).

Analysis of dubbing into Italian

In this section, I present a selection of examples taken from the sitcoms *Jessie* and its spin-off *Bunk'D* (Disney Channel) and *How to Be Indie* (YTV), which, at different levels, manage to convey the multicultural identity of the characters.

Accents

As stated in the previous section, accent is only one of the aspects which distinguish geographical dialects, although it is one of the most visible in a ST. However, when dealing with AVT, it is a feature which is typically lost, for various practical constraints (Chiaro 2009: 158). In the sitcoms under investigation, accents typical of dialectal varieties are also neutralised.

In *How to Be Indie*, Indie's mother, father and grandfather – first- and second-generation immigrants from India – have a strong Indian English accent. In the Italian dubbed version, they invariably speak unmarked Italian, without any specific accent. On the other hand, Indira (Indie) and her friend Abigail (Abi) from the Philippines, third-generation immigrants, speak American and Canadian English, which is normalised in the TT, without conveying any geographical hint.

Similarly, in Disney's *Jessie*, while most characters speak American English in the ST and unmarked Italian in the TT, there is one character who is highly connoted for his dialectal variety: Ravi, the 10-year-old boy adopted from India, who has an Indian accent in the ST and uses contractions very rarely. In the Italian dubbed text, Ravi speaks unmarked Italian. Zuri, the 6-year-old girl adopted from Uganda, sometimes speaks with a Black English accent,[4] which is normalised in the Italian translation. Jessie, the 18-year-old nanny of the Ross children, also speaks with a Texan accent, which is not reproduced in the TT through a dialectal choice.

However, despite the use of neutralisation at the phonological level, the characters' identity is also conveyed through lexico-grammatical choices and the visual code; therefore, the translation loss is not particularly problematic, as the following section aims to show.

Lexico-grammar

Cultural traditions

Words that refer to specific socio-cultural, religious as well as culinary traditions of the source culture are often employed in the STs. In the TTs, non-translation mainly occurs, thus a strategy of foreignisation is used, which maintains the multiple identity of the characters.

For instance, in *Jessie*, the name of a typical Indian garment is featured in both the ST and the Italian dubbed version, as in:

Table 11.1 From Disney's *Jessie*, episode 1x11

Character	ST	TT	BT (Back Translation)
Ravi	Hello, good family! Who is ready to get their learn on?	*Salve, bella famiglia! Chi è pronto a imparare qualcosa?*	Hello, good family! Who is ready to learn something?
Jessie	Oh, my... What you wearing?	*Oh mio... Ma come ti sei vestito?*	Oh my... But how have you dressed up?
Ravi	It is my **sherwani**, only worn on very special occasions.	*Questo è il mio **sherwani** e lo indosso soltanto in occasioni molto importanti.*	This is my **sherwani** and I just wear it on very special occasions.

In the example in Table 11.1, the name of *sherwani* – a man's knee-length coat buttoning up to the neck – which Ravi is proud to wear on his first school day to show his origins, is also combined with the visual code. Linguistically, the referential pronoun 'it', translated into the determiner *questo* ('this'), contributes to clarifying that Ravi is talking about his bright yellow piece of Indian clothing. The following scene plays on the mispronunciation of the word, thus combining the phonological and lexico-grammatical levels.

It also occurs that non-English words are limited to the verbal code, as in the case of an expression with religious connotations related to a character's background heritage, which is found in *Jessie*:

Table 11.2 From Disney's *Jessie*, episode 1x13

Character	ST	TT	BT
Luke (as Lucas)	Hey! That's D.J. Half-Wit Master Flex to you! I'm available for birthdays, **bar mitzvahs**, and witch burnings.	*Ehi! Qui è DJ Strambo Master Flex che vi sta parlando! Disponibile per compleanni, **bar mitzvah**, roghi di streghe.*	Hey! It's Funny DJ Master Flex speaking! Available for birthdays, **bar mitzvahs**, witch burnings.

In the example in Table 11.2, Luke, the adopted son of Jewish origin from Detroit, mentions a typical religious ceremony, whose Hebrew name is also maintained in the Italian version.

How to Be Indie includes many references to typical Indian dishes, through their original Hindi names or in combination with English words. Those items are always kept in the TT, not only when in combination with the visual code but also when limited to the verbal code. For example, on the occasion of the 'Wonderful World O' Food Day' that celebrates cultural diversity, the South Asia Booth will offer special dishes such as *pani puri*, '*biryani* cones', '*tandoori* chicken' and 'onion *pakoras*', which have been translated in the TT as *pani puri, coni biryani, pollo tandoori* and *pakora di cipolla*. A culinary culture specific item is also included in the title of the same episode, "How to Have your Samosa and Eat it Too" (episode 1x02), translated as *Come ottenere il tuo samosa e mangiartelo*" [How to obtain your *samosa* and eat it], where *samosa* is a triangular envelope of pastry, stuffed with spiced vegetables or meat and fried crisp, typical of Indian cuisine.

Greetings

Interestingly, there are lexico-grammatical choices which represent both a geographical origin and a character's idiolect, and also intersect with tenor, as in the following example:

Table 11.3 From Disney's *Jessie*, episode 1x11

Character	ST	TT	BT
Ravi	Ravi K. Ross, pleased to meet you! **Cheerio**, fellow pupil!	*Ravi Ross, lieto di conoscerti!* **Cheerio**, *caro compagno di scuola!*	Ravi Ross, pleased to meet you! *Cheerio*, dear schoolmate!

In the instance offered in Table 11.3, Ravi uses a formal and polite way of greeting such as 'pleased to meet you' when he first meets a schoolmate and combines it with a farewell greeting such as 'cheerio', with a humorous effect. In the TT, the formality is conveyed and the English word is also retained, producing a foreignising effect. Although it is likely that the Italian young viewer does not understand the type of greeting, s/he will probably perceive and appreciate an idiolectal way of speaking.

Proverbs and idioms

Significantly, foreignisation does not only concern isolated lexical items but also entire structures. An interesting example is found in *Jessie*:

Table 11.4 From Disney's *Jessie*, episode 1x15

Character	ST	TT	BT
Ravi	Yes. Back in my village, we would say Bertram appears to be a few chickpeas short of a samosa.	*Al mio villaggio direbbero che è un piatto di legumi senza samosa.*	In my village [they] would say that it is a pulse dish without any *samosa*.

In the ST in Table 11.4, Ravi, the Indian boy, compares the butler, Bertram, to "a few chickpeas short of a samosa", referring to the same Indian dish mentioned earlier. However, not only is the Hindi word transferred into the TT, but also the whole clause. Whether real or invented, and presumably meaning 'strange' or 'crazy', the expression sounds culture specific and as a typical 'translation' from a different dialectal variety. The 'foreignising' effect is also maintained in the Italian version, preserving the multicultural nature of the character.

In *How to Be Indie*, a similar strategy concerns a proverb, which appears as a calque from one of the Indian languages:

Table 11.5 From *How to Be Indie/Essere Indie*, episode 1x01

Character	ST	TT	BT
Bhaba Ji	The bruisest banana is quite often the sweetest.	*La banana ammaccata spesso è la più dolce.*	The bruised banana is often the sweetest.

The scene suggests that the instance in Table 11.5 is meant not to be comprehensible, and the same effect has been maintained in the TT.

In *Jessie*, the rendering of a simile imbued with Indianness has been tackled with a similar foreignising strategy:

Table 11.6 From Disney's *Jessie*, episode 1x15

Character	ST	TT	BT
Ravi	Shield your eyes, siblings! She will make you sing **like a Malayan Night Heron**.	*Chiudete gli occhi [0]! O vi farà cantare* **come un airone notturno malese**, *fidatevi.*	Shield your eyes [0]! Or she will make you sing **like a Malayan night heron**, trust me.

In the example in Table 11.6, the TT is extremely close to the ST. The verb 'sing', used in a figurative way and meaning 'confess', has been rendered in Italian with its direct equivalent, also working idiomatically in the TL. A 'localising' translation such as 'dotty' or an omission of the geographical reference have been avoided. The comparison with 'a Malayan night heron', a medium-sized heron found in Asia, has been maintained, with a foreignising effect.

Metalanguage

English is also used as a metalanguage to talk about the characters' identity, as in:

Table 11.7 From Disney's *Jessie*, episode 1x11

Character	ST	TT	BT
Ravi	Clearly, you are not smart enough to recognize a phony Indian accent.	*Be', è ovvio che non sei abbastanza sveglio per riconoscere un vero* [0] *indiano da uno fasullo.*	Well, it is obvious that you are not smart enough to recognize a real Indian [0] from a phony one.

In the example shown in Table 11.7, Ravi comments on his own accent. Given that such an accent is not practically reproduced in the TT, the character's identity is expressed with respect to his nationality ('a real Indian') through an omission, although the global effect is essentially conveyed.

In a final example taken from *Bunk'D*, the omission is even greater:

Table 11.8 From Disney's *Bunk'D*, episode 1x01

Character	ST	TT	BT
Xander	You understood him?	*Hai capito che ha detto?*	Have you understood what he said?
Emma	Ravi panics a lot, so I picked up a little Hindi.	*Ravi va sempre nel panico, posso immaginarlo . . .*	Ravi always panics, I can imagine it . . .

In this specific case shown in Table 11.8, the reference to Hindi language is totally omitted in the TT and substituted with the comment 'I can imagine it', probably also linked to synchronisation problems, which are typical of dubbing.

Discussion

For its very nature of replacing a source language sound track with a target language one, dubbing typically involves adaptation, for at least two main reasons. Firstly, the technical constraints imposed by the channel, such as the synchronisation between the actors' voices and their lips' movement, often require semantic changes in the dubbed version. Secondly, the television industry tends to privilege globalised products for the marketplace. In the specific case of the small screen, as Steemers (2016: 54) points out, children's television is one of the most globalised AV products, and translation practices act accordingly. When it comes to language variation, the adoption of strategies of neutralisation and omission is often the norm.

TV series which feature the use of dialectal varieties certainly pose major challenges for AVT translation and dubbing in particular. On the one hand, strategies of localisation and neutralisation will eliminate crucial aspects related to cultural identity. On the other hand, preservation of language variation might lead to incomprehension and non-natural effect in dialogues.

It is important to point out that objections have been raised in the media, for example to Ravi's accent in ST *Jessie*, condemned as 'fake', 'stereotypical' and 'exaggerated' (Lakshmi 2018). This attack reflects a wider critical attitude, voiced in media studies, towards Indian accents in US film and television, which are viewed as 'racial performance' (Davé 2013). As Bednarek (2018: 76) observes, this issue has also attracted criticism from linguists, who observe how 'telecinematic discourse' contributes to constructing and perpetuating cultural stereotypes. However, when dealing with multicultural/multiethnic sitcoms for younger viewers, one should consider the different functions that language variation in AV products may fulfil. If in multilingual films the function may be 'realistic rendering', 'conflict' and 'confusion of lingua-cultural identities' (De Bonis 2014: 243), when it comes to television series it may well be an imitation of spontaneous language for the sake of realism, a resource for humorous purposes or a tool for characterisation. Starting with the assumption that the language of screen is fictional and thus based on 'fictive dialogues' (Brumme and Espunya 2012: 7), it may be argued that naturalness is not necessarily such a relevant issue when coping with dubbing of multicultural sitcoms for a younger audience. From this perspective, the most common strategies of AVT may be reinterpreted. The usual poles of 'incoherent localisation' and 'banalising neutralisation' (Ranzato 2010: 109) might be seen from a different viewpoint. Normalisation, which is typical of TV products for a younger audience, may result in homologation of cultures. Conversely, foreignisation may represent a means to preserve cultural diversity rather than defective rendering of real speech. Significantly, what sounds as non-natural in the shape of a calque (as examples in Tables 11.4, 11.5 and 11.6 demonstrated) may be considered an effective means of communication. Therefore, the much-debated issue of spoken dialogue vs. naturally occurring interaction (e.g., Pavesi 2008), which is valid for other AV products, may be overcome.

Conclusion

This chapter has dealt with multiethnic/multicultural tween-sitcoms dubbed into Italian, although its claims might also hold true for other language combinations. It aimed to show the advantages of an SFL approach for the analysis of dialectal variation in AVT and its translation.

Firstly, from a strictly linguistic point of view, such an approach helps to solve the ambiguity between the issues of 'dialect' and 'accent', which do not necessarily overlap. Consequently, neutralisation at the level of phonological aspects does not necessarily exclude the preservation of multicultural identity, which may also be expressed through lexico-grammatical choices.

Secondly, from the perspective of discourse analysis and TS, such a model is comprehensive of the whole range of linguistic variation, that is, geographical and social dialects, idiolect, standard and non-standard dialects. Although such categories sometimes happen to be related, by adopting a use-user oriented model of language variation, each of them is clearly distinguished. By employing an SFL approach, other types of dialect may also be accounted for. For example, the recreation of a youth's speech may be tackled as an example of idiolectal variation, while a character's speech which conveys class origin may be analysed as a social dialect. The latter aspect is strictly related to the close link between dialectal variation and the use-related tenor, the Hallidayan contextual variable that realises the interpersonal metafunction, determined by the relationship between and among characters.

Furthermore, the SFL notion of 'standard' and 'non-standard' dialect is particularly relevant when dealing with multicultural television products, given that it only considers intelligibility as a parameter. Therefore, diversity and otherness are also advocated from a theoretical point of view. In other words, a character who uses a geographical variety to characterise his or her identity is not necessarily viewed as 'non-standard', with respect to a supposedly 'superior' variety. Widening the horizons to include ideology and world view, an SFL approach seems to help overcome prejudices, especially when dealing with a text-type that is centred on championing cultural diversity.

Notes

1 At the time of writing, only *Kim's Convenience* has not been dubbed for Italian television or web.
2 For an overview, see Ranzato and Zanotti (2019: 1).
3 Halliday, M.A.K. (1985). *An Introduction to Functional Grammar*. London: Edward Arnold (revised 2nd edition 1994; revised 3rd edition, with C.M.I.M. Matthiessen, 2004; Halliday, M.A.K., rev. by Matthiessen, C.M.I.M., 4th edition 2014).
4 The so-called 'Black English', or African American vernacular English, which is a variety spoken by many African Americans in the United States, displays some marked phonological features, although it also involves lexico-grammatical choices.

References

Bednarek, M. (2010) *The Language of Fictional Television: Drama and Identity*, London: Continuum.
Bednarek, M. (2018) *Language and Television Series: A Linguistic Approach to TV Dialogue*, Cambridge: Cambridge University Press.
Beltrán, M. C. and Fojas, C. (eds.) (2008) *Mixed Race Hollywood*, New York: New York University Press.
Beseghi, M. (2017) *Multilingual Films in Translation: A Sociolinguistic and Intercultural Study of Diasporic Films*, Oxford: Peter Lang.
Beseghi, M. (2019) 'The representation and translation of identities in multilingual TV series: *Jane the Virgin*, a case in point', in *Multilingüismo y representación de las identidades en textos audiovisuales/Multilingualism and representation of identities in*

audiovisual texts, MonTI, Monografías de Traducción e Interpretación. M. Pérez L. de Heredia and I. Higes Andino (eds.), special issue. pp. 145–172. doi:10.6035/MonTI.2019.ne4.5 (Accessed: 3 February, 2020).

Bleichenbacher, L. (2008) *Multilingualism in the Movies: Hollywood Characters and Their Language Choices*, Tübingen: Francke.

Brumme, J. and Espunya, A. (2012) 'Background and justification: Research into fictional orality and its translation', in *The Translation of Fictive Dialogue*. J. Brumme and A. Espunya (eds.), Amsterdam and New York: Rodopi. pp. 7–31.

Catford, J. C. (1965) *A Linguistic Theory of Translation*, Oxford: Oxford University Press.

Chiaro, D. (2009) 'Issues in audiovisual translation', in *The Routledge Companion to Translation Studies*. J. Munday (ed.), London and New York: Routledge. pp. 141–165.

Corrius Gimbert, M. (2005) 'The third language: A recurrent textual restriction that translators come across in audiovisual translation', *Cadernos de tradução* 2(16): 147–160.

Corrius Gimbert, M. and Zabalbeascoa, P. (2011) 'Language variation in source texts and their translations: The case of L3 in film translation', *Target* 23(1): 113–130.

Davé, S. S. (2013) *Indian Accents: Brown Voice and Racial Performance in American Television and Film*, Champaign, IL: University of Illinois Press.

De Bonis, G. (2014) 'Dubbing multilingual films between neutralisation and preservation of lingua-cultural identities: A critical review of the current strategies in Italian dubbing', in *The Languages of Dubbing: Mainstream Audiovisual Translation in Italy*. M. Pavesi, M. Formentelli and E. Ghia (eds.), Bern: Peter Lang. pp. 243–266.

Dwyer, T. (2005) 'Universally speaking: Lost in translation and polyglot cinema', in *Fictionalising Translation and Multilingualism: Linguistica Antverpiensia, New Series*. D. Delabastita and R. Grutman (eds.), Vol. 4. pp. 295–310. Available at: https://lans-tts.uantwerpen.be/index.php/LANS-TTS/issue/view/9

Espindola, E. (2012) 'Systemic functional linguistics and audiovisual translation studies: A conceptual basis for the study of the language of subtitles', *D.E.L.T.A.* 28: 495–513.

Federici, F. M. (ed.) (2009) *Translating Regionalised Voices in Audiovisuals*, Roma: Aracne.

Gregory, M. J. (1967) 'Aspects of varieties differentiation', *Journal of Linguistics* 3(2): 177–198.

Gregory, M. J. (1980) 'Perspectives on translation from the Firthian tradition', *Meta* 25(4): 455–466.

Gregory, M. J. and Carroll, S. (1978) *Language and Situation: Language Varieties and Their Social Contexts*, London, Henley, and Boston: Routledge and Kegan Paul.

Halliday, M. A. K. (1978) *Language as Social Semiotic: The Social Interpretation of Language and Meaning*, London: Arnold.

Halliday, M. A. K. (1985) *An Introduction to Functional Grammar*, London: Arnold.

Halliday, M. A. K. (1994) *An Introduction to Functional Grammar* (2nd ed.), London: Arnold.

Halliday, M. A. K. and Hasan, R. (1985/1989) *Language, Context and Text: Aspects of Language in a Social-Semiotic Perspective*, Geelong, Vic., Australia: Deakin University Press/Oxford: Oxford University Press.

Halliday, M. A. K. and Matthiessen, C. M. I. M. (2004) *An Introduction to Functional Grammar* (3rd ed.), London: Arnold.

Halliday, M. A. K., revised by Matthiessen, C. M. I. M. (2014) *Halliday's Introduction to Functional Grammar* (4th ed.), London and New York: Routledge.

Halliday, M. A. K., McIntosh, A. and Strevens, P. (1964) *The Linguistic Sciences and Language Teaching*, London: Longman.

Hatim, B. and Mason, I. (1990) *Discourse and the Translator*, London and New York: Longman.

Heiss, C. (2004) 'Dubbing multilingual films: A new challenge?', *Meta* 49(1): 208–220.

Lakshmi, K. (2018) 'Casual racism in media', *The Voice*, 18 May. Available at: https://presentationvoice.com/all-posts/ae/2018/05/18/casual-racism-in-media/ (Accessed: 30 September, 2019).

Manfredi, M. (2018) 'How to be Indian in Canada, *How to be Indie* in Italy: Dubbing a TV sitcom for teenagers', in *Fast-Forwarding with Audiovisual Translation*. J. Díaz-Cintas and K. Nikolić (eds.), Bristol, UK and Blue Ridge Summit, PA, USA: Multilingual Matters. pp. 31–46.

Mubenga, K. S. (2010) 'Towards an integrated approach to cohesion and coherence in interlingual subtitling', *Stellenbosch Papers in Linguistics PLUS* 40: 39–54.

Munday, J. and Zhang, M. (2015) 'Introduction', *Discourse Analysis in Translation Studies, Target* special issue 27(3): 325–334.

Pavesi, M. (2008) 'Spoken language in film dubbing: Target language norms, interference and translational routines', in *Between Text and Image: Updating Research in Screen Translation*. D. Chiaro, C. Heiss and C. Bucaria (eds.), Amsterdam and Philadelphia: John Benjamins. pp. 79–99.

Piazza, R., Bednarek, M. and Rossi, F. (eds.) (2011) *Telecinematic Discourse: Approaches to the Language of Films and Television Series*, Amsterdam: John Benjamins.

Ranzato, I. (2006) 'Tradurre dialetti e socioletti nel cinema e nella televisione', in *Translating Voices, Translating Regions*. N. Armstrong and F. M. Federici (eds.), Roma: Aracne. pp. 143–162.

Ranzato, I. (2010) 'Localising Cockney: Translating dialect into Italian', in *New Insights into Audiovisual Translation and Media Accessibility*. J. Díaz-Cintas, A. Matamala and J. Neves (eds.), Leiden, Netherlands: Brill. pp. 109–122.

Ranzato, I. and Zanotti, S. (eds.) (2019) *Reassessing Dubbing: Historical Approaches and Current Trends*, Amsterdam and Philadelphia: John Benjamins.

Steemers, J. (2016) 'The context of localization: Children's television in Western Europe and the Arabic-speaking world', in *Media across Borders: Localizing TV, Film, and Video Games*. A. Esser, M. Á. Bernal-Merino and I. R. Smith (eds.), New York and London: Routledge. pp. 53–67.

Taylor, C. J. (2000) 'The subtitling of film: Reaching another community', in *Discourse and Community*. E. Ventola (ed.), Tübingen: Gunther Narr. pp. 309–327.

Taylor, C. J. (2006) 'The translation of regional variety in the films of Ken Loach', in *Translating Voices, Translating Regions*. N. Armstrong and F. M. Federici (eds.), Roma: Aracne. pp. 37–52.

Taylor, C. J. (2017) 'Reading images (including moving ones)', in *The Routledge Handbook of Systemic Functional Linguistics*. T. Bartlett and G. O'Grady (eds.), London and New York: Routledge. pp. 575–590.

Zabalbeascoa, P. and Voellmer, E. (2014) 'Accounting for multilingual films in translation studies: Intratextual translation in dubbing', in *Media and Translation: An Interdisciplinary Approach*. D. Abend-David (ed.), New York and London: Bloomsbury. pp. 25–51.

Filmography

Ae Fond Kiss. K. Loach. UK. 2004.
Bend it Like Beckham. G. Chadha. USA/UK/Germany. 2002.
The Bing Bang Theory. USA, CBS. 2007–2019.

Gran Torino. C. Eastwood. USA. 2008.
Jane the Virgin. USA, The CW/Netflix. 2014–2019.
Kim's Convenience. Canada, CBC/Netflix. 2016–.
Lizzie McGuire. USA, Disney Channel. 2001–2004.
Narcos. USA/Columbia, Netflix. 2015–2017.
One Day at a Time. USA, Netflix. 2017–.
Orange Is the New Black. USA, Netflix. 2013–2019.
The Simpsons. USA, FOX. 1989–.
Spanglish. J. L. Brooks. USA. 2004.
Ugly Betty. USA, ABC. 2006–2010.

Primary sources

Bunk'D. P. Eeells O'Connell. USA, Disney Channel. 2015: First season. [*Summer Camp.* ITA, Disney Channel. 2016. Dubbing dialogue adapter: R. Manzi].
How to Be Indie. V. Santamaria, J. May and S. Bolch. Canada, YTV. 2009: First season. [*Essere Indie.* ITA, DeAKids. 2010. Dubbing director: F. Danti].
Jessie. P. Eeells O'Connell. USA: Disney Channel. 2011–2012: First season. [*Jessie.* ITA, Disney Channel. 2011–2012. Dubbing dialogue adapter: R. Manzi].

Acknowledgement:

Special thanks to ©Disney Enterprises Inc. for the permissions granted for the use of the textual excerpts in Examples 1, 2, 3, 4, 6, 7, 8, and ITA, DeAKids and DHX Media in Example 5 of this chapter.

Index

accent 212, 215–216, 220–221
affect (appraisal theory) 26–27, 118, 135, 170–171, 175
agency 2, 26, 41–43, 46, 51, 59, 65, 95, 97, 125, 151
agent 4, 86, 95–97, 103
appellative function 5, 190–196, 201–205, 209
appraisal 4, 26–32, 36, 45, 65, 111, 116, 118, 125, 131, 135–137, 146, 170–171, 174; appraisal theory 3–5, 25–28, 36, 65, 132, 134–135, 170, 174
attitude (appraisal theory) 27–29, 30–31, 36, 42, 44, 51, 70–71, 77, 111, 114, 116–119, 120–121, 124, 131, 135, 141–142, 144, 146, 166, 170–171, 176–178, 180–182, 191, 194, 211
audience design 123
audiovisual translation (AVT) 212–216, 221
authorial voice 140, 142–145; external voice 136, 143, 145

Baker, M. 5, 10, 40, 44, 65, 67, 69, 85, 108, 134, 151, 155, 159, 170, 172–173
BBC Chinese 5, 152–155, 158–166
Belt and Road 2, 10–11, 12, 14–15, 20, 22

conceptual narratives 67–71
concordance 13, 19–23, 50–51, 86, 88, 152, 155
conference interpreting 2, 24–25, 28, 36
corpus linguistics 13, 19, 28, 44–46, 151, 155; corpus-based critical discourse analysis (corpus-based CDA) 29, 40–41, 44–45, 58, 60, 110, 151–155, 166–167; corpus-based discourse analysis 2, 6, 68
critical points 3, 28, 36, 59, 65–66, 75, 79

decision-making 3, 28, 65, 76, 78
dialect 6, 215, 221–222; geographical 216; non-standard 216, 222; standard 216
discourse analysis 1–6, 10, 13, 24–25, 28–29, 44, 214, 222; corpus-based critical discourse analysis (corpus-based CDA) 29, 40–41, 44–45, 58, 60, 110, 151–155, 166–167; corpus-based discourse analysis 2, 6, 68; critical discourse analysis (CDA) 3–6, 10, 24–26, 28–29, 36, 40–45, 51, 58, 60, 106–107, 110–111, 123, 125, 135, 150–153, 155, 166–167; multimodal discourse analysis 192, 214
distance 119–120; social distance 193–194, 196, 200
dubbing 213–216, 220–221

engagement (appraisal theory) 27–28, 42, 49, 111, 114–116, 118–120, 124, 135–136, 143, 171
evaluation 2–3, 25–27, 29–36, 59, 64, 71, 103, 118, 133–134, 137–143, 145–147, 160–161, 171–172, 175–176, 182, 190
experiential function 85–86, 90, 95, 103

Fairclough, N. 10, 24, 43, 47, 55, 110–111, 134, 151
focus (appraisal theory) 27, 116
force (appraisal theory) 27, 116
framing 4, 22, 131–134, 136–137, 144, 146–147, 172–176, 193; (re)framing 40–41, 48, 55, 58–59

gatekeeping 4, 106–125
government press conferences (GPC), China 4, 106

graduation (appraisal theory) 27–31, 36, 111, 114, 116–117, 123, 135, 171

Halliday, M.A.K. 25–27, 42, 58, 66, 85, 87, 90, 92, 98, 103, 111, 114–115, 121, 135, 192
Hong Kong 5, 55, 70, 93, 102, 150–166
Hunston, S. 25–26, 171

ideational metafunction 108, 192
identity 1, 5–6, 58–59, 65, 114, 117–118, 131, 152, 212–222
ideological alignment 116, 120, 124
ideology 1–3, 7, 10, 41–46, 58, 68, 75, 78, 110–111, 125, 150–152, 222
image 2, 4–5, 11, 13, 15, 17–19, 21–22, 41–43, 45, 47, 49, 58–59, 90, 103, 121, 124, 131, 134, 137–139, 140–141, 143–146, 163, 189–190, 192, 193–196, 201–202, 205, 208–209
interpersonal function 5, 90–91, 103, 190, 192–194, 196, 200–205, 208–209
interpersonal metafunction 26, 108, 111, 192–193, 222
interpreters' choices 3, 64–68, 72–78

judgement 118, 135, 175

keywords analysis 28, 161
Kress, G. 5, 190, 192–195, 201

labelling 13–15, 21–22, 41, 173, 175–176, 179–180
linguistic resources 2, 24–25, 27–28, 32, 36, 113, 119, 136, 175

Martin, J.R. and White, P.R. 4–5, 26, 29, 132, 135, 170
material process 4, 86, 97–98, 101–103
Matthiessen, C. 26, 90–92, 98, 103, 111, 114, 193
meaning potential 5, 26, 189
mediation 1–2, 4, 9, 22, 28, 41–51, 58–59, 106, 131–137, 145–147, 181
mental process 93, 97–98, 102
metadiscourse 41–49, 57–59, 166
metadiscursive (re)construction 3, 40, 54, 59
meta-narratives 3, 67, 69, 78
metaphor: co-textual metaphors 137, 143, 145–146; metaphorical image 138, 140–143; metaphor translation 133, 136–137; political metaphors 132–135, 142, 145–147
military interpreting 65–66, 78–79
modalisation 91–94
modality 25, 42, 91–94, 192–196, 200–201, 208–209
modulation 4, 91, 103, 195
mood 77, 91, 111, 114, 121–125
multimodal discourse analysis 192, 214
Munday, J. 1–2, 6, 10, 24–26, 28–29, 36, 45, 59, 64–66, 111, 135, 174, 191, 215

narrative theory 3, 5, 42, 65–67, 172, 174
news translation 4, 107, 134–135, 150–160, 167, 170, 173; media translation 4, 131–133, 145, 147

participation framework 111–112, 125
perception 2, 9, 10–11, 14–15, 17, 20–22
polarity 91
political discourse 2, 4, 9–10, 12–13, 41, 45, 50, 58, 88, 90, 106, 117, 131–133, 135
political speeches 4, 28, 131–134, 145, 147
positioning 22, 26, 28, 110, 134, 135–137, 142–147; co-textual positioning 144
Premier-Meets-the-Press conferences 41, 106
presentation 2, 9, 10, 13, 22, 43, 58–59
public narratives 67–72, 76
public notices 5, 28, 189–209

relational process 97–98, 102
reported speech 132, 134, 136, 142–147
reporting verb 28, 142, 156
re-presentation 2, 9, 10–11, 13–15, 17, 21–22
representation 1, 5, 6, 54–55, 132, 146, 151, 193–196, 200–201, 209, 212

Schäffner, C. 10, 24, 64, 131, 133, 146
selective appropriation 44, 173–176
semantic prosody 13, 19–20, 21–22, 161
semiotic(s) 2, 5, 25–26, 44, 171, 189–190, 192–193, 209, 214
shifts in translation 4–5, 24–31, 36, 45–46, 66, 72, 75, 108, 110–125, 152, 158, 161, 166–167
sitcom 212–214

speech function 111, 114, 116–117, 121, 123, 125
stance 4–5, 25–28, 43, 45, 49, 58–59, 64, 66, 110, 113, 115–116, 119–124, 131–139, 142–147, 160, 166, 170–172, 174–183
systemic functional linguistics (SFL) 4–6, 25–26, 36, 44, 65–66, 85, 87, 90–91, 95, 108, 110–111, 123, 125, 135, 171, 212, 214–216, 221–222

textual metafunction 108, 192–193
Thompson, G. 25–26, 171
transitivity 25, 95, 97

Valdeón, R. A. 134–135, 152, 174
van Leeuwen, T. 5, 190, 192–195, 201
variety 214, 216; dialectal 216–217; geographical 222; language 214
visual social semiotics 5, 190, 192–193, 209

Wodak, R. 10, 24, 44, 155
word frequency 156, 158
Word Sketch 156, 161; thesaurus sketch 13, 17–18
World Economic Forum (WEF) 2, 12, 24, 29, 36, 132, 144

Zhang, M. 2, 10, 24–25, 174, 215